Published by:

Invincible Publishers

201A, SAS Tower, Sector 38, Gurugram, Haryana – 122003

Phone: +91-124-4034247, +91 9599066061

Website : www.invinciblepublishers.com

Sales Office : - 4760-61/23, Basement, Pratap Street, Ansari Road,

Daryaganj, New Delhi - 110002

Phone: +91-11-40198405

Email: invinciblepublishers@gmail.com

ISBN : 978-93-94200-83-8

Book Name : Deepadiary Joyful Learning

First Edition: January 2023

Price: Rs. 299/-

Cover design by Dr. Deepa Gupta
Book design by Dr. Deepa Gupta

Dr. Deepa Gupta
Visit my website at Home | Deepa Diary deepadiary.com

Dedicated

To

My Husbend

Pawan Kumar

And

My sons

Bipul &Mridul

Deepa

Dedicated

To
My Husband
Nageswara Rao
and
My children
Siddhartha, Manjeera
Radharani

Table of Contents

प्रिय पाठक

इस किताब को पढ़ने से पहले दो शब्द

हमलोगों ने इस किताब को लिखने से पहले कई किताबों का अध्ययन किया जो हिंदी से तेलुगु या तेलुगु से हिंदी सिखाते हैं।उनका लक्ष्य केवल एक भाषा को ही सिखाना होता है परंतु यहाँ हमारा लक्ष्य हिंदी व तेलुगु का समान रूप से अध्ययन करना तथा हिंदी के माध्यम से तेलुगु व तेलुगु के माध्यम से आसानी से हिंदी सिखाना है। यह किताब हिंदी तेलुगु के साथ अंग्रेजी सीखने में भी सहायक होगी।

हिंदी व तेलुगु के वर्णमाला में तनिक भिन्नता है। उन शब्दों को सरलता व सहजता से उच्चारण के लिए तुलनात्मक रूप से लिखा गया है तथा बारहखड़ी में उसके दीर्ध उच्चारण के लिए उसके ऊपर रेफ लगाया गया है।पाठों का वर्गीकरण क्रमबद्ध तरीके से किया गया है।वर्ण से शब्द□शब्द से वाक्य फिर वार्तालाप का सिलसिलेवार वर्णन किया गया है।इस कारण एक के बाद एक क्रमश□पाठों का अध्ययन करना चाहिए और अगले पाठ में तभी जाना है जब पिछले पाठ से पूरी तरह अभ्यस्त हो जाए।किताब को पढ़ने के साथ-साथ लोगों से बातें करना□सिनेमा देखना व अखबार पढ़ने की कोशिश करते रहनी चाहिए।

इस किताब में दैनिक जीवन में प्रयोग होने वाली सभी घटनाओं का विस्तृत वर्णन किया गया है। विशेष स्थान पर वार्तालाप करने से पहले यदि उसे दृष्टि में रखा जाए तो काफी सहायता मिलेगी। समझने में आसानी हो इस कारण साथ ही अंग्रेजी में अनुवाद भी दिया गया है□साथ ही जो हिंदी या तेलुगु के माध्यम से अंग्रेजी सीखना चाहते है उसके लिए भी बहुत उपयोगी है।भाषाओं का ज्ञान आत्मविश्वास व कर्मशक्ति को मजबूत बनाता है।

हँसते मुस्काते सीखें |

ప్రియ పాఠకులకు,

పుస్తకం చదివే ముందు....

హిందీ నుంచి తెలుగు నేర్చుకొనే , తెలుగు నుంచి హిందీ నేర్చుకునే ఎన్నో పుస్తకాలు మనం చూసి వుంటాం. ఈ పుస్తకం ప్రత్యేకత ఏమిటంటే దీని ద్వారా తెలుగు తెలిసినవారు హిందీ నేర్చుకోగలరు మరియు హిందీ తెలిసినవారు తెలుగు నేర్చుకోగలరు. అదనంగా ఆంగ్లభాషలో కూడా వివరణ ఇవ్వబడింది.

పాఠాలన్నీ అత్యంత జాగ్రత్తగా ప్రారంభదశ నుంచి భాషపై పట్టు సాధించే దిశగా ఒక క్రమ పద్ధతిలో అమర్చబడ్డాయి..

వర్ణమాల మొదలుకొని పదాలు, పదబంధాలు ఆ పై వాక్యాలు ఈ పుస్తకం లో పొందుపరచ బడ్డాయి.

పాఠకులు గరిష్ఠ ప్రయోజనం పొందాలంటే మొదటి పాఠం నుంచీ చివరి పాఠం వరకు వారి ఆసక్తి అనుసారం ఒక క్రమ పద్ధతిలో నేర్చుకుంటే భాష మీద పట్టు సాధించవచ్చు. ప్రతి పాఠాన్నీ చదివి అభ్యాసం చేసిన తరువాతనే దాని తరువాతి పాఠానికి వెళ్ళవలసిందిగా మా సలహా.

ఇలా ఈ పుస్తకానికే పరిమితం కాకుండా ఆయా భాషలు తెలిసిన వారితో సంభాషించటం మరియు చలనచిత్రాలు చూడటం ద్వారా కూడా భాష మీద మరింత పట్టు సాధించవచ్చు.

ఈ పుస్తకం లో మేము మన దైనందిన జీవితంలో ఎదురయ్యే అన్ని రకాల సంభాషణలను పొందుపరిచే ప్రయత్నం చేసాము. ఈ పుస్తకం ఒక విషయసూచిక లా కూడా ఉపయోగపడుతుంది. ప్రతిచోటా ఆంగ్లభాషానువాదం కూడా ఇవ్వబడింది.

హిందీ తెలిసిన వారు తెలుగు, తెలుగు తెలిసిన వారు హిందీయే కాకుండా ఆయా భాషల ద్వారా ఆంగ్లం నేర్చుకోవటానికి కూడా ఈ పుస్తకం ఉపయోగపడుతుందని చెప్పటానికి మేము సంతోషిస్తున్నాము. చదవండి. చదివించండి. ఇతర భాషలను నేర్చుకోండి. మీ ఆలోచనాపరిధిని పెంచుకోండి. ఇతర భాషలు మాట్లాడేవారితో సంబంధబాంధవ్యాలు పెంపొందించుకోండి.

శుభాభినందనలతో,

Before you Begin

We have come across many books which try to teach either Hindi or Telugu. However, most of the books deal either Telugu or Hindi separately. This book deals holistically with both Hindi and Telugu languages. It will prove to be equally helpful for both Hindi, Telugu or English speakers to learn the other language (Hindi, Telugu or English).

The lessons have been carefully planned in a systematical manner, gradually ascending from beginner level to advanced level to develop fluency. The course starts from letters (Varnamala), and progressively builds into words, phrases and finally sentences. For the maximum benefit, the reader is strongly advised to start reading the book in a systematical manner from the first chapter to the last chapter. They are advised to proceed to the next section only after they are comfortable with the previous sections. We also advise the reader to not to limit themselves to this book and try to participate in conversations and explore movies in other languages as much as possible to extract the maximum benefit from the book.

We can assure you the book covers nearly every detail of a language that the reader is likely to encounter. It can also function as useful reference book. We have also included English translations to help improve understanding. Also, this book can prove to be instrumental for those who are trying to learn English as well, either through Hindi or Telugu. Read and make others read this book. Learn other languages and increase the scope of your thinking and connect better with the people who speak other languages.
Happy learning!

About Deepa Gupta

NAME: Dr. Deepa Gupta

PLACE OF BIRTH:Ramanujganj,Balarampur Dist.,Chattisgarh

EDUCATIONAL QUALIFICATION: M.A.(Hindi,English)), LLB(goldmedalist),B.Ed.,Ph.D.(Hindi)

FATHER: Late Madan Prasad Gupta

MOTHER: Sharada Devi

HUSBAND: Pawan Kumar Gupta

CHILDREN: Bipul, Mridul

PAST WORK EXPERIENCE: Hindi lecturer(10years)–MVR degree college, Visakhapatnam-26

PRESENT PROFESSION: Advocate, freelance writer

EMAIL:deepawan99@gmail.com**WEBSITE**:www.deepadiary.com

PUBLICATIONS: Pawan...Ek Jhonka (Hindi Poetry Collection) – 2014

Mrigtrishna (Hindi stories collection) –2016

Aahuti (Hindi stories collection) - 2021

AWARDS: Bharat-Bharti Samman (Jabalpur, Madhya Pradesh) Yuva Sahityakar Shatabdi (Bihar Hindi Sahitya Sammelan, Patna), Visakha Hindi Ratna (Visakha Hindi Parishad), Mahaveer Prasad Dwivedi Samman

About Radharani

NAME: Mrs. M. Radha Rani

PLACE OF BIRTH: Visakhapatnam, Andhra Pradesh

EDUCATIONAL QUALIFICATION: Grad IETE

FATHER:G. Narayana Rao

MOTHER: Ammaji Rao

HUSBAND:M. Nageswara Rao

CHILDREN: Siddhartha, Manjeera

PASTWORK EXPERIENCE: Teaching

PRESENT PROFESSION: freelancing

EMAIL:radha.mudda@gmail.com

वर्णमाला	వర్ణమాల	ALPHABET
स्वर	**అచ్చులు**	
अ-	అ	A
आ- ा	ఆ ా	AA
इ- ि	ఇ ి	I
ई- ी	ఈ ీ	EE
उ- ु	ఉ ు	U
ऊ- ू	ఊ ూ	OO
ऋ- ृ	ఋ ృ	RI
ए- े	ఎ ె	AE
ए-	ఏ ే	AEE
ऐ- ै	ఐ ై	AI
ओ- ो	ఒ ొ	O
ओ- ो	ఓ ో	O
औ- ौ	ఔ ౌ	OW
अं- ं	అం ం	AM
अः- ः	అః ః	AHA

व्यंजन	హల్లులు
क- क्‍	క – ్క
ख- ख्‍	ఖ – ్ఖ
ग -ग्‍	గ – ్గ
घ - घ्‍	ఘ హా– ్ఘ
ङ -	ఙ
च -च्‍	చ – ్చ
छ - छ्	ఛ – ్ఛ
ज - ज्‍	జ – ్జ
झ -झ्‍	ఝ –
ञ	ఞ
ट-ट्	ట – ్ట
ठ-ठ्	ఠ – ్ఠ
ड-ड्	డ – ్డ
ढ-ढ्	ఢ –
ण-ण्‍	ణ – ్ణ
त-त्‍	త – ్త
थ-थ्‍	థ – ్థ
द-द्	ద – ్ద
ध-ध्‍	ధ – ్ధ
न-न्‍	న – ్న
प-प्‍	ప – ్ప
फ-फ्‍	ఫ – ్ఫ
ब-ब्‍	బ – ్బ
भ-भ्‍	భ – ్భ

म-म्‍	మ - ్మ
य-य्‍	య - ్య
र-र्	ర - ్ర
ल-ल्‍	ల - ్ల
व-व्‍	వ - ్వ
श-श्‍	శ - ్శ
ष-ष्‍	ష - ్ష
स-स्‍	స - ్స
ह-ह्‍	హ - ్హ
ळ-ळ्‍	ళ - ్ళ
क्ष-क्ष्‍	క్ష -
त्र-त्र्‍	త్ర
ज्ञ-ज्ञ्	జ్ఞ

स्वर   అచ్చులు

अ	आ	इ	ई	उ	ऊ	ऋ	ऋ
అ	ఆ	ఇ	ఈ	ఉ	ఊ	ఋ	ౠ
A	AA	I	EE	U	OO	RI	RI

ए	ए	ऐ	ओ	ओ	औ	अं	अः
ఎ	ఏ	ఐ	ఒ	ఓ	ఔ	అం	అః
E	E	AI	O	O	AU	AN	AHA

व्यंजन **హల్లులు**

क	ख	ग	घ	ङ
క	ఖ	గ	ఘ	ఙ
KA	KHA	GA	GHA	ANG
च	छ	ज	झ	ञ
చ	ఛ	జ	ఝ	ఞ
CHA	CHA	JA	HA	YN
ट	ठ	ड	ढ	ण
ట	ఠ	డ	ఢ	ణ
TA	THA	DA	DHA	NA
त	थ	द	ध	न
త	థ	ద	ధ	న
TA	THA	DA	DHA	NA
प	फ	ब	भ	म
ప	ఫ	బ	భ	మ
PA	PHA	BA	BHA	MA
य	र	ल	व	श
య	ర	ల	వ	శ
YA	RA	LA	VA	SH
ष	स	ह	ळ	क्ष

ష	స	హ	ళ	క్ష
SHA	SA	HA	ALA	KSHA
त्र	ज्ञ			
త్ర	జ్ఞ			
TRA	GYNA			

बारहखड़ी గుణింత

क	का	कि	की	कु	कू	कृ	कृ	के	के
క	కా	కి	కీ	కు	కూ	కృ	కౄ	కె	కే
K	KA	KI	KEE	KU	KOO	KRI	KRU	KE	KE

कै	को	को	कौ	कं	कः
కై	కొ	కో	కౌ	కం	కః
KAI	KO	KO	KAU	KAN	KAHA

ख	खा	खि	खी	खु	खू	खृ	खृ	खे	खे
ఖ	ఖా	ఖి	ఖీ	ఖు	ఖూ	ఖృ	ఖౄ	ఖె	ఖే
KH	KHA	KHI	KHEE	KHU	KHOO	KHRI	KHRU	KHE	KHE

खै	खो	खो	खौ	खं	खः
ఖై	ఖొ	ఖో	ఖౌ	ఖం	ఖః
KHAI	KHO	KHO	KHAU	KHAN	KHAHA

ग	गा	गि	गी	गु	गू	गृ	गृ	गे	गे
గ	గా	గి	గీ	గు	గూ	గృ	గౄ	గె	గే
GA	GAA	GI	GEE	GU	GOO	GRI	GRU	GE	GE

गै	गो	गो	गौ	गं	गः
గై	గొ	గో	గౌ	గం	గః
GAI	GO	GO	GAU	GUN	GAHA

घ	घा	घि	घी	घु	घू	घृ	घृ	घे	घे
ఘ	ఘా	ఘి	ఘీ	ఘు	ఘూ	ఘృ	ఘౄ	ఘె	ఘే
GHA	GHAA	GHI	GHEE	GHU	GHOO	GHRI	GHRU	GHE	GHE

घै	घो	घो	घौ	घं	घः
ఘై	ఘొ	ఘో	ఘౌ	ఘం	ఘః
GHI	GHO	GHO	GHOW	GHAN	GAHA

च	चा	चि	ची	चु	चू	चृ	चॄ	चे	चे
చ	చా	చి	చీ	చు	చూ	చృ	చౄ	చె	చే
CHA	CHAA	CHE	CHEE	CHU	CHOO	CRI	CRU	CE	CE

चै	चो	चो	चौ	चं	चः
చై	చొ	చో	చౌ	చం	చః
CHAI	CHO	CHO	CHAU	CHAN	CHAHA

छ	छा	छि	छी	छु	छू	छृ	छॄ	छे	छे
ఛ	ఛా	ఛి	ఛీ	ఛు	ఛూ	ఛృ	ఛౄ	ఛె	ఛే
CHA	CHAA	CHI	CHEE	CHU	CHOO	CHRI	CHRU	CHE	CHE

छै	छो	छो	छौ	छं	छः
ఛై	ఛొ	ఛో	ఛౌ	ఛం	ఛః
CHAI	CHO	CHO	CHAU	CHAN	CHAHA

ज	जा	जि	जी	जु	जू	जृ	जॄ	जे	जे
జ	జా	జి	జీ	జు	జూ	జృ	జౄ	జె	జే
JA	JAA	JI	JEE	JU	JOO	JRI	JRU	JE	JE

जै	जो	जो	जौ	जं	जः
జై	జొ	జో	జౌ	జం	జః
JAI	JO	JO	JAU	JAN	JAHA

झ	झा	झि	झी	झु	झू	झृ	झॄ	झे	झे
ఝ	ఝా	ఝి	ఝీ	ఝు	ఝూ	ఝృ	ఝౄ	ఝె	ఝే
JHA	JHAA	JHI	JHEE	JHU	JHOO	JHRI	JHRU	JHE	JHE

झै	झो	झो	झौ	झं	झः
ఝై	ఝొ	ఝో	ఝౌ	ఝం	ఝః
JHAI	JHO	JHO	JHAU	JHAN	JHAHA

ट	टा	टि	टी	टु	टू	टृ	टॄ	टे	टे
ట	టా	టి	టీ	టు	టూ	టృ	టౄ	టె	టే

TA	TAA	TI	TEE	TU	TOO	TRI	TRU	TE	TE

टै	टो	टो	टौ	टं	टः
టై	టొ	టో	టౌ	టం	టః
TAI	TO	TO	TAU	TAN	TAHA

ठ	ठा	ठि	ठी	ठु	ठू	ठृ	ठृ	ठे	ठे
ఠ	ఠా	ఠి	ఠీ	ఠు	ఠూ	ఠృ	ఠౄ	ఠె	ఠే
THA	THAA	THI	THEE	THU	THOO	THRI	THRU	THE	THE

ठै	ठो	ठो	ठौ	ठं	ठः
ఠై	ఠొ	ఠో	ఠౌ	ఠం	ఠః
THAI	THO	THO	THAU	THAN	THAHA

ड	डा	डि	डी	डु	डू	डृ	डृ	डे	डे
డ	డా	డి	డీ	డు	డూ	డృ	డౄ	డె	డే
DA	DAA	DI	DEE	DU	DOO	DRI	DRU	DE	DE

डै	डो	डो	डौ	डं	डः
డై	డొ	డో	డౌ	డం	డః
DAI	DO	DO	DAU	DAN	DAHA

ढ	ढा	ढि	ढी	ढु	ढू	ढृ	ढृ	ढे	ढे
ఢ	ఢా	ఢి	ఢీ	ఢు	ఢూ	ఢృ	ఢౄ	ఢె	ఢే
DHA	DHAA	DHI	DHEE	DHU	DHOO	DHRI	DHRU	DHE	DHE

ढै	ढो	ढो	ढौ	ढं	ढः
ఢై	ఢొ	ఢో	ఢౌ	ఢం	ఢః
DHAI	DHO	DHO	DHAU	DHAN	DHAHA

त	ता	ति	ती	तु	तू	तृ	तृ	ते	ते
త	తా	తి	తీ	తు	తూ	తృ	తౄ	తె	తే
TA	TAA	TI	TEE	TU	TUOO	TRI	TRU	TE	TE

तै	तो	तो	तौ	तं	तः
తై	తొ	తో	తౌ	తం	తః

TAI	TO	TO	TAU	TAN	TAHA

थ	था	थि	थी	थु	थू	थृ	थॄ	थे	थे
థ	థా	థి	థీ	థు	థూ	థృ	థౄ	థె	థే
THA	THAA	THI	THEE	THU	THOO	THRI	THRU	THE	THE

थै	थो	थो	थौ	थं	थः
థై	థొ	థో	థౌ	థం	థః
THAI	THO	THO	THAU	THAN	THAHA

द	दा	दि	दी	दु	दू	दृ	दॄ	दे	दे
ద	దా	ది	దీ	దు	దూ	దృ	దౄ	దె	దే
DA	DAA	DI	DEE	DU	DOO	DRI	DRU	DE	DE

दै	दो	दो	दौ	दं	दः
దై	దొ	దో	దౌ	దం	దః
DAI	DO	DO	DAU	DAN	DAHA

ध	धा	धि	धी	धु	धू	धृ	धॄ	धे	धे
ధ	ధా	ధి	ధీ	ధు	ధూ	ధృ	ధౄ	ధె	ధే
DHA	DHAA	DHI	DHEE	DHU	DHOO	DHRI	DHRU	DHE	DHE

धै	धो	धो	धौ	धं	धः
ధై	ధొ	ధో	ధౌ	ధం	ధః
DHAI	DHO	DHO	DHAU	DHAN	DHAHA

न	ना	नि	नी	नु	नू	नृ	नॄ	ने	ने
న	నా	ని	నీ	ను	నూ	నృ	నౄ	నె	నే
NA	NAA	NI	NEE	NU	NOO	NRI	NRU	NE	NEE

नै	नो	नो	नौ	नं	नः
నై	నొ	నో	నౌ	నం	నః
NAI	NO	NO	NAU	NAN	NAHA

प	पा	पि	पी	पु	पू	पृ	पृ	पे	पे
ప	పా	పి	పీ	పు	పూ	పృ	పౄ	పె	పే
PA	PAA	PI	PEE	PU	POO	PRI	PRU	PE	PEE

पै	पो	पो	पौ	पं	पः
పై	పొ	పో	పౌ	పం	పః
PAI	PO	PO	PAU	PAN	PAHA

फ	फा	फि	फी	फु	फू	फृ	फृ	फे	फे
ఫ	ఫా	ఫి	ఫీ	ఫు	ఫూ	ఫృ	ఫౄ	ఫె	ఫే
PHA	PHAA	PHI	PHEE	PHU	PHOO	PHRI	PHRU	PHE	PHE

फै	फो	फो	फौ	फं	फः
ఫై	ఫొ	ఫో	ఫౌ	ఫం	ఫః
PHAI	PHO	PHO	PHAU	PHAN	PHAHA

ब	बा	बि	बी	बु	बू	बृ	बृ	बे	बे
బ	బా	బి	బీ	బు	బూ	బృ	బౄ	బె	బే
BA	BAA	BI	BEE	BU	BOO	BRI	BRU	BE	BE

बै	बो	बो	बौ	बं	बः
బై	బొ	బో	బౌ	బం	బః
BAI	BO	BO	BAU	BAN	BAHA

भ	भा	भि	भी	भु	भू	भृ	भृ	भे	भे
భ	భా	భి	భీ	భు	భూ	భృ	భౄ	భె	భే
BHA	BHAA	BHI	BHEE	BHU	BHOO	BHRI	BHRU	BHE	BHE

भै	भो	भो	भौ	भं	भः
భై	భొ	భో	భౌ	భం	భః
BHAI	BHO	BHO	BHAU	BHAN	BHAHA

म	मा	मि	मी	मु	मू	मृ	मृ	मे	मे
మ	మా	మి	మీ	ము	మూ	మృ	మౄ	మె	మే
MA	MAA	MI	MEE	MU	MOO	MRI	MRU	ME	ME

मै	मो	मो	मौ	मं	मः				
మై	మొ	మో	మౌ	మం	మః				
MAI	MO	MO	MAU	MAN	MAHA				
य	या	यि	यी	यु	यू	यृ	यृ	ये	ये
య	యా	యి	యీ	యు	యూ	యృ	యౄ	యె	యే
YA	YA	YI	YEE	YU	YOO	YRI	YRU	YE	YE
यै	यो	यो	यौ	यं	यः				
యై	యొ	యో	యౌ	యం	యః				
YAI	YO	YO	YAU	YAN	YAHA				
र	रा	रि	री	रु	रू	रृ	रृ	रे	रे
ర	రా	రి	రీ	రు	రూ	రృ	రౄ	రె	రే
RA	RAA	RI	REE	RU	ROO	RRI	RRU	RE	RE
रै	रो	रो	रौ	रं	रः				
రై	రొ	రో	రౌ	రం	రః				
RAI	RO	RO	RAU	RAN	RAHA				
ल	ला	लि	ली	लु	लू	लृ	लृ	ले	ले
ల	లా	లి	లీ	లు	లూ	లృ	లౄ	లె	లే
LA	LAA	LI	LEE	LU	LOO	LRI	LRU	LE	LE
लै	लो	लो	लौ	लं	लः				
లై	లొ	లో	లౌ	లం	లః				
LAI	LO	LO	LAU	LAN	LAHA				
ळ	ळा	ळि	ळी	ळु	ळू	ळृ	ळृ	ळे	ळे
ళ	ళా	ళి	ళీ	ళు	ళూ	ళృ	ళౄ	ళె	ళే
LH	LHAA	LHI	LHEE	LHU	LHOO	LHRI	LHRU	LHE	LHE
ळै	ळो	ळो	ळौ	ळं	ळः				
ళై	ళొ	ళో	ళౌ	ళం	ళః				
LHAI	LHO	LHO	LHAU	LHAN	LHAHA				

व	वा	वि	वी	वु	वू	वृ	वृ	वे	वे
వ	వా	వి	వీ	వు	వూ	వృ	వౄ	వె	వే
VA	VAA	VI	VEE	VU	VOO	VRI	VRU	VE	VE
वै	वो	वो	वौ	वं	वः				
వై	వొ	వో	వౌ	వం	వః				
VAI	VO	VO	VAU	VAN	VAHA				
श	शा	शि	शी	शु	शू	शृ	शृ	शे	शे
శ	శా	శి	శీ	శు	శూ	శృ	శౄ	శె	శే
SHA	SHAA	SHI	SHEE	SHU	SHOO	SHRI	SHRU	SHE	SHE
शै	शो	शो	शौ	शं	शः				
శై	శొ	శో	శౌ	శం	శః				
SHAI	SHO	SHO	SHAU	SHAN	SHAHA				
ष	षा	षि	षी	षु	षू	षृ	षृ	षे	षे
ష	షా	షి	షీ	షు	షూ	షృ	షౄ	షె	షే
SHA	SHAA	SHI	SHEE	SHU	SHOO	SHRI	SHRU	SHE	SHE
षै	षो	षो	षौ	षं	षः				
షై	షొ	షో	షౌ	షం	షః				
SHAI	SHO	SHO	SHAU	SHAN	SHAHA				
स	सा	सि	सी	सु	सू	सृ	सृ	से	से
స	సా	సి	సీ	సు	సూ	సృ	సౄ	సె	సే
SA	SAA	SI	SEE	SU	SOO	SRI	SRU	SE	SE
सै	सो	सो	सौ	सं	सः				
సై	సొ	సో	సౌ	సం	సః				
SAI	SO	SO	SAU	SAN	SAHA				
ह	हा	हि	ही	हु	हू	हृ	हृ	हे	हे
హ	హా	హి	హీ	హు	హూ	హృ	హౄ	హె	హే
HA	HAA	HI	HEE	HU	HOO	HRI	HRU	HE	HE
है	हो	हो	हौ	हं	हः				

హై	హొ	హో	హౌ	హం	హః
HAI	HO	HO	HAU	HAN	HAHA

क्ष	क्षा	क्षि	क्षी	क्षु	क्षू	क्षृ	क्षृ	क्षे	क्षे
క్ష	క్షా	క్షి	క్షీ	క్షు	క్షూ	క్షృ	క్షౄ	క్షె	క్షే
KSH	KSHA	KSHI	KSHEE	KSHU	KSHOO	KSHRI	KSHRU	KSHE	KSHE

क्षै	क्षो	क्षो	क्षौ	क्षं	क्षः
క్షై	క్షొ	క్షో	క్షౌ	క్షం	క్షః
KSHAI	KSHO	KSHO	KSHAU	KSHAN	KSHAHA

त्र	त्रा	त्रि	त्री	त्रु	त्रू	त्रृ	त्रृ	त्रे	त्रे
త్ర	త్రా	త్రి	త్రీ	త్రు	త్రూ	త్రృ	త్రౄ	త్రె	త్రే
TR	TRAA	TRI	TREE	TRU	TROO	TRRI	TRRU	TRE	TRE

त्रै	त्रो	त्रो	त्रौ	त्रं	त्रः
త్రై	త్రొ	త్రో	త్రౌ	త్రం	త్రః
TRAI	TRO	TRO	TRAU	TRAN	TRAHA

ज्ञ	ज्ञा	ज्ञि	ज्ञी	ज्ञु	ज्ञू	ज्ञृ	ज्ञृ	ज्ञे	ज्ञे
జ్ఞ	జ్ఞా	జ్ఞి	జ్ఞీ	జ్ఞు	జ్ఞూ	జ్ఞృ	జ్ఞౄ	జ్ఞె	జ్ఞే
GYN	GYNA	GYNI	GYNEE	GYNU	GYNOO	GYNRI	GYNRU	GYNE	GYNE

ज्ञै	ज्ञो	ज्ञो	ज्ञौ	ज्ञं	ज्ञः
జ్ఞై	జ్ఞొ	జ్ఞో	జ్ఞౌ	జ్ఞం	జ్ఞః
GYNAI	GYNO	GYNO	GYNAU	GYNAN	GYNAHA

अंक			అంకెలు		NUMBERS
१	एक	ओकटी	ఒకటి	ఏక్	ONE
२	दो	रेंडु	రెండు	దో	TWO
३	तीन	मूडु	మూడు	తీన్	THREE
४	चार	नालुगु	నాలుగు	చార్	FOUR
५	पाँच	ऐदु	ఐదు	పాంచ్	FIVE
६	छः	आरु	ఆరు	ఛః	SIX
७	सात	एडु	ఏడు	సాత్	SEVEN
८	आठ	एनिमिदि	ఎనిమిది	ఆఠ్	EIGHT
९	नौ	तोम्मिदि	తొమ్మిది	నౌ	NINE
१०	दस	पदि	పది	దస్	TEN
११	ग्यारह	पदकोंडु	పదకొండు	గ్యారహ్	ELEVEN
१२	बारह	पन्नेंडु	పన్నెండు	బారహ్	TWELVE
१३	तेरह	पदमुडु	పదమూడు	తేరహ్	THIRTEEN
१४	चौदह	पध्नालुगु	పధ్నాలుగు	చౌదహ్	FOURTEEN
१५	पंद्रह	पदिहेनु	పదిహేను	పంద్రహ్	FIFTEEN
१६	सोलह	पदाहारु	పదహారు	సోలహ్	SIXTEEN
१७	सत्रह	पदिहेडु	పదిహేడు	సత్రహ్	SEVENTEEN
१८	अठारह	पध्दनिमिदि	పద్దెనిమిది	అఠారహ్	EIGHTEEN
१९	उन्नीस	पंतोम्मिदि	పంతొమ్మిది	ఉన్నీస్	NINETEEN
२०	बीस	इरवै	ఇరవై	బీస్	TWENTY
२१	इक्कीस	इरवै ओकटी	ఇరవై ఒకటి	ఇక్కీస్	TWENTY ONE
२२	बाईस	इरवै रेंडु	ఇరవై రెండు	బాఈస్	TWENTY TWO
२३	तेइस	इरवै मुडु	ఇరవై మూడు	తేఈస్	TWENTY THREE
२४	चौबीस	इरवै नालुगु	ఇరవై నాలుగు	చౌబీస్	TWENTY FOUR
२५	पच्चीस	इरवै ऐदु	ఇరవై ఐదు	పచ్చీస్	TWENTY FIVE
२६	छब्बीस	इरवै आरु	ఇరవై ఆరు	ఛబ్బీస్	TWENTY SIX
२७	सत्ताईस	इरवै एडु	ఇరవై ఏడు	సత్తాఈస్	TWENTY SEVEN
२८	अट्ठाईस	इरवै एनिमिदि	ఇరవై ఎనిమిది	అఠాఈస్	TWENTY EIGHT
२९	उनतीस	इरवै तोम्मिदि	ఇరవై తొమ్మిది	ఉన్‌తీస్	TWENTY NINE
३०	तीस	मुप्फै	ముప్ఫై	తీస్	THIRTY
३१	इकतीस	मुप्फै ओकटी	ముప్ఫై ఒకటి	ఇక్‌తీస్	THIRTY ONE
३२	बत्तीस	मुप्फै रेंडु	ముప్ఫై రెండు	బత్తీస్	THIRTY TWO

३३	तैंतीस	मुप्फै मूडु	ముప్పై మూడు	తైంతీస్	THIRTY THREE
३४	चौंतीस	मुप्फै नालुगु	ముప్పై నాలుగు	చౌంతీస్	THIRTY FOUR
३५	पैंतीस	मुप्फै ऐदु	ముప్పై ఐదు	పైంతీస్	THIRTY FIVE
३६	छत्तीस	मुप्फै आरु	ముప్పై ఆరు	ఛత్తీస్	THIRTY SIX
३७	सैंतीस	मुप्फै एडु	ముప్పై ఏడు	సైంతీస్	THIRTY SEVEN
३८	अड़तीस	मुप्फै एनिमिदि	ముప్పై ఎనిమిది	అడ్తీస్	THIRTY EIGHT
३९	उनतालीस	मुप्फै तोम्मिदि	ముప్పై తొమ్మిది	ఉన్తీస్	THIRTY NINE
४०	चालीस	नलभै	నలభై	చాలీస్	FORTY
४१	इकताली	नलभै ओकटी	నలభై ఒకటి	ఇక్తాలీస్	FORTY ONE
४२	बयालीस	नलभै रेंडु	నలభై రెండు	బయాలీస్	FORTY TWO
४३	तैतालीस	नलभै मूडु	నలభై మూడు	తైంతాలీస్	FORTY THREE
४४	चवालीस	नलभै नालुगु	నలభై నాలుగు	చవాలీస్	FORTY FOUR
४५	पैंतालीस	नलभै ऐदु	నలభై ఐదు	పైంతాలీస్	FORTY FIVE
४६	छियालीस	नलभै आरु	నలభై ఆరు	ఛైయాలీస్	FORTY SIX
५७	सैंतालीस	नलभै एडु	నలభై ఏడు	సైంతాలీస్	FORTY SEVEN
४८	अड़तालीस	नलभै एनिमिदि	నలభై ఎనిమిది	అడ్తాలీస్	FORTY EIGHT
४८	उनचास	नलभै तोम्मिदि	నలభై తొమ్మిది	ఉన్చాస్	FORTY NINE
५०	पचास	याभै	ఏభై	పచాస్	FIFTY
५१	इक्यावन	याभै ओकटी	ఏభై ఒకటి	ఇక్యావన్	FIFTY ONE
५२	बावन	याभै रेंडु	ఏభై రెండు	బావన్	FIFTY TWO
५३	तिरपन	याभै मूडु	ఏభై మూడు	తిర్పన్	FIFTY THREE
५४	चौवन	याभै नालुगु	ఏభై నాలుగు	చౌవన్	FIFTY FOUR
५५	पचपन	याभै ऐदु	ఏభై ఐదు	పచ్పన్	FIFTY FIVE
५६	छप्पन	याभै आरु	ఏభై ఆరు	ఛప్పన్	FIFTY SIX
५७	सत्तावन	याभै एडु	ఏభై ఏడు	సత్తావన్	FIFTY SEVEN
५८	अट्ठावन	याभै एनिमिदि	ఏభై ఎనిమిది	అఠావన్	FIFTY EIGHT
५९	उनसठ	याभै तोम्मिदि	ఏభై తొమ్మిది	ఉన్సఠ్	FIFTY NINE
६०	साठ	अरवै	అరవై	సాఠ్	SIXTY
६१	इकसठ	अरवै ओकटी	అరవై ఒకటి	ఇక్సఠ్	SIXTY ONE
६२	बासठ	अरवै रेंडु	అరవై రెండు	బాసఠ్	SIXTY TWO
६३	तिरसठ	अरवै मूडु	అరవై మూడు	తిర్సఠ్	SIXTY THREE
६४	चौंसठ	अरवै नालुगु	అరవై నాలుగు	చౌసఠ్	SIXTY FOUR
६५	पैंसठ	अरवै ऐदु	అరవై ఐదు	పైంసఠ్	SIXTY FIVE
६६	छियासठ	अरवै आरु	అరవై ఆరు	ఛియాసఠ్	SIXTY SIX
६७	सड़सठ	अरवै एडु	అరవై ఏడు	సడ్సఠ్	SIXTY SEVEN
६८	अड़सठ	अरवै एनिमिदि	అరవై ఎనిమిది	అడ్సఠ్	SIXTY EIGHT

६९	उनहत्तर	अरवै तोम्मिदि	అరవై తొమ్మిది	ఉన్‌హత్తర్	SIXTY NINE
७०	सत्तर	डेभ्बै	డెబ్బై	సత్తర్	SEVENTY
७१	इकहत्तर	डेभ्बै ओकटी	డెబ్బై ఒకటి	ఇక్‌హత్తర్	SEVENTY ONE
७२	बहत्तर	डेभ्बै रेंडु	డెబ్బై రెండు	బహత్తర్	SEVENTY TWO
७३	तिहत्तर	डेभ्बै मूडु	డెబ్బై మూడు	తిహత్తర్	SEVENTY THREE
७४	चौहत्तर	डेभ्बै नालुगु	డెబ్బై నాలుగు	చౌహత్తర్	SEVENTY FOUR
७५	पचहत्तर	डेभ्बै ऐदु	డెబ్బై ఐదు	పచ్‌హత్తర్	SEVENTY FIVE
७६	छिहत्तर	डेभ्बै आरु	డెబ్బై ఆరు	ఛిహత్తర్	SEVENTY SIX
७७	सतहत्तर	डेभ्बै एडु	డెబ్బై ఏడు	సత్‌హత్తర్	SEVENTY SEVEN
७८	अट्ठहत्तर	डेभ्बै एनिमिदि	డెబ్బై ఎనిమిది	అఠ్‌హత్తర్	SEVENTY EIGHT
७९	उन्नासी	डेभ्बै तोम्मिदि	డెబ్బై తొమ్మిది	ఉన్యాసి	SEVENTY NINE
८०	अस्सी	एनभै	ఎనభై	అస్సీ	EIGHTY
८१	इक्यासी	एनभै ओकटी	ఎనభై ఒకటి	ఇక్యాసీ	EIGHTY ONE
८२	बयासी	एनभै रेंडु	ఎనభై రెండు	బయాసీ	EIGHTY TWO
८३	तिरासी	एनभै मूडु	ఎనభై మూడు	తిరాసీ	EIGHTY THREE
८४	चौरासी	एनभै नालुगु	ఎనభై నాలుగు	చౌరాసీ	EIGHTY FOUR
८५	पचासी	एनभै ऐदु	ఎనభై ఐదు	పచాసీ	EIGHTY FIVE
८६	छियासी	एनभै आरु	ఎనభై ఆరు	ఛియాసీ	EIGHTY SIX
८७	सत्तासी	एनभै एडु	ఎనభై ఏడు	సతాసీ	EIGHTY SEVEN
८८	अट्ठासी	एनभै एनिमिदि	ఎనభై ఎనిమిది	అఠాసీ	EIGHTY EIGHT
८९	नवासी	एनभै तोम्मिदि	ఎనభై తొమ్మిది	నవాసీ	EIGHTY NINE
९०	नब्बे	तोंभै	తొంభై	నబ్బే	NINETY
९१	इंक्यानवे	तोंभै ओकटी	తొంభై ఒకటి	ఇక్యానబే	NINETY ONE
९२	बानवे	तोंभै रेंडु	తొంభై రెండు	బానబే	NINETY TWO
९३	तिरानवे	तोंभै मूडु	తొంభై మూడు	తిరానబే	NINETY THREE
९४	चौरानवे	तोंभै नालुगु	తొంభై నాలుగు	చౌరానబే	NINETY FOUR
९५	पंचानवे	तोंभै ऐदु	తొంభై ఐదు	పంచానబే	NINETY FIVE
९६	छियानवे	तोंभै आरु	తొంభై ఆరు	చియానబే	NINETY SIX
९७	संतानवे	तोंभै एडु	తొంభై ఏడు	సంతానబే	NINETY SEVEN
९८	अंट्ठानवे	तोंभै एनिमिदि	తొంభై ఎనిమిది	అంఠానబే	NINETY EIGHT
९९	निन्यानवे	तोंभै तोम्मिदि	తొంభై తొమ్మిది	నిన్యానబే	NINETY NINE
१००	एक सौ	वन्दा	వంద	ఏక్ సౌ	HUNDRED

हजार	वेइ	వేయి	హజార్	ONE THOUSAND

लाख	लक्षा	లక్ష	లాఖ్	ONE LAKH
करोड़	कोटि	కోటి	అరబ్అరచ్కరోడ్	ONE CRORE
अरब/सौ करोड	सतकोटि	శతకోటి	సౌకరోడ్	HUNDRED CRORES
खरब/हजार करोड	सहस्र कोटि	సహస్రకోటి	ఖరబ్హజార్కరోడ్	THOUSAND CRORES

पाव	पाऊ	పావ్	పావు	QUARTER
आधा	अरा	అర	ఆదా	HALF
पौने	मूप्पावु	ముప్పావు	పౌనే	THREE QUARTERS
सवा	ओकटिंपाऊ	ఒకటింపావు	సవా	ONE AND QUARTER
डेढ़	ओकटिन्नरा	ఒకటిన్నర	డేఢ్	ONE AND HALF
पौने दो	ओकटि मूप्पवु	ఒకటి ముప్పావు	పౌనే దో	ONE AND THREE QUARTERS
सवा दो	रेंडुमपावु	రెండుంపావు	సవా దో	TWO AND QUARTER
ढाई	रेंडुन्नरा	రెండున్నర	ఢాఈ	TWO AND HALF
पौने तीन	रेंडुमप्पवु	రెండుముప్పావు	పౌనే తీన్	TWO AND THREE QUARTERS
सवा तीन	मुडुमपावु	మూడుంపావు	సవా తీన్	THREE AND QUARTER
साढ़े तीन	मुडुन्नरा	మూడున్నర	సాఢే తీన్	THREE AND HALF
पौने चार	मुडुमूप्पवु	మూడు ముప్పావు	పౌనే చార్	THREE AND THREE QUARTERS
सवा चार	नालुगुमपावु	నాలుగుం పావు	సవా చార్	FOUR AND QUARTER
साढ़े चार	नालुगुन्नरा	నాలుగున్నర	సాఢే చార్	FOUR AND HALF
पौनें पांच	नालुगु मूप्पवु	నాలుగు ముప్పావు	పౌనే పాంచ్	FOUR AND THREE QUARTE
सवा पांच	ऐदु पावु	ఐదుంపావు	సవా పాంచ్	FIVE AND QUARTER
सौढ़े पांच	ऐदुन्नरा	ఐదున్నర	సాడే పాంచ్	FIVE AND HALF
पौने छः	ऐदुं मूप्पवु	ఐదు ముప్పావు	పౌనే ఛే	FIVE AND THREE QUARTERS

श्रृंखला **వరుసక్రమం** **SEQUENCE**

अव्वल/पहला	मोदटी/ओकटवा	మొదటి/ఒకటవ	పహలా/అవ్వల్	FIRST
दूसरा	रेंडवा	రెండవ	దూస్‌రా	SECOND
तीसरा	मूड़वा	మూడవ	తీస్‌రా	THIRD
चौथा	नालुगवा	నాలుగవ	చౌథా	FOURTH
पाँचवाँ	ऐदवा	ఐదవ	పాంచ్‌వా	FIFTH
छठवाँ	आरवा	ఆరవ	ఛర్‌వా	SIXTH
सातवाँ	एड़वा	ఏడవ	సాత్‌వా	SEVENTH
आठवाँ	एनिमिदवा	ఎనిమిదవ	ఆర్‌వా	EIGHTH
नौवाँ	तोम्मिदवा	తొమ్మిదవ	నౌవా	NINETH
दसवाँ	पदवा	పదవ	దస్‌వా	TENTH
ग्यारहवाँ	पदकोंडवा	పదకొండవ	గ్యారహ్‌వా	ELEVENTH
बारहवाँ	पन्नेंडवा	పన్నెండవ	బారహ్‌వా	TWELTH
तेरहवाँ	पदमूडवा	పదమూడవ	తేరహ్‌వా	THIRTEENTH
चौदहवाँ	पदनालुगवा	పద్నాలుగవ	చౌదహ్‌వా	FOURTEENTH
पंद्रहवाँ	पदिहेनवा	పదిహేనవ	పంద్రహ్‌వా	FIFTEENTH
सौवाँ	वंदवा	వందవ	సౌవా	HUNDREDTH
हजारवाँ	वेय्यवा	వెయ్యవ	హజార్‌వా	THOUSANDTH
दोनों	इद्दरु	ఇద్దరు	దోనో	BOTH
तीनों	मुग्गुरु	ముగ్గురు	తీనో	ALL THREE
चारों	नलुगुरु	నలుగురు	చారో	ALL FOUR
पाँचों	ऐदुगुरु	ఐదుగురు	పాంచో	ALL FIVE
छवों	आरुगुरु	అరుగురు	ఛవో	ALL SIX
सातों	एडुगुरु	ఏడుగురు	సాతో	ALL SEVEN
आठों	एनिमिदिमंदि	ఎనిమిదిమంది	ఆఠో	ALL EIGHT
नवों	तोमिदिमंदि	తొమ్మిదిమంది	నావో	ALL NINE
दसों	पदिमंदि	పదిమంది	దసో	ALL TEN
ग्यारहों	पदकोंडुमंदि	పదకొండుమంది	గ్యారహో	ALL ELEVEN
बारहों	पन्नेंडुमंदि	పన్నెండుగురు	బారహో	ALL TWELEVE
तेरहों	पदमुग्गुरु	పదముగ్గురు	తేరహో	ALL THIRTEEN
चौदहवों	पदनालुगुमंदि	పద్నాలుగుమంది	చౌదహో	ALL FOURTEEN
पंद्रहवों	पदहेनुमंदि	పదిహేనుమంది	పంద్రహో	ALL FIFTEEN

सौवो	वंदमंदि	వందమంది	సౌవో	ALL HUNDRED
हजारवों	वेय्यिमंदि	వెయ్యిమంది	హజారవో	ALL THOUSAND
लाखों	लक्षमंदि	లక్షమంది	లాఖో	ALL LAKH

अभ्यास(एक अक्षर)		అభ్యాసము		PRACTICE
आ	रा	ఆ	రా	COME
जा	वेल्लु	జా	వెళ్లు	GO
खा	तिनु	ఖా	తిను	EAT
सो	पडुको	సో	పడుకో	SLEEP
पी	तागु	పీ	తాగు	DRINK
दे	इव्वु	దే	ఇవ్వు	GIVE
ले	तीसुको	లే	తీసుకో	TAKE
छू	ताकु	ఛూ	తాకు	TOUCH
ला	ते	లా	తే	BRING
पे	पै/मीदा	పే	పై/మీద	OVER/ON

अभ्यास(दो अक्षर) రెండక్షరాల పదాల అభ్యాసము PRACTICE

पत्र	उत्तरमु	ఉత్తరము	పత్ర్	LETTER
थोडा	कोंचेमु	కొంచెము	థోడా	SOME
जल्दी	त्वरगा	త్వరగా	జల్దీ	FAST
बात	माटा	మాట	బాత్	TALK
भाषा	भाषा	భాష	భాషా	LANGUAGE
घास	गड्डि	గడ్డి	ఘాస్	GRASS
वर्ग	वर्गमु	వర్గము	వర్గ్	SECTION
अग्नि	अग्नि	అగ్ని	అగ్నీ	FIRE
भाई	सोदरुडु	సోదరుడు	భాఈ	BROTHER
देश	दोशमु	దేశము	దేశ్	COUNTRY
काम	पनि	పని	కామ్	WORK
अच्छा	मंचि	మంచి	అచ్ఛా	GOOD
बुरा	चेडु	చెడు	బురా	BAD
पक्का	तप्पकुंडा	తప్పకుండా	పక్కా	SURE
कच्चा	पच्चि	పచ్చి	కచ్చా	RAW
कुर्सी	कुर्चि	కుర్చీ	కుర్సీ	CHAIR
मेज	मेजाबल्ला	మేజాబల్ల	మేజ్	TABLE
ठग	मोसगाडु	మోసగాడు	ఠగ్	FRAUD
ताली	चप्पट्लु	చప్పట్లు	తాలీ	CLAP
ईर्ष्या	ईर्ष्या	ఈర్ష్య	ఈర్ష్యా	JEALOUSY
रस	रसमु	రసము	రస్	JUICE
क्षण	क्षणमु	క్షణము	క్షణ్	MINUTE
छल	मोसमु	మోసము	ఛల్	CHEATIN
पेटी	पेट्टे	పెట్టె	పేటీ	BOX
फूट	विरगटम	విరగటం	ఫూట్	BLAST
पति	भर्ता	భర్త	పతి	HUSBAND

अभ्यास(तीन अक्षर) ముంాడక్షరాలపదాల అభ్యాసము PRACTICE

अनंत	अनंतमु	అనంతము	అనంత్	INFINITY
ईश्वर	ईश्वरुडु	ఈశ్వరుడు	ఈశ్వర్	GOD
प्रार्थना	प्रार्थना	ప్రార్ధన	ప్రార్ధనా	PRAYER
सफेद	तेलुपु	తెలుపు	సఫేద్	WHITE
कहानी	कथा	కధ	కహానీ	STORY
चिड़िया	पक्षि	పక్షి	చిడియా	BIRD
अंग्रेजी	आंग्लमु	ఆంగ్లము	అంగ్రేజీ	ENGLISH
मैदान	मैदानमु	మైదానము	మైదాన్	GROUND
जुकाम	जलुभु	జలుబు	జుకామ్	COLD
दिमाग	बुद्धि	బుద్ధి	దిమాగ్	BRAIN
पहले	मुंदु	ముందు	పహలే	BEFORE
बीमार	अनारोग्यमु	అనారోగ్యము	బీమార్	SICK
आराम	विश्रांति	విశ్రాంతి	ఆరామ్	RELAXATION
लकड़ी	कर्रा	కర్ర	లకడీ	STICK
लड़की	अम्मायि	అమ్మాయి	లడకీ	GIRL
कीमत	धरा	ధర	కీమత్	COST
सवारी	प्रयाणम्/प्रयाणिकुडु	ప్రయాణం/ ప్రయాణికుడు	సవారి	RIDE/PASSENGER
शांति/अमन	शांति	శాంతి	శాంతి	PEACE
अशुभ	अशुभमु	అశుభము	అశుభ్	INAUSPICIOUS
आग्रह	अभ्यर्दना	అభ్యర్ధన	ఆగ్రహ్	REQUEST
आगोश	कौगिलि	కౌగిలి	ఆగోశ్	LAPPED
इज्जत/आबरू	गौरवमु	గౌరవము	ఆబరూ/ఇజ్జత్	RESPECT
गिरोह/समूह	समूहमु	సమూహము	గిరోహ్	GROUP
चखना	रुचि चूचुटा	రుచిచూచుట	చఖ్నా	TO TASTE
छप्पन	याभै आरू	యాభై ఆరు	ఛప్పన్	FIFTTY-SIX
झुकना	वंगुटा	వంగుట	ఝుక్నా	BEND

अभ्यास(चार अक्षर) నాలుగక్షరాల పదాల అభ్యాసము PRACTICE

भगवान	भगवंतुडु	భగవంతుడు	భగవాన్	GOD
छरहरा	सन्ननि	సన్నని	ఛర్‌హరా	PETITE/SLIM
झिलमिल	मेरिसे	మెరిసే	ఝిల్‌మిల్	TWINKLING
जानवर	जंतुवु	జంతువు	జాన్‌వర్	ANIMAL
वफादार	नम्मकस्तुडु	నమ్మకస్తుడు	వఫాదార్	RELIABLE
पुरस्कार	बहुमति	బహుమతి	పురస్కార్	PRIZE
परिश्रम	श्रमा	శ్రమ	పరిశ్రమ్	HARDWORK
नारियल	कोब्बरिकाया	కొబ్బరికాయ	నారియల్	COCONUT
ठहराव	कुदुरुगा	కుదురుగా	ఠహరావ్	STABILITY
दहकना	प्रज्वरिल्लु	ప్రజ్వరిల్లు	దహక్‌నా	BLAZING
धडकन	गुंडेचप्पुडु	గుండెచప్పుడు	ధడ్‌కన్	HEARTBEAT
दशानन	दशाननुडु	దశాననుడు	దశానన్	KING RAVAN
दस्तावेज	दस्तावेजु	దస్తావేజు	దస్తావేజ్	DOCUMENT
दमदार	शक्तिवंतुडु	శక్తివంతుడు	దమ్‌దార్	POWERFUL
नगरीय	पट्टणपु	పట్టణపు	నగరీయ్	URBAN
जादूगर	मायाजालकुडु	మాయాజాలకుడు	జాదూగర్	MAGICIAN
डरावना	भयानकमु	భయానకము	డరావ్‌నా	SCARY
रमणीय	अंदमैना	అందమైన	రమణీయ్	PLEASANT
लहराना	ऊपडम	ఊపడం	లహ్‌రానా	TO WAVE

संयुत्काक्षर సంయుక్తాక్షరములు combined letters

आंध्रप्रदेश	आंध्रप्रदेश	ఆంధ్రప్రదేశ్	ఆంధ్రప్రదేశ్	ANDHRA PRADESH
स्त्री	स्त्री	స్త్రీ	స్త్రీ	LADY
भार्या	भार्या	భార్య	భార్యా	WIFE
वृक्ष	वृक्षमु	వృక్షము	వృక్ష్	TREE
दृष्टि	दृष्टि	దృష్టి	దృష్టి	SIGHT
ज्वाला	ज्वाला	జ్వాలా	జ్వాలా	HIGH FLAME
न्यायाधीश	जड्जि	జడ్జి	న్యాయాధీశ్	JUDGE
न्याय	न्यायमु	న్యాయము	న్యాయ్	JUSTICE
भक्त	भक्तुडु	భక్తుడు	భక్త్	DEVOTEE
ज्योति	ज्योति	జ్యోతి	జ్యోతి	FLAME
चर्म	चर्ममु	చర్మము	చర్మ్	SKIN
शुध्दि	शुध्दि	శుద్ధి	శుద్ధి	CLEANING
मंत्रि	मंत्रि	మంత్రి	మంత్రి	MINISTER
खर्च	खर्चु	ఖర్చు	ఖర్చ్	SPENDING
राष्ट्रपति	राष्ट्रपति	రాష్ట్రపతి	రాష్ట్రపతి	PRESIDENT
वस्त्र	वस्त्रमु	వస్త్రము	వస్త్ర్	CLOTH
कीर्ति	कीर्ति	కీర్తి	కీర్తి	FAME
चक्र	चक्रमु	చక్రము	చక్ర్	WHEEL
संतुष्ठ	संत्रुप्ति	సంతృప్తి	సంతుష్ట్	SATISFACTION
लक्ष्मी	लक्षमी	లక్ష్మి	లక్ష్మీ	LAKSHMI
इंद्र	इंद्रडु	ఇంద్రుడు	ఇంద్ర్	INDRA
कृष्ण	कृष्णुडु	కృష్ణుడు	కృష్ణ్	KRISHNA
धृतराष्ट्र	धृतराष्ट्रडु	ధృతరాష్ట్రుడు	ధృతరాష్ట్ర్	DHRITRASTRA
वक्ता	वत्ता	వక్త	వక్తా	SPEAKER
अग्नि	अग्नि	అగ్ని	అగ్ని	FIRE
स्वतंत्र	स्वतंत्रमु	స్వతంత్రము	స్వతంత్ర్	FREE
सत्य	सत्यमु	సత్యము	సత్య్	TRUTH
मरम्मत	मरम्मत्तु	మరమ్మత్తు	మరమ్మత్	REPAIR

प्याज	वुल्लिपाया	వుల్లిపాయ	ప్యాజ్	ONION
ह्रस्व	ह्रस्वमु	హ్రస్వము	హ్రస్వ	SHORT
संस्कृत	संस्कृतमु	సంస్కృతము	సంస్కృత్	SANSKRIT
श्री	श्री	శ్రీ	శ్రీ	SRI
ब्रह्मा	ब्रह्मा	బ్రహ్మ	బ్రహ్మా	BRAHMA
योग्य	योग्यमु	యోగ్యము	యోగ్య	ELIGIBLE
अन्नपूर्णा	अन्नपूर्णा	అన్నపూర్ణ	అన్నపూర్ణ	ANNAPURNA

फल పండ్లు FRUITS

आम	मामिडि पंडु	మామిడిపండు	ఆమ్	MANGO
अमरूद	जामा पंडु	జామపండు	అమ్‌రూద్	GUAVA
अनार	दानिम्मा पंडु	దానిమ్మపండు	అనార్	POMEGRANATE
नारंगी/संतरा	कमला पंडु	కమలాపండు	నారంగీ/సంత్‌రా	ORANGE
अनानास	अनासा पंडु	అనాసపండు	అనాన్నస్	PINEAPPLE
अंगूर	द्राक्षा पंडु	ద్రాక్షపండు	అంగూర్	GRAPES
केला	अरटि पंडु	అరటిపండు	కేలా	BANANA
सेब	अपिल पंडु	ఆపిల్‌పండు	సేబ్	APPLE
चीकू	सपोटा पंडु	సపోటాపండు	చీకూ	SAPOTA
पपीता	बोप्पाइयि	బొప్పాయి	పపీతా	PAPAYA
जामुन	नेरेडु पंडु	నేరేడుపండు	జామూన్	BLACK-BERRY
बेर	रेगुपंडु	రేగుపండు	బేర్	INDIAN PLUM
कटहल कोवा	पनसा पंडु	పనసపండు	కట్‌హల్	JACK-FRUIT
खजूर	खर्जूर पंडु	ఖర్జూరపండు	ఖజూర్	DATES
ईख/गन्ना	चेरकु	చెరకు	గన్నా	SUGARCANE
सीताफल	सीताफलमु	సీతాఫలము	సీతాఫల్	CUSTARD-APPLE
चेरी	चेर्री पंडु	చెర్రీపండు	చెరీ	CHERRY
अंजीर	अत्तिपंडु	అత్తిపండు	అంజీర్	FIG
खूबानी	खूबानी	ఖూబాని	ఖూబాని	APRICOT
तरबूज	पुच्चाकाया	పుచ్చకాయ	తర్‌బూజ్	WATER-MELON
मौसंबी	बत्ताइ पंडु	బత్తాయిపండు	మౌసంబీ	SWEET-LIME
नासपाती	सीमरैगु	సీమరేగు	నాస్‌పతీ	PEAR

फूल | పూవులు/పుష్పములు | FLOWERS

कमल	तामर पुव्वु	తామర పువ్వు	కమల్	LOTUS
गुलाब	गुलाबी पुव्वु	గులాబి పువ్వు	గులాబ్	ROSE
गुडहल	मंदरा पुव्वु	మందార పువ్వు	గుడ్‌హల్	HIBISCUS
चमेली	मल्ले पुव्वु	మల్లె పువ్వు	చమేలీ	JASMINE
बेली	नंदिवर्दनमु	నందివర్ధనము	బేలీ	CRAPE JASMINE
रजनीगंधा	लिल्ली पुव्वु	లిల్లీ పువ్వు	రజనీగంద్	LILLY
चंपा	देवगन्नेरु	దేవగన్నేరు	చంపా	MAGNOLIA
सुरजमुखी	प्रोद्दुतिरूगुडु पुव्वु	ప్రొద్దుతిరుగుడు పువ్వు	సురజ్‌ముఖీ	SUN FLOWER
जूही	सन्नाजाजी	సన్నజాజి	జూహీ	STAR JASMINE
गेंदा	बन्ति पुव्वु	బంతి పువ్వు	గేందా	MARIGOLD
कंद पुष्प	ट्यूलिप	ట్యూలిప్	కంద్ పుష్ప్	TULIP
कनेर	गन्नेरु पुव्वु	గన్నేరు	కనేర్	NERIUM
सदा बहार	बिल्लागन्नेरु	బిళ్ళ గన్నేరు	సదా బహార్	PERIWINKLE
केवड़ा	मोगलि पुव्वु	మొగలి పువ్వు	కేవడా	KEWRA

रंग రంగులు COLOURS

लाल	एरुपु	ఎరుపు	లాల్	RED
पीला	पसुपु	పసుపు	పీలా	YELLOW
हरा	आकुपच्चा	ఆకుపచ్చ	హరా	GREEN
नीला	नीलमु	నీలము	నీలా	BLUE
गुलाबी	गुलाबी रंगु	గులాబి రంగు	గులాబి	PINK
सफेद	तेलुपु	తెలుపు	సఫేద్	WHITE
काला	नलुपु	నలుపు	కాలా	BLACK
आसमानी	आकाश वर्णमु	ఆకాశవర్ణము	ఆస్మానీ	INDIGO
केसरिया/नारंगी	काषाया रंगु	కాషాయ రంగు	నారంగి	SAFFRON
बैंगनी	ऊदा रंगु	ఊదారంగు	బైంగనీ	PURPLE/VIOLET
भूरा/गेहुंआ	गोधुमा रंगु	గోధుమ రంగు	భూరా	BROWN
सुनहरा	बंगारु रंगु	బంగారురంగు	సున్‌హరా	GOLDEN
सांवला	चामनछाया	చామనఛాయ	సావ్‌లా	WHEATISH
चमकीला	प्रकाशवंतमैना	ప్రకాశవంతమైన	చమ్‌కీలా	BRIGHT
धुंघला	मसका	మసక	దుంధ్‌లా	DIM
केसर	काषाय रंगु	కాషాయరంగు	కేసర్	SAFFRON

सब्जियाँ   కాయగూరలు   VEGETABLES

आलू	बंगालदुंपा	బంగాళదుంప	ఆలూ	POTATO
प्याज	उल्लिपाय	ఉల్లిపాయ	ప్యాజ్	ONION
टमाटर	टमाटा	టమాట	టమాటర్	TOMATO
भिंडी	बेंडकाया	బెండకాయ	భిండీ	LADY FINGER
गाजर	केरेट	క్యారట్	గాజర్	CARROT
बरबट्टी	बरबाटि	బర్‌బాటీ	బర్‌బట్టీ	STING BEANS
परवल	पोटल्स	పోటల్స్	పరవత్	POINTED GOURD
नेनुआ	नेतबीरकाया	బీరకాయ	నేనూవా	RIDGE GOURD
सेम	चिक्कुडुकाया	చిక్కుడుకాయ	సేమ్	BEANS
सहजन/मुनगा	मुनागकाया	మునగకాయ	సహ్‌జన్/ మునగా	DRUMSTICK
करेला	काकरकाया	కాకరకాయ	కరేలా	BITTERGOURD
केला	अरटिकाया	అరటికాయ	కేలా	RAWBANANA
फूलगोभी	कालीफ्लावर	కాలీఫ్లవర్	ఫూల్‌గోభీ	CAULIFLOWER
पत्तागोभी	केबेजी	కేబేజ్	పత్తాగోభీ	CABBAGE
कुम्हडा/कद्दू	गुम्मडिकाय	గుమ్మడికాయ	కుహాడా/కద్దూ	PUMPKIN
लौकी	आनपकाय	ఆనపకాయ	లౌకీ	BOTTLE GOURD
गवार फली	गोरुचिक्कुडुकाया	గోరుచిక్కుడుకాయ	గవార్‌ఫలీ	CLUSTER BEANS
शलगम	एर्र मुल्लंगि	ఎర్రముల్లంగి	షల్‌గమ్	TURNIP
कुन्दुरू	दोंडकाया	దొండకాయ	కుందురు	TINDOORA/ GHERKINS
हरिमिर्च	पच्चिमिरपकाया	పచ్చిమిరపకాయ	హరీమిర్చ్	GREEN CHILLI
नारियल	कोब्बारिकाया	కొబ్బరికాయ	నారియల్	COCONUT
बैंगन	वंकाया	వంకాయ	బైంగన్	BRINJAL
मटर	बठानिलु	బఠాణీలు	మటర్	PEAS
शिमला मिर्च	बेंगुलूरु मिरपकाया	బెంగుళూరు మిరపకాయ	సిమ్లామిర్చ్	CAPSICUM
लहसून	वेल्लुल्लि	వెల్లులి	లహ్‌సూన్	GARLIC
नींबू	निम्मकाया	నిమ్మకాయ	నీంబూ	LEMON
फ्रेंच बीन	फ्रेंच बीन्सु	ఫ్రంచ్ బీన్సు	ఫ్రెంచ్‌బీన్స్	FRENCH BEANS
चिचिंदा	पोट्लाकाया	పొట్లకాయ	చిచిందా	SNAKE GOURD
पेक्ची	चेंमदुम्पा	చేమదుంప	పేక్చీ	COLOCASIAROOT

मशरूम/ खुखड़ी	पुट्टागोडुगु	పుట్టగొడుగు	మష్‌రూమ్/ఖుఖుడీ	MUSHROOMS
अदरक	अल्लमु	అల్లము	అదరక్	GINGER
ककड़ी	दोसकाया	దోసకాయ	కకడీ	ARMENIAN CUCUMBER
खीरा	कीरादोसकाया	కీర దోసకాయ	ఖీరా	CUCUMBER
मूली	मुल्लंगि	ముల్లంగి	మూలీ	RADISH
तुई/तुराई/झिंगी	बीराकाया	బీరకాయ	తురయీ	RIDGE GOURD
शकरकंद	चिलकडादुंपा	చిలకడదుంప	శకర్‌కంద్	SWEET POTATO
हराप्याज	वुल्लिकाडलु	వుల్లికాడలు	హరాప్యాజ	SPING ONIONS

साग		ఆకుకూరలు		LEAFY VEGETABLES
पालक	पालाकूरा	పాలకూర	పాలక్	SPINACH
मेथी	मेंतिकूरा	మెంతికూర	మెథీ	FENUGREEK
धनिया पत्ति	कोत्तिमीरा	కొత్తిమీర	ధనియాపత్తి	CORIANDER
लकड़ा	गोंगूरा	గోంగూరలక్డ		SORREL
तुलसी	तुलसि	తులసీ	తులసి	BASIL
मनहारीभाजी	तोटकूरा	తోటకూర	మన్హారీభాజీ	AMARANATH LEAVES
पुदीना	पुदीना	పుదీనా	పుదీనా	MINT LEAVES
सरसों का साग	आव आकुलु	ఆవఆకులు	సరసోంకాసాగ్	MUSTARD LEAVES
कड़ी पत्ता	करिवेपाकु	కరివేపాకు	కడీపత్తా	CURRY LEAVES

अंगो के नाम　　శరీర భాగములు　　PARTS OF BODY

शरीर	शरीरमु	శరీరము	శరీర్	BODY
बाल	जुट्टु	జుట్టు	బాల్	HAIR
सिर	तला	తల	శిర్	HEAD
माथा/ललाट	नुदुरु	నుదురు	మాథా/లలాట్	FOREHEAD
भौहं	कनुबोम्मलु	కనుబొమ్మలు	భౌహ్	EYEBROWS
आँख	कल्लु	కళ్లు	ఆంఖ్	EYES
पलक	कनुरेप्पा	కనురెప్ప	పలక్	EYELID
नाक	मुक्कु	ముక్కు	నాక్	NOSE
नाखून	गोरु	గోరు	నాఖూన్	NAIL
गाल	बुग्गा	బుగ్గ	గాల్	CHEEK
कान	चेवुलु	చెవులు	కాన్	EARS
ठोढ़ी	चुबुकमु	చుబుకము	ఠోఢీ	CHIN
मुँह	नोरु	నోరు	ముహ్	MOUTH
दाँत	पल्लु	పళ్లు	దాంత్	TEETH
होंठ	पेदवुलु	పెదవులు	హోంఠ్	LIPS
कोहनी	मोचेइ	మోచేయి	కోహ్నీ	ELBOW
जीभ	नालुका	నాలుక	జీభ్	TONGUE
मूँछ	मीसालु	మీసాలు	మూఛ్	MOUSTACHE
दाढ़ी	गड्डमु	గడ్డం	దాఢీ	BEARD
टांग	कालु	కాలు	టాంగ్	LEG
मसूढ़ा	चिगुल्लु	చిగుళ్ళు	మసూఢా	GUMS
गला	कंठम	కంఠము	గలా	THROAT
गर्दन	मेडा	మెడ	గర్దన్	NECK
खोपड़ी	कपालमु	కపాలము	ఖోపడీ	SKULL
कंधा	भुजमु	భుజము	కంధా	SHOULDER
बाँह	चेतुलु	చేతులు	బాహ్	ARMS
कलाई	मणिकट्टु	మణికట్టు	కలాఈ	WRIST

हाथ	चेइ	చేయి	హాథ్	HAND
उँगली	वेलु	వేలు	ఉంగ్‌లీ	FINGER
अँगूठा	बोटनवेलु	బొటనవేలు	అంగూఠా	THUMB
हथेली	हस्तमु	హస్తము	హథేలీ	PALM
छाती	छाती	ఛాతీ	ఛాతీ	CHEST
नाभि	बोड्डु	బొడ్డు	నాభి	NAVEL
हृदय	गुंडे	గుండె	హృదయ్	HEART
पेट	कडुपु	కడుపు	పేట్	STOMACH
पीठ	वीपु	వీపు	పీఠ్	BACK
कमर	नडुमु	నడుము	కమర్	WAIST
नितम्बं	पिरुदुलु	పిరుదులు	నితంబ్	BUTTOCKS
कूल्हा	पिर्र	పిర్ర	కూల్హా	HIP
जाँघ	तोडा	తొడ	జాంఘ్	THIGH
घुटना	मोकालु	మోకాలు	ఘుటనా	KNEE
पैर	पादमु	పాదము	పైర్	FOOT
एड़ी	मडमा	మడమ	ఎడీ	HEEL
तलवा	अरिकालु	అరికాలు	తల్‌వా	SOLE
गुर्दा	मूत्रपिंडमु	మూత్రపిండము	గుర్దా	KIDNEY
आँत	प्रेगु	ప్రేగు	ఆంత్	INTESTINE
तिल	पुट्टुमच्चा	పుట్టుమచ్చ	తిల్	MOLE
हड्डी	एमुका	ఎముక	హడ్డీ	BONE
मांस	मांसमु	మాంసము	మాంస్	FLESH
नस	नरमु	నరము	నస్	VEIN
खून/रक्त	रक्तमु	రక్తము	ఖూన్	BLOOD
पसली	प्रक्कटेमुका	ప్రక్కటెముక	పస్‌లీ	RIB
मल	मलमु	మలము	మల్	BOWEL
मूत्र	मुत्रमु	మూత్రము	మూత్ర	URINE
वीर्य	वीर्यमु	వీర్యము	వీర్య్	SEMEN
जोड	कीलु	కీలు	జోడ్	JOINT
स्तन	स्तनमु	స్తనము	స్తన్	BREAST
पैर की उंगली	कालिवेलु	కాలివేళ్లు	పైర్‌కీ వుంగలీ	TOES

नथुना	नसिकारंध्रमु	నాసికారంధ్రము	నథునా	NOSTRIL
सींग	कोम्मु	కొమ్ము	సీంగ్	HORN
पूंछ	तोका	తోక	పూంఛ్	TAIL
शिश्न	पुरुषांगमु	పురుషాంగము	శిశ్న్	PENIS
योनि	जननांगमु	జననాంగము	యోని	VAGINA
गुदा	गुदमु	గుదము	గుదా	ANUS
अनामिका	उंगरपु वेलु	ఉంగరపువేలు	అనామిక	RING-FINGER
काँख	चंका	చంక	కాంఖ్	ARM-PIT
गोद	ओडि	ఒడి	గోద్	LAP
त्वचा/चमडा/खाल	चर्ममु	చర్మము	త్వచా, చమ్డా	SKIN
चूचुक	चूचुकमु	చూచుకము	చూచుక్	NIPPLE
जिगर	कालेयमु	కాలేయము	జిగర్	LIVER
मुट्ठी	पिडिकिलि	పిడికిలి	ముట్ఠీ	FIST
टखना	चीलमंडा	చీలమండ	టఖనా	ANKLE
जबड़ा	दवडा	దవడ	జబ్డా	JAW

पेड़-पौधे　　చెట్లు-మొక్కలు　　TREES-PLANTS

आम	मामिडिपंडु	మామిడిపండు	ఆమ్	MANGO
जामुन	नेरेडुपंडु	నేరేడుపండు	జాముున్	LACK BERRY
कटहल	पनस	పనస	కట్‌హల్	JACK FRUIT
बबूल	नल्लतुम्मा	నల్లతుమ్మ	బబూల్	BABOOL
नीम	वेप	వేప	నీమ్	NEEM
सागौन	टेकु	టేకు	సాగౌన్	TEAK
बरगद	मर्रि	మర్రి	బర్‌గద్	BANYAN
बेल	मारेडु	మారేడు	బేల్	BAEL
अमरूद	जामा	జామ	అమ్‌రూద్	GUAVA
अंजीर	अंजीरा	అంజీర	అంజీర్	FIG
चीकू	सपोटा	సపోట	చీకూ	SAPODILLA
कचनार	देवकांचनम्	దేవకాంచనం	కచ్‌నార్	BAUHINIA
महुआ	विप्पा	విప్ప	మహువా	MAHUA
कनेर	बिल्लगन्नेरू	బిళ్లగన్నేరు	కనేర్	OLEANDER
बेर	रेगु	రేగు	బేర్	JUJUBE
नारियल	कोब्बरि	కొబ్బరి	నారియల్	COCONUT
मेहंदी	गोरिंटाकु	గోరింటాకు	మేహందీ	HENNA
सेम	चिक्कुडु	చిక్కుడు	సేమ్	BEANS
बरबट्टी	बरबाटी	బర్‌బాటీ	బర్‌బట్టీ	LONGYARDBEANS
गुलाब	गुलाबी	గులాబీ	గులాబ్	ROSE
गुडहल	मंदारा	మందార	గుడ్‌హల్	HIBISCUS
ताड़	ताटिचेट्टु	తాటిచెట్టు	తాడ్	PALM TREE

जानवर		జంతువులు		ANIMALS
मछली	चेपा	చేప	మఛిలీ	FISH
मगरमच्छ	मोसलि	మొసలి	మగర్‌మచ్ఛ్	CROCODILE
केकड़ा	पीता	పీత	కేకడా	CRAB
कछुआ	ताबेलु	తాబేలు	కఛువా	TORTOISE
घोंघा	नत्ता	నత్త	ఘోంఘా	SNAIL
कुत्ता	कुक्का	కుక్క	కుత్తా	DOG
खरगोश	कुंदेलु	కుందేలు	ఖర్‌గోశ్	RABBIT
गिलहरी	उडुता	ఉడుత	గిల్‌హరీ	SQUIRREL
गाय	आवु	ఆవు	గాయ్	COW
घोड़ा	गुर्रमु	గుర్రము	ఘోడా	HORSE
बैल	एद्दु	ఎద్దు	బైల్	OX
चीता	चिरुता	చిరుత	చీతా	LEOPARD
चूहा	एलुका	ఎలుక	చూహా	RAT
ऊँट	ओंटे	ఒంటె	వూంట్	CAMEL
हाथी	एनुगु	ఏనుగు	హాథీ	ELEPHANT
नेवला	मुंगीसा	ముంగిస	నేవ్‌లా	MANGOOSE
सुअर	पंदि	పంది	సువర్	PIG
शेर	सिंहमु	సింహము	షేర్	LION
हिरण	लेडि	లేడి	హిరణ్	DEER
सांड	वृषभमु	వృషభము	సాంఢ్	BULL
भेड़िया	गोर्रेलु	గొర్రెలు	భేడియా	SHEEP
भालू	एलुगुबंटि	ఎలుగుబంటి	భాలూ	BEAR
भैंस	गेदे	గేదె	భైంస్	BUFFALO
बछड़ा	दूडा	దూడ	బఛ్‌డా	CALF
बिल्ली	पिल्लि	పిల్లి	బిల్లీ	CAT

बकरा	मेका	మేక	బకరా	GOAT
बंदर	कोति	కోతి	బందర్	MONKEY
बाघ	पुलि	పులి	బాఘ్	TIGER
पिल्ला	कुक्का पिल्ला	కుక్కపిల్ల	పిల్లా	PUPPY
छिपकली	बल्लि	బల్లి	ఛిప్‌కలీ	LIZARD
सांप	पामु	పాము	సాంప్	SNAKE
बिच्छू	तेलु	తేలు	బిచ్ఛూ	SCORPION
गधा	गाडिदा	గాడిద	గధా	ASS
गेंडा	खड्ग़मृग़म	ఖడ్గమృగము	గేండా	RHENOCEROS

चिडिया-पक्षी		పక్షులు		BIRDS
कबूतर	पावुरमु	పావురము	కబూతర్	PIGEON
कौवा-कौआ	काकि	కాకి	కౌవా	CROW
तोता	चिलुका	చిలుక	తోతా	PARROT
मैना	मैना	మైనా	మైనా	MAINA
हंस	हंसा	హంస	హంస్	SWAN
बत्तख/बगुला	बातु	బాతు	బత్తఖ్	DUCK
गीद्ध	राबंदु	రాబందు	గీద్ధ	VULTURE
गौरैया	पिच्चुका	పిచ్చుక	గౌరైయా	SPARROW
मुर्गी	कोडी	కోడి	ముర్గీ	HEN
मोर	नेमली	నెమలి	మోర్	PEACOCK
मुर्गा	कोडिपुंजु	కోడిపుంజు	ముర్గా	COCK
मक्खी	ईगा	ఈగ	మక్ఖీ	FLY
मच्छर	दोमा	దోమ	మచ్ఛర్	MOSQUITO
सारस	कोंगा	కొంగ	సారస్	CRANE
पक्षी	पक्षी	పక్షి	పక్షి	BIRD
उल्लू	गुड्लगूबा	గుడ్లగూబ	ఉల్లూ	OWL
चमागादड़	गब्बिलमु	గబ్బిలము	చమ్‌గాదడ్	BAT
कोयल	कोयिला	కోయిల	కోయల్	SWALLOW
बगुला	कोंगा	కొంగ	బగులా	HERON

अनाज व अन्य खाद्य पदार्थ ధాన్యములు-చిరుధాన్యములు FOOD-GRAIN

धान	धन्यमु	ధాన్యము	ధాన్	GRAIN
चावल	बिय्यमु	బియ్యము	చావల్	RICE
दाल	पप्पू	పప్పు	దాల్	PULSES
लोबिया	बोब्बर्लु	బొబ్బర్లు	లోబియా	LOBIA
ज्वार	झोन्नलु	జొన్నలు	జ్వార్	SORGHUM
बाजरा	सज्ञलु	సజ్జలు	బాజ్‌రా	PEARLMILLET
मूंग	पेसलु	పెసలు	మూంగ్	GREEN GRAM
चना	**सेनग़लू**	శెనగలు	చనా	BENGAL GRAM
राई	आवालु	ఆవాలు	రాయీ	MUSTARD
सरसों	आवालु	ఆవాలు	సరసోం	MUSTARD
तिल	नुव्वुलु	నువ్వులు	తిల్	SESAME SEEDS
मटर	बठाणीलु	బఠాణీలు	మటర్	PEAS
गेहूँ	गोधुमलु	గోధుమలు	గేహు	WHEAT
उरद	मिनप्पप्पु	మినపప్పు	వురద్	BLACK GRAM
अरहर/रहर	कंदिपप्पु	కందిపప్పు	రాహర్	TOORDAL
मसूर	एर्रकंदिपप्पु	ఎర్ర కందిపప్పు	మసూర్	MASOORDAL
मूँगफली	वेरूसेनगपप्पु	వేరుశెనగపప్పు	మూంగ్‌ఫలీ	GROUND NUT
बादाम	बादहमपप्पु	బాదంపప్పు	బాదామ్	ALMOND
सोयाबीन	सोयाबीन्सु	సోయాబీన్సు	సోయాబీన్	SOYABEANS
धनियाँ	धनियालु	ధనియాలు	ధనియా	CORIANDER
गुड़	बेल्लमु	బెల్లము	గుడ్	JAGGERY
कालीमिर्च	मिरियालु	మిరియాలు	కాలీమిర్చ్	PEPPER
जीरा	जीलकर्रा	జీలకర్ర	జీరా	CUMIN
मेथी	मेंतुलु	మెంతులు	మేథీ	FENUGREEK SEEDS
लौंग	लवंगालु	లవంగాలు	లౌంగ్	CLOVES

इलाइची	यालकुलु	యాలకులు	ఇలాయిాచీ/ఇలాఇచి	CARDAMOM
दालचीनी	दालचिनाचेक्का	దాల్చినచెక్క	దాల్‌చినీ	CINNAMON
इमली	चिंतपंडु	చింతపండు	ఇమలీ	TAMARIND
नारियल	कोब्बरिकाया	కొబ్బరికాయ	నారియల్	COCONUT
मिट्टीतेल	किरसनायलु	కిరసనాయలు	మిట్టీతేల్	KEROSENE
रीठा	कुंकुंडिकायलु	కుంకుడుకాయలు	రీఠా	SOAPNUTS
अचार	ऊरागाया	ఊరగాయ	అచార్	PICKLE
आटा	गोदुमपिंडि	గోధుమపిండి	ఆటా	WHEAT FLOUR
बेसन	सनगपिंडि	శనగపిండి	బేసన్	BENGALGRAM FLOUR
मैदा	मइदा	మైదా	మైదా	MAIDA
सूजी	गोधुमरव्वा	గోధుమరవ్వ	సుజీ	SEMOLIN
अंडा	गुड्डु	గుడ్డు	అండా	EGG
चाय	तेनीरू	తేనీరు	చాయ్	TEA
कॉफी	काफी	కాఫీ	కాఫీ	COFFEE
चटनी	चटनी	చట్నీ	చటనీ	CHUTNEY
तेल	नूने	నూనె	తేల్	OIL
दही	पेरुगु	పెరుగు	దహీ	CURD
दूध	पालु	పాలు	దూధ్	MILK
मट्ठा	मज्जिगा	మజ్జిగ	మట్టా	BUTTERMILK
घी	नेय्यि	నెయ్యి	ఘీ	CLARIFIED BUTTER
नमक	उप्पु	ఉప్పు	నమక్	SALT
चीनी	पंचदारा	పంచదార	చీనీ	SUGAR
पानी	नीरु	నీరు	పానీ	WATER
मक्खन	वेन्ना	వెన్న	మక్ఖన్	BUTTER
सांभर	सांबार	సాంబార్	సాంభార్	SAMBAR
रोटी	रोट्टे	రొట్టె	రోటి	ROTI
सब्जी	कूरा	కూర	సబ్జీ	CURRY
मांस	मांसमु	మాంసము	మాంస్	MEAT
चिप्स	चिप्स	చిప్స్	చిప్స్	CHIPS

पापड	अप्पडम्	అప్పడం	పాపడ్	PAPAD
दाल	पप्पु	పప్పు	దాల్	DAL
सरबत	षरबत	షర్బత్	సర్‌బత్	SHERBAT
लस्सी	लस्सी	లస్సీ	లస్సీ	LASSI
ठंडई	ठंड़ई	ఠండఈ	ఠండాఈ	THANDAI
भांग	भंगु	భంగు	భాంగ్	CANNAABIS
समोसा	समोसा	సమోసా	సమోసా	SAMOSA
आलूचाप	आलुबोंडा	ఆలూబోండా	ఆలూచాప్	ALUBONDA
रसगुल्ला	रसगुल्ला	రసగుల్లా	రస్‌గుల్లా	RASGOLLA
पेडा	कोवा	పేడా	కోవా	KHOVA
बरफी	बरफी	బర్ఫీ	బర్ఫీ	BURFI
निमकी	मुरुकुलु	మురుకులు	నిమ్‌కీ	SAVORY
झरुआ/सेव	कारप्पूसा	కారప్పూస	ఝురువా-సేవ్	SEV
दही वड़ा	पेरगुगारे	దహీవడా పెరుగుగారె		DAHIVADA
गुलाब जामुन	गुलाबजामुन	గులాబ్ జామున్	గులాబ్ జామున్	GULABJAMUN
कलाकंद	कलाकंद	కలాకండ్	కలాకంద్	KALAKAND
लड्डू	लड्डु	లడ్డు	లడ్డు	LADOO
चिक्की	अच्चु	అచ్చు	చిక్కీ	CHIKKI
चकली	चक्कीलालु	చక్కిలాలు	చకలీ	MURUKUL
सौंफ	सोपु	సోపు	సౌంఫ్	ANISEEDS
पान	किल्ली	కిళ్లీ	పాన్	PAAN
कसैली	वक्का	వక్క	కసైలీ	BEETLENUT
चटनी	पच्चडि/चट्नी	పచ్చడి	చటనీ	SAUCE
चुड़ा/पोहा	अटुकुलु	అటుకులు	చుడా-పోహా	BEATENRICE
मैदा	मैदापिंडि	మైదాపిండి	మైదా	REFINDFLOUR

पेशा/रोजगार		వృత్తులు/పనులు		PROFESSIONS/
अभियंता	इंजनीयर	ఇంజనీరు	అభియంత	ENGINEER
अधिवक्ता/वकील	वकीलु	వకీలు	అధివక్తా/వకీల్	LAWYER
शिक्षक	अध्यापकुडु	అధ్యాపకుడు	శిక్షక్	TEACHER
सैनिक	सैनिकुडु	సైనికుడు	సైనిక్	SOLDIER
कर्मचारी	कार्मिकुडु	కార్మికుడు	కర్మచారీ	WORKER
व्यपारी	व्यापारी	వ్యాపారి	వ్యాపారీ	BUSINESSMAN
दुकानदार	दुकानदारुडु	దుకాణదారుడు	దుకాణ్‌దార్	SHOPKEEPER
धोबी	चाकलि	చాకలి	ధోభీ	WASHERMAN
बहेलिया	वेटागाडु	వేటగాడు	బహేలియా	HUNTER
कुम्हार	कुम्मारि	కుమ్మరి	కుమ్‌హర్	POTTER
बढ़ाई	वड्रंगि	వడ్రంగి	బఢయీ	CARPENTER
सुनार	कंसालि	కంసాలి	సునార్	GOLDSMITH
चमार	चर्मकारुडु	చర్మకారుడు	చమార్	COBBLER
रसोइया	वंटवाडु	వంటవాడు	రసోఇయా	COOK
लेखक	रचयिता	రచయిత	లేఖక్	WRITER
कवि	कवि	కవి	కవి	POET
नौकर	पनिवाडु	పనివాడు	నౌకర్	SERVENT
पटवारी	पटवारी	పట్వారి	పట్‌వారీ	PATVARI
दर्जी	टैलरु	టైలరు	దర్జీ	TAILOR
तेली	तेलुकलवाडु	తెలుకలవాడు	తేలీ	OIL-MAN
नाई	मंगलि	మంగలి	నాయీ	BARBER
कुली	कूली	కూలీ	కూలీ	COOLIE
हकीम	वैद्युडु	వైద్యుడు	హకీమ్	DOCTOR
जुलाहा	सालेवाडु	సాలెవాడు	జులాహీ	WEAVER
राज मेस्त्री	मेस्त्री	మేస్త్రీరాజ్	మేస్త్రీ	MASON
खरीददार	कोनुगोलुदारूडु	కొనుగోలుదారుడు	ఖరీద్‌దార్	BUYER
आयात	दिगुमति	దిగుమతి	ఆయాత్	IMPORT
निर्यात	एगुमति	ఎగుమతి	నిర్యాత్	EXPORT
मेहतर	ऊड्चेवाडु	ఊడ్చేవాడు	స్వీపర్	SWEEPER
कामवाली	पनिमनिषि	పనిమనిషి	కామ్‌వాలీ	SERVANT MAID
फुग्गावाला	बेन्लुअम्मेवाडु	బెలూన్లుఅమ్మేవాడు	ఫుగ్గావాలా	BALLON SELLER

फलवाला	पंड्लुअम्मेवाडु	పండ్లుఅమ్మేవాడు	ఫల్‌వాలా	FRUIT SELLER
मलहोरी/फुलवाला	फुलविक्रेता	పూలవిక్రేత	మలహోరి/ఫూల్‌వాలా	FLOWER SELLER
ग्वाला	पालवाडु	పాలవాడు	గ్వాలా	MILK MAN
डाकू	दोपिडिदारु	దోపిడిదారు	డాకూ	DECOIT
चोर	दोंगा	దొంగ	చోర్	THIEF
जादूगर	इंद्रजालिकुडु	ఇంద్రజాలికుడు	జాదూగర్	MAGICIAN
लिपिक/बाबु	गुमस्ता	గుమస్తా	లిపిక్/బాబూ	CLERK
चपरासी	बंट्रोतु	బంట్రోతు	చప్‌రాసీ	PEON
चिकित्सक	वैद्युडु/डाक्टरु	వైద్యుడు/డాక్టరు	వైద్య్	DOCTOR
पहरेदार	कापलादारु	కాపలదారు	పహేరేదార్	WATCHMAN

मनोभाव		మనోభావాలు		FEELINGS
हँसना	नव्वुटा	నవ్వుట	హస్నా	TO LAUGH
रोना	एड्वुटा	ఏడ్చుట	రోనా	TO CRY
प्रेम	प्रेमा	ప్రేమ	ప్రేమ్	LOVE
धोखा	मोसमु	మోసము	ధోఖా	DECEPTION
उदास	उदासिनमु	ఉదాసీనము	ఉదాస్	DEJECTED
शांत	निश्शब्दम्	నిశ్శబ్దము	శాంత్	QUIET
शोर	शब्दम्	శబ్దము	షోర్	NOISE
आशा	अशाभावमु	ఆశాభావం	ఆశా	HOPEFUL
निराशा	निराशा	నిరాశ	నిరాశా	DESPAIR
दुखी	बाधा	బాధ	దుఖీ	SAD
सुख	सुखमु	సుఖము	సుఖ్	HAPPINESS
शोक	दुखमु	దుఖము	శోక్	MOURNING
लालच	अत्याशा	అత్యాశ	లాలచ్	GREED
दया	दया	దయ	దయా	KINDNESS
कोमलता	सुनितत्वम्	సున్నితత్వము	కోమలతా	SOFTNESS
डर-भय	भयमु	భయము	భయ్	FEAR
संतोष	संतोषमु	సంతోషము	సంతోష్	HAPPY
हिम्मत/साहस	धैर्यमु	ధైర్యము	హిమ్మత్	BRAVE
वेग	वेगमु	వేగము	వేగ్	SPEED
मित्रता/दोस्ती	स्नेहमु	స్నేహము	దోస్తీ	FRIENDLY
चिढ़चिढ़ाना	चिकाकु	చికాకు	చిడ్‌చిడానా	IRRITATION
खुशी/आनंद	आनंदमु	ఆనందము	ఖుషీ/ఆనంద్	HAPPY
अनुमान	वूहा	ఊహ	అనుమాన్	GUESS
हलचल	गोडवा	గొడవ	హల్‌చల్	STIR
खामोश	मौनम्	మౌనం	ఖామోష్	SILENT
आशंका/संदेह	अनुमानमु	అనుమానము	ఆశంకా	DOUBTFUL
घृणा/नफरत	द्वेषमु	ద్వేషము	నఫ్రత్	HATRED

गुमसुम/चुपचाप	निशब्द	నిశ్శబ్దం	చుప్‌చాప్	SILENT
विचार	आलोचना	ఆలోచన	విచార్	THOUGHT
गंभीर	गंभीरमु	గంభీరము	గంభీర్	SERIOUS
व्याकुल	व्याकुलता	వ్యాకులత	వ్యాకుల్	DISTRAUGHT
प्रसन्नचित	संतुष्टि	సంతుష్టి	ప్రసన్నచిత్	CONTENTED
निर्दयता	क्रूरम्	క్రూరం	నిర్దయతా	UNKIND
निराश	निराश	నిరాశ	నిరాశ్	DISAPPOINTED
आवाज	ध्वनि	ధ్వని	ఆవాజ్	SOUND
गुस्सा	कोपमु	కోపము	గుస్సా	FEDUP/ANGER
जलन	असूया	అసూయ	జలన్	ENVY
उत्सुक	जिज्ञास	జిజ్ఞాస	ఉత్సుక్	CURIOUS
गर्वित	गर्वमु	గర్వము	గర్విత్	PROUD
समझदार	विवेकमु	వివేకము	సమఝ్‌దార్	SENSIBLE
परेशान	कलता	కలత	పరేషాన్	UPSET
अकेला	वंटारितनमु	వంటరితనము	అకేలా	LONELY
सावाधान	जाग्रता	జాగ్రత్త	సావధాన్	CAREFUL
निष्पक्ष	निष्पक्षापातमु	నిష్పక్షపాతము	నిష్పక్ష్	FAIR/IMPARTIAL
निर्दोष	निर्दोषि	నిర్ధోషి	నిర్ధోష్	INNOCENT
नाराज	क्रोधमु	క్రోధము	నారాజ్	ANNOYED
असहाय	असहायता	అసహయత	అసహయ్	HELPLESS
पागल	पिच्चि	పిచ్చి	పాగల్	MAD
हैरान	हैराना	హైరానా	హైరాన్	SHOCKED
बुरा	चेड्डु	చెడు	బురా	NASTY
दोषी	दोषि	దోషి	దోషి	GUILTY
थकान	अलसटा	అలసట	థకాన్	TIRED
आशावादी	अशावादि	ఆశావాది	ఆశావాదీ	OPTMISTIC

रिश्तेदार   బంధువులు   RELATIVES

माँ	अम्मा	అమ్మ	మా	MOTHER
नानी	अम्मम्मा	అమ్మమ్మ	నానీ	GRAND MOTHER
पापा	नान्ना	నాన్న	పాపా	FATHER
बेटी	अम्मायि	అమ్మాయి	బేటీ	DAUGHTER
बेटा	कोडुकु	కొడుకు	బేటా	SON
नाना/दादा	तातय्या	తాతయ్య	నానా/దాదా	GRAND FATHER
दादी	नानम्मा	నానమ్మ	దాదీ	PATEMALGRANDMOTHER
नाती/पोता	मनवडु	మనవడు	నాతీ/పోతా	GRAND SON
बहू	कोडलु	కోడలు	బహు	DAUGHTER-IN-LAW
जीजाजी	बावगारु	బావగారు	జీజాజీ	BROTHER-IN-LAW
मामा	मावय्या	మావయ్య	మామా	UNCLE
भतीजा	मेनल्लुडु	మేనల్లుడు	భతీజా	NEPHEW(MOTHER'S SON)
बुआ	मेनत्ता	మేనత్త	బువా	AUNT(FATHER'S SISTER)
फूफा	मेनमामा	మేనమామ	ఫుఫా	UNCLE(FATHER'S BROTHER)
मौसा/चाचा	चिन्नाना	చిన్నాన్న	చాచా	UNCLE(FATHER'S BROTHER)
मौसी/चाची	पिन्नि	పిన్ని	చాచీ	AUNT(MOTHER'S SISTER)
बडे पापा	पेदानान्ना	పెదనాన్న	బడే పాప	UNCLE/ FATHERS ELDER BROTHER
बडी मां	पेद्दम्मा	పెద్దమ్మ	బడీ మా	AUNT
भैया	अन्नय्या	అన్నయ్య	భైయ్యా	ELDER BROTHER
बहन	चेल्लि	చెల్లి	బహన్	YOUNGER SISTER
दीदी	अक्का	అక్క	దీదీ	ELDER SISTER
भांजा	मेनल्लुडु	మేనల్లుడు	భాంజా	NEPHEW(SISTER'S SON)
भाभी	वदिना	వదిన	భాభీ	SISTER-IN-LAW(BROTHER'S WIFE)
सास	अत्ताय्या	అత్తయ్య	సాస్	MOTHER-IN-LAW
दामाद	अल्लुडु	అల్లుడు	దామాద్	SON-IN-LAW
साला/देवर	मरिदी	మరిది	దేవర్	HUSBANDS YOUNGER BROTHER
साली/देवरानी	मरदलु	మరదలు	దేవ్‌రానీ	HUSBAND'S WIFE
जेठ	बावगारु	బావగారు	జేఠ్	HUSBANDS ELDER BROTHER
जेठानी	तोडिकोडलु	తోడికోడలు	జేఠానీ	HUSBANDS BROTHERS WIFE
ससुर	मावय्या	మావయ్య	ససుర్	HUSBANDS FATHER-IN-LAW
ननद	आडपडुचु	ఆడపడుచు	ననద్	HUSBANDS SISTER-IN-LAW

बच्ची	आडपिल्ला	ఆడపిల్ల	బచ్చీ	GIRL CHILD
बगलवाली	पक्काइंटीवारु	పక్కఇంటివారు	బగల్‌వాలీ	NEIGHBOURS IN ADJACENT HOUSE
सामनेवाली	एदूरिंटीवारु	ఎదురింటివారు	సామ్‌నేవాలీ	NEIGHBOURS IN OPPISITE HOUSE
पड़ोसी	इरुगु-पोरुगु	ఇరుగు-పొరుగు	పడోసి	NEIGHBOURS
दुल्हन	पेल्लिकुतुरु	పెండ్లికూతురు	దుల్హన్	BRIDE
दुल्हा	पेल्लिकोडुकू	పెండ్లికొడుకు	దూల్హా	BRIDE-GROOM
कन्या	कन्या	కన్య	కన్యా	UNMARRIED GIRL
लडकी	बालिका	బాలిక	లడకీ	GIRL
औरत	स्त्री	స్త్రీ	ఔరత్	WOMAN
पुरुष	पुरुशुडु	పురుషుడు	పురుష్	MAN
भाई	सोदरुडु	సోదరుడు	భాఈ	YOUNGER BROTHER
सहोदरी/बहिन	सोदरी	సోదరి	బహిన్	SISTER

समय		సమయము		TIME
वार्षिक	प्रतिसंवत्सरमु	ప్రతిసంవత్సరము	వార్షిక్	ANNUAL
वर्षगांठ	वार्षिकोत्सवमु	వార్షికోత్సవము	వర్షగాంఠ్	ANNIVERSARY
शिशिर	शिशिररूतुवु	శిశిరఋతువు	శిశిర్	AUTUMN
सतक	शताब्दम्	శతాబ్దం	సతక్	CENTURY
जलवायु	शीतोष्णस्थिति	శీతోష్ణస్థితి	జల్‌వాయూ	CLIMATE
ठंडा	चलि	చలి	ఠండా	COLD
दिनांक	तेदी	తేదీ	దినాంక్	DATE
दशाब्दि	दशब्दमु	దశాబ్దము	దశాబ్ది	DECADE
संध्या	संध्याकालमु	సంధ్యాకాలము	సంధ్యా	DUSK
पूर्णिमा	पौर्नमि	పౌర్ణమి	పూర్ణిమ	FULLMOON
भविष्य	भविष्यत्तु	భవిష్యత్తు	భవిష్య్	FUTURE
पखवाड़ा	पक्षमु	పక్షము	పఖ్‌వాడా	FORTNIGHT
घंटा	गंटा	గంట	ఘంటా	HOUR
अमावस्या	अमावास्या	అమావాస్య	అమావస్య	NEWMOON
बरसात	वर्षाकालमु	వర్షాకాలము	బర్‌సాత్	RAINYSEASON
ऋतु	ऋतुवु	ఋతువు	ఋతు	SEASON
सूर्योदय	सूर्योदयमु	సూర్యోదయము	సూర్యోదయ్	SUNRISE
सूर्योस्त	सूर्यास्तमयमु	సూర్యాస్తమయము	సూర్యాస్త్	SUNSET
आज	इवाला	ఇవాళ	ఆజ్	TODAY
आज की रात	ई रात्रि	ఈ రాత్రి	ఆజ్‌కీరాత్	TONIGHT
ठंड का मौसम	चलिकालमु	చలికాలం	ఠండ్ కా మౌసమ్	WINTER
सप्ताह	वारमु	వారము	సప్తాహ్	WEEK
साप्ताहिक	प्रतिवारमु	ప్రతివారము	సాప్తాహిక్	WEEKLY
मौसम	वातावरणमु	వాతావరణము	మౌసమ్	WEATHER
वार्षिक	प्रतिसंवत्सरमु	ప్రతిసంవత్సరము	వార్షిక్	YEARLY
दिन	पगलु	పగలు	దిన్	DAY
रात	रात्रि	రాత్రి	రాత్	NIGHT
शाम	सायंत्रमु	సాయంత్రం	షామ్	EVENING
सुबह	उदयमु	ఉదయము	సుబహ్	MORNING
प्रातः	वेकुवजामु	వేకువజాము	ప్రాతః	EARLY MORNING

दोपहर	मध्यानमु	మధ్యాహ్నము	దోపహర్	AFTERNOON
वर्ष	संवत्सरमु	సంవత్సరము	వర్ష్	YEAR
महीना	नेला	నెల	మహీనా	MONTH
घंटा	गंटा	గంట	ఘంటా	HOUR
मिनट	निमिषमु	నిమిషము	మినీట్	MINUTE
सेकंड	सेकनु	సెకను	సెకండ్	SECOND
गोधूलि	सन्ध्याकालमु	సంధ్యాకాలము	గోధూళి	SUNSET
कल	रेपु	రేపు	కల్	TOMORROW
कल	निन्ना	నిన్న	కల్	YESTERDAY
परसों	मोन्ना	మొన్న	పరశోం	DAY BEFORE YESTERDAY

चैत्र	चौत्रमु	చైత్రము	చైత్ర్	MARCH-APRIL
वैशाख	वौशाखमु	వైశాఖము	వేశాఖ్	APRIL-MAY
ज्येष्ठ	ज्येष्टमु	జ్యేష్ఠము	జ్యేష్ఠ	MAY-JUNE
आषाढ़	आषाढमु	ఆషాడము	ఆషాడ్	JUNE-JULY
सावन	श्रावणमु	శ్రావణము	సావన్	JULY-AUGUST
भाद्रो	भाद्रापदमु	భాద్రపదము	భాదో	AUGUST-SEPTEMBER
कुवार/अश्विन	अश्वियुजमु	ఆశ్వీయుజము	ఆశ్విన్	SEPTEMBER-OCTOBER
कार्तिक	कार्तिकमु	కార్తీకము	కార్తీక్	OCTOBER-NOVEMBER
अगहन	मार्गशिरमु	మార్గశిరము	అగహన్	NOVEMBER-DECEMBER
पूस/पौष	पुष्यमु	పుష్యము	పౌష్	DECEMBER-JANUARY
माघ	माघमु	మాఘము	మాఘ్	JANUARY-FEBUARY
फागुन/फाल्गुन	फलगुणमु	ఫాల్గుణము	ఫాగున్	FEBUARY-MARCH
रविवार	आदिवारमु	ఆదివారము	రవివార్	SUNDAY
सोमवार	सोमवारमु	సోమవారము	సోమవార్	MONDAY
मंगलवार	मंगलवारमु	మంగళవారము	మంగలవార్	TUESDAY
बुघवार	बुधवारमु	బుధవారము	బుధవార్	WEDNESDAY
गुरूवार	गुरुवारमु	గురువారము	గురువార్	THURSDAY
शुक्रवार	शुक्रवारमु	శుక్రవారము	శుక్రవార్	FRIDAY
शनिवार	शनिवारमु	శనివారము	శనివార్	SATURDAY

मौसम-ऋतु		ఋతువులు		SEASONS
बसंत	वसंतरूतुवु	వసంతఋతువు	బసంత్	MAR-APRIL
ग्रीष्म	ग्रीष्मरूतुवु	గ్రీష్మఋతువు	గ్రీష్మ్	MAY-JUNE
वर्षा	वर्षारूतुवु	వర్షఋతువు	వర్షా	JULY-AUGUST
शरद	शरद्रुतु	శరదృతువు	శరద్	SEPT-OCTOBER
हेमंत	हेमंतरूतुवु	హేమంతఋతువు	హేమంత్	NOV-DEC
शिशिर	शिशिररूतुवु	శిశిరఋతువు	శిశిర్	JAN-FEBUARY
धूप	एंडा	ఎండ	ధూప్	SUNNY
हवा	गाली	గాలి	హవా	AIR
बादल	मेघम	మేఘం	బాదల్	CLOUD

दिशायें दిక్కులు DIRECTIONS

पूरब	तूर्पु	తూర్పు	పూరబ్	EAST
पश्चिम	पडमरा	పడమర	పశ్చిమ్	WEST
उत्तर	उत्तरमु	ఉత్తరము	ఉత్తర్	NORTH
दक्षिण	दक्षिणमु	దక్షిణము	దక్షిణ్	SOUTH
दायाँ	कुडि	కుడి	దాయా	RIGHT
बायाँ	एडमा	ఎడమ	బాయా	LEFT
ऊपर	मीदा	మీద	ఊపర్	UP
नीचे	क्रिंदा	క్రింద	నీచే	DOWN
आगे	मुंदु	ముందు	ఆగే	BEFORE
पीछे	वेनुका	వెనుక	పీచే	AFTER
मध्य	मध्या	మధ్య	మధ్య్	MIDDLE
ओर	तरपु	తరపు	ఓర్	TOWARDS
भीतर	लोपला	లోపల	భీతర్	INSIDE
बाहर	बयटा	బయట	బాహర్	OUTSIDE
बगल	प्रक्कना	ప్రక్కన	బగల్	SIDE
दूर	दूरंगा	దూరంగా	దూర్	FAR
पास/निकट	दग्गरगा	దగ్గరగా	పాస్/నికట్	NEAR
इधर	इक्कड़ा	ఇక్కడ	ఇధర్	HERE
उधर	अक्कड़ा	అక్కడ	ఉధర్	THERE
यहाँ	इक्कड़ा	ఇక్కడ	యహా	HERE
वहाँ	अक्कड़ा	అక్కడ	వహా	THERE
कहाँ	एक्कड़ा	ఎక్కడ	కహా	WHERE
जहाँ	अक्कड़ा	అక్కడ	జహా	HITHER
तहाँ	इक्कड़ा	ఇక్కడ	తహా	THITHER

कामकाज　　　పని　　　WORK

कारखाना	कर्मागारमु	కర్మాగారము	కార్‌కానా	FACTORY
दफ्तर	कार्यालयमु	కార్యాలయము	దఫ్తర్	OFFICE
अधिकारी	अधिकारी	అధికారి	అధికారి	OFFICER
नौकर	बंट्रोतु	బంట్రోతు	నౌకర్	PEON
मजदूर	कूली	కూలీ	మజ్‌దూర్	LABOR
काम	पनि	పని	కామ్	WORK
पेशा	वृत्ति	వృత్తి	పేషా	OCCUPATION
आमदनी	संपादन	సంపాదన	ఆమ్‌దనీ	INCOME
सहायक	सहायकुडु	సహాయకుడు	సహాయక్	HELPER
कमाई	संपादन	సంపాదన	కమాఈ	EARNINGS
अनशन	निराहारदीक्षा	నిరాహారదీక్ష	అన్‌షన్	HUNGER STRIKE
हड़ताल	सम्मे	సమ్మె	హడ్‌తా	STRIKE
डाकघर	तपाला कार्यालयमु	తపాలాకార్యాలయము	డాక్‌ఘర్	POST-OFFICE
चिट्ठी	उत्तरमु	ఉత్తరము	ఛిట్టీ	LETTER
पता	चिरुनामा	చిరునామా	పతా	ADDRESS
तार	तंति	తంతి	తార్	WIRE
पार्सल	पोट्लम्	పొట్లం	పార్సల్	PARCEL
रजिस्टर	रजिस्टरु	రిజిస్టరు	రిజిష్టర్	REGISTER
कार्ड	कार्डु	కార్డు	కార్డ్	CARD
लिफाफा	कवरु	కవరు	లిఫాఫా	ENVELOPE
मनीआर्डर	मनीआर्डरु	మనియార్డరు	మనీఆర్డర్	MONEY ORDER
मुहर/छापा	शीलु	సీలు	ముహర్/ఛాపా	SEAL
छापाखाना	मुद्रणालयमु	ముద్రణాలయము	ఛాపాఖన	PRINTING PRESS
अख़बार	वार्तापत्रिका	వార్తాపత్రిక	అఖ్‌బార్	NEWSPAPER
अलमारी	आलमारु	అలమారు	అల్‌మారీ	ALMIRAH

आलपिन	गुंडुसूदि	గుండుసూది	ఆల్‌పిన్	PIN
कलम	कलम	కలము	కలమ్	PEN
कलमतराश	पेनाकत्ति	పేనాకత్తి	కలమ్‌తరాస్	PEN KNIFE
कागज	कागितमु	కాగితము	కాగజ్	PAPER
कागजदाब	पेपरबरुवु	పేపరు-బరువు	కాగజ్‌దాబ్	PAPER WEIGHT
काली स्याही	नल्लइंकु	నల్లఇంకు	కాలీస్యాహీ	BLACK-INK
फाइल	फाइलु	ఫైలు	ఫైల్	FILE
गोंद	जिगुरु	జిగురు	గోంద్	GUM
चिमटी	क्लिप्पु	క్లిప్పు	చిమటీ	CLIP
दवात	सिराबुड्डि	సిరాబుడ్డీ	దవాత్	INKPOT
नकल कागज	कार्बनपेपरु	కార్బన్ పేపరు	నకల్ కాగజ్	CARBON PAPER
निमन्त्रण पत्र	आह्वान पत्रमु	ఆహ్వానపత్రము	నిమంత్రణ్ పత్ర్	INVITATION CARD

घर	इल्लु	ఇల్లు	ఘర్	HOUSE
दिवार	गोड़ा	గోడ	దివార్	WALL
दरवाजा	तलुपु	తలుపు	దర్వాజా	DOOR
खिड़की	किटिकी	కిటికీ	ఖిడ్కీ	WINDOW
मेज़	बल्ला	బల్ల	మేజ్	TABLE
कुर्सी	कुर्ची	కుర్చీ	కుర్సీ	CHAIR
खाट	मंचम	మంచం	ఖాట్	COT
पलंग	पक्का	పక్క	పలంగ్	BED
अलमारी	सोरुगू/अलमारु	అలమారు	అల్మారీ	ALMIRAH
आंगन	वरंडा	వరండా	ఆంగన్	VERANDAH
छत	इंटिकप्पु	ఇంటికప్పు	ఛత్	ROOF
सीढ़ी	मेट्लु	మెట్లు	సీఢీ	STAIRS
बिस्तर	परुपु	పరుపు	బిస్తర్	MATTRESS
किला	कोटा	కోట	కిలా	FORT
महल	महलु	మహలు	మహల్	PALACE
कमरा	गदि	గది	కమరా	ROOM
झोपड़ी	गुडिसे	గుడిసె	ఝోపడీ	HUT
चुल्हा	पोय्यि	పొయ్యి	చూల్హా	STOVE
कोयला	बोग्गु	బొగ్గు	కోయలా	COAL
अंगारा	निप्पु	నిప్పు	అంగారా	FIRE
लकड़ी	कर्रा	కర్ర	లకడీ	STICK
मिट्टीतेल	किरसनायिलु	కిరసనాయిలు	మిట్టీతేల్	KEROSENE
थाली	पल्लेमु	పళ్లెము	థాలీ	PLATE
गिलास	ग्लासु	గ్లాసు	గిలాస్	TUMBLER
कटोरी	कप्पु	కప్పు	కటోరీ	CUP
तस्तरी	प्लेट	ప్లేట్	తస్తరీ	PLATE
चम्मच	चम्चा	చెంచా	చమ్మచ్	SPOON
कड़ाही	पेनम्	పెనం	కడాహీ	GRIDDLE
ढक्कन	मूता	మూత	దక్కన్	LID
बरतन	गिन्नेलु	గిన్నెలు	బర్తన్	BOWL

रसोई घर	वंटिल्लु	వంటిల్లు	రసోఈఘర్	KITCHEN
स्नानी	स्नाला गदि	స్నానాలగది	స్నానీ	BATH ROOM
आईना	अद्दम्	అద్దం	ఆఈనా	MIRROR
कंघी	दुव्वेना	దువ్వెన	కంఘీ	COMB
तेल	नूने	నూనె	తేల్	OIL
सलाई	अग्गिपेट्टि	అగ్గిపెట్టి	సలాఈ	MATCH BOX
झंझरा	चिल्लुलुगलचेम्चा	సిబ్బిరేకు	ఝంఝరా	PERFORATED SPOON
कलछुल	गरिटा	గరెటె	కల్‌ఛుల్	LADLE
डेकची	डेगिसा	డేగిసా	డేక్‌చీ	CAULDHON
घड़ी	गडियारमू	గడియారము	ఘడీ	CLOCK
कमीज	चोक्का	చొక్కా	కమీజ్	SHIRT
पजामा	पैजमा	పైజమా	పజామా	PAJAMA
पतलून	पांटु	పాంటు	పత్‌లూన్	PANTS
लुंगी	लुंगी	లుంగీ	లుంగీ	LUNGI
कच्छा	ड्रायरु	డ్రాయరు	కచ్ఛా	SHORTS
बनियान	बनियनु	బనియను	బనియాన్	BANIAN
समीज	समीजु	సమీజు	సమీజ్	WOMEN'S TOP
सलवार	सलवारु	సల్వారు	సల్‌వార్	SHALWAR
चुन्नी/दुपट्टा	दुपट्टा	చున్నీ/దుపట్టా	దుపట్టా	STOLE
तौलिया	तुव्वालु	తువ్వాలు	తౌలియా	TOWEL
थैला	संचि	సంచి	థైలా	BAG

धातु లోహములు METALS

सोना	बंगारम	బంగారం	సోనా	GOLD
चाँदी	वेंडि	వెండి	చాందీ	SLIVER
लोहा	इनुमु	ఇనుము	లోహా	IRON
ताँबा	रागि	రాగి	తాంబా	COPPER
पीतल	इत्तडि	ఇత్తడి	పీతల్	BRASS
शीशा	गाजु	గాజు	సీసా	GLASS
हीरा	डैमंड	డైమండ్	హీరా	DIAMOND
जस्ता	जिंकु	జింకు	జస్తా	ZINC
टिन	रेकु	రేకు	టిన్	TIN
प्लेटिनम	प्लाटिनमु	ప్లాటినము	ప్లాటినమ్	PLATINUM
रेडियम	रेडियमू	రేడియం	రేడియమ్	RADIUM
इस्पात	उक्कु	ఉక్కు	ఇస్పాత్	STEEL

## नाप	కొలతలు	MEASUREMENTS

लंबा	पोडवु	పొడవు	లంబా	LENGTH
चौड़ा	वेडल्पु	వెడల్పు	చౌడా	BREADTH
अधिक	एक्कुवा	ఎక్కువ	అధిక్	MORE
कम	तक्कुवा	తక్కువ	కమ్	LESS
छोटा	चिन्ना	చిన్న	ఛోటా	SMALL
बड़ा	पेद्दा	పెద్ద	బడా	BIG
हल्का	तेलिका	తేలిక	హల్కా	LIGHT
भारी	बरुवैना	బరువైన	భారీ	HEAVIER
वजन	बरुवु	బరువు	వజన్	HEAVY
भार	भारम्	భారం	భార్	BURDEN
गोल	गुंड्रमु	గుండ్రము	గోల్	ROUND
गज	गजमु	గజము	గజ్	YARD
खाली	खाली	ఖాళీ	ఖాళీ	EMPTY

पढ़ाई से संबंधित   విద్యా సంబంధితము   EDUCATION

विद्यार्थी	विद्यार्थि	విద్యార్థి	విద్యార్థి	STUDENT
शिक्षक	उपाद्यायुडु	ఉపాధ్యాయుడు	శిక్షక్	TEACHER
विद्यालय	पाठशाला	పాఠశాల	విద్యాలయ్	SCHOOL
पाठ	पाठमु	పాఠము	పాఠ్	LESSON
पाठ्यक्रम	पीठिका	పీఠిక	పాఠ్యక్రమ్	INDEX
किताब	पुस्तकमु	పుస్తకము	కితాబ్	BOOK
कलम	पेन्नु	పెన్ను	కలమ్	PEN
परीक्षा	परीक्षा	పరీక్ష	పరీక్ష	EXAMINATION
छात्र	विद्यार्थि	విధ్యార్థి	ఛాత్ర్	BOY STUDENT
छात्रा	विद्यार्थिनि	విధ్యార్థిని	ఛాత్రా	GIRL STUDENT
शोधार्थी	परिशोधकुडु	పరిశోధకుడు	శోధార్థి	RESEARCHER(M)
शोधार्थीनी	परिशोधकुरालु	పరిశోధకురాలు	శోధార్థిని	RESEARCHER(FE)
कापी	नकलु	నకలు	కాపీ	COPY
पेन्सिल	पेन्सिलु	పెన్సిలు	పెన్సిల్	PENCIL
रबर	रब्बरु	రబ్బరు	రబర్	ERASER
कंपास	दिकसूचि	దిక్సూచి	కంపాస్	COMPASS
संगणक	कंप्यूटरु	కంప్యూటరు	సంగణక్	COMPUTER
एटलस	भौगोलिकपटम्	భౌగోళికపటం	ఎట్‌లాస్	ATLAS
कागज	कागितमु	కాగితము	కాగజ్	PAPER
छुट्टी	सेलवु	సెలవు	ఛుట్టీ	HOLIDAY
वेतन	जीतमु	జీతము	వేతన్	SALARY
प्रधानाचार्य	प्रधानोपाद्यायुडु	ప్రధానోపాధ్యాయుడు	ప్రధాన్‌చార్య్	HEAD MASTER
व्याख्याता	लेक्चररु	లెక్చరరు	వ్యాఖ్యతా	LECTURER
आचार्य	उपाद्यायुडु	ఉపాధ్యాయుడు	ఆచార్య్	TEACHER
प्राचार्य	प्रिन्सपालु	ప్రిన్సిపాలు	ప్రాచార్య్	PRINCIPAL
कवि	कवि	కవి	కవి	POET
लेखक	रचयिता	రచయిత	లేఖక్	AUTHOR
वैज्ञानिक	शस्त्रवेत्ता	శాస్త్రవేత్త	వైజ్ఞానిక్	SCIENTIST
साहित्यकार	सहित्यकारुडु	సాహిత్యకారుడు	సాహిత్యకార్	WRITTER
पाठक	पाठकुडु	పాఠకుడు	పాఠక్	READER

संपादक	संपादकुडु	సంపాదకుడు	సంపాదక్	EDITOR
कुलपति	कुलपति	కులపతి	కుల్‌పతి	CHANCELLOR
सचीव	कार्यदर्शि	కార్యదర్శి	సచీవ్	SECRETARY
अध्यक्ष	अध्यक्षुडु	అధ్యక్షుడు	అధ్యక్ష్	DIRECTOR
शिक्षाधिकारी	विद्याशाखाधिकारी	విద్యాశాఖాధికారి	శిక్షాధికారి	EDUCATION OFFICER
शिक्षा मंत्री	विद्यामंत्री	విద్యామంత్రి	శిక్షామంత్రి	EDUCATION MINISTER
शिक्षा आयोग	विद्याकमिटि	విద్యాకమిటీ	శిక్షాఆయోగ్	EDUCATION COMMITTE
शिक्षित	विद्यावंतुडु	విద్యావంతుడు	శిక్షిత్	EDUCATOR
गृहकार्य	इंटिपनि	ఇంటిపని	గృహ్‌కార్య్	HOMEWORK
गर्मी छुट्टी	वेसवि सेलवुलु	వేసవిసెలవులు	గర్మీఛుట్టీ	SUMMER HOLIDAYS
मध्यान भोजन	मद्यान भोजनम्	మధ్యాహ్నభోజనం	మధ్యాహ్నభోజన్	MIDDAY MEALS
पिटाई	कोट्टुटा	కొట్టుట	పిటాయి	BEATING
दण्ड	दंडना	దండన	దండ్	PUNISHMENT
कविता	कविता	కవిత	కవితా	POEM
कहानी	कधा	కథ	కహానీ	STORY
लेख	रचना	రచన	లేఖ్	ARTICLE
मुद्रण	मुद्रणा	ముద్రణ	ముద్రణ్	PRINTING
प्रकाशित	प्रचुरिंचु	ప్రచురించు	ప్రకాశిత్	TO PUBLISH
प्रकाशक	प्रचुरणकर्ता	ప్రచురణకర్త	ప్రకాశక్	PUBLISHER
भाषण	उपन्यासम	ఉపన్యాసం	భాషణ్	LECTURE
वक्ता	उपन्यासकुडु	ఉపన్యాసకుడు	వక్తా	ORATOR
श्रोता	श्रोता	శ్రోత	శ్రోతా	LISTENER
संगीत	संगीतमु	సంగీతము	సంగీత్	MUSIC
गायक	गायकुडु	గాయకుడు	గాయక్	SINGER
वाद्ययंत्र	वायिद्यमु	వాయిద్యము	వాద్యయంత్ర్	MUSIC INSTRUMENT
वीणा	वीण	వీణ	వీణా	VEENA
सारंगी	सारंगि	సారంగి	సారంగీ	SARANGI

वचन వచనములు (SINGULAR-PLURAL) NUMBERS

मैं-हम	नेनु-मनमु	నేను-మనము	మై-హమ్	I-WE
तुम-तुमलोग	नीवु-मीरु	నీవు-మీరు	తుమ్-తుమ్‌లోగ్	YOU-YOU
वह-वे	इतडु/ईमे/वीरु	ఇతడు-ఈమె-వీరు	వహ్-వే	HE/SHE-THEY
यह-ये	अतडु/आमे/वारु	అతడు-ఆమె-వారు	యహ్-యే	HE/SHE-THEY
बच्चा-बच्चे	पिल्ला-पिल्ललु	పిల్ల-పిల్లలు	బచ్చా-బచ్చే	CHILD-CHILDREN
लड़का-लड़के	बालुडु-बालुरु	బాలుడు-బాలురు	లడకా-లడకే	BOY-BOYS
लड़की-लड़कियाँ	बालिका-बालिकलु	బాలిక-బాలికలు	లడకీ-లడకీయా	GIRL-GIRLS
लता-लताएं	लता-लतलु	లత-లతలు	లతా-లతాయే	CREEPER-CREEPERS
कुआँ-कुएँ	बावि-बावुलु	బావి-బావులు	కుఆ-కుఎ	WELL-WELLS
किताब-	पुस्तकमु-	పుస్తకము-	కితాబ్-	BOOK-
किताबें	पुस्तकमुल	పుస్తకములు	కితాబే	BOOKS
दो-दीजिए	इव्वु-इव्वंडि	ఇవ్వు-ఇవ్వండి	దో-దీజిఎ	GIVE-GIVE
आओ-आइये	रा-रंडि	రా-రండి	ఆవో-ఆఇయే	COME-COME
करो-कीजिए	चेयु-चेयंडि	చేయు-చేయండి	కరో-కీజిఎ	DO-DO
लिखो-लिखिए	व्रायु-व्रायंडि	వ్రాయు-వ్రాయండి	లిఖో-లిఖిఎ	WRITE-WRITE
कहो-कहिए	चेप्पु-चेप्पंडि	చెప్పు-చెప్పండి	కహో-కహిఎ	TELL-TELL
सुनो-सुनिए	विनु-विनंडि	విను-వినండి	సునో-సునిఎ	LISTEN-LISTEN
डिबिया-डिबियाँ	डब्बा-डब्बालु	డబ్బా-డబ్బాలు	డిబియా-డిబియాం	TIN-TINS
मकान-मकानें	इल्लु-इल्लु	ఇల్లు-ఇళ్ళు	మకాన్-మకానేం	HOUSE-HOUSES
बात-बातें	माटा-माटलु	మాట-మాటలు	బాత్-బాతేం	WORD-WORDS
नीति-नीतियाँ	नीति-नीतुलु	నీతి-నీతులు	నీతి-నీతియా	MORAL-MORALS
साड़ी-साड़ियाँ	चीरा-चीरलु	చీర-చీరలు	సాడీ-సాడియా	SAREE-SAREES
माता-माताएं	तल्लि-तल्लुलु	తల్లి-తల్లులు	మాతా-మాతాఎం	MOTHER-MOTHERS

लिंग		లింగములు		GENDER
माता-पिता	तल्लि-तंड्रि	తల్లి-తండ్రి	మాతా-పిత	MOTHER-FATHER
भाई-बहन	सोदरुडु-सोदरि	సోదరుడు-సోదరి	భాయి-బహన్	BROTHER-SISTER
गाय-बैल	आवु-एद्दु	ఆవు-ఎద్దు	గాయ్-బైల్	COW-OX
दादा-दादी	तातय्या-नानम्मा	తాతయ్య-నానమ్మ	దాదా-దాదీ	GRANDFATHER/MOTHER
चाचा-चाची	बाबायि-पिन्नि	బాబాయి-పిన్ని	చాచా-చాచీ	UNCLE-AUNT
घोड़ा-घोड़ी	मगा गुर्रम्-आडा गुर्रम्	మగగుర్రం-ఆడగుర్రం	ఘోడా-ఘోడీ	HORSE-MARE
शेर-शेरनी	मगा सिंहम्-आडा सिंहम्	మగసింహం-ఆడసింహం	షేర్-షేర్నీ	LION-LOINESS
मोर-मोरनी	मगा नेमलि-आडा नेमलि	మగనెమలి-ఆడనెమలి	మోర్-మోర్నీ	PEACOCK-PEAHEN
वर-वधु	वरुडु-वधुवु	వరుడు-వధువు	వర్-వధు	BRIDE GROOM-BRIDE
कबूतर-कबूतरी	मगा पावुरमु-आडा पावुरम	మగపావురము-ఆడపావురము	కబూతర్-కబూతరీ	COCK-HEN
कुत्ता-कुतिया	मगा कुक्का-आडा कुक्का	మగకుక్క-ఆడకుక్క	కుత్తా-కుత్తియా	DOG-BITCH
पंडित-पंडिताइन	पंडितुडु-पंडितुरालु	పండిత-పండితురాలు	పండిత్-పండితాయిన్	PRIEST-PRIESTESS
धोबी-धोबिन	चाकलिवाडु-चाकलिआम	చాకలివాడు-	ధోబీ-ధోబిన్	WASHERMAN/
गायक-गायिका	गायकुडु-गायिनि	గాయకుడు-గాయకి	గాయక్-గాయికా	SINGER-SONGSTRESS
कवि-कवियित्री	कवि-कवियित्रि	కవి-కవయిత్రి	కవి-కవయిత్రి	POET-POETESS
लेखक-लेखिका	लेखकुडु-लेखिकुरालु	లేఖకుడు-లేఖికురాలు	లేఖక్-లేఖికా	AUTHOR-AUTHORESS
विदुषि-विद्वान	विद्वांसुडु-विदुषि	విద్వాంసుడు-విదుషి	విద్వాన్-విదుషీ	SCHOLAR-LADY SCHOLAR
नेता-नेत्री	नायकुडु-नायकुरालु	నాయకుడు-నాయకురాలు	నేత-నేత్రీ	MALE LEADER-FEMALE LEADER
अभिमेता-अभिनेत्री	नटुडु-नटि	నటుడు-నటి	అభినేత-అభినేత్రి	ACTOR-ACTRESS
शिक्षक-शिक्षिका	शिक्षकुडु-शिक्षकुरालु	శిక్షకుడు-	శిక్షక్-శిక్షికా	TEACHER-

		శిక్షకురాలు		SCHOOL MISTRESS
महोदय-महोदया	आर्या-अम्मा	ఆర్యా-అమ్మా	మహోదయ-మహోదయా	SIR-MADAM
श्रीमान-श्रीमती	श्री-श्रीमति	శ్రీ-శ్రీమతి	శ్రీమాన్-శ్రీమతి	MR-MRS
श्री-सुश्री	श्री-कुमारी	శ్రీ-కుమారి	శ్రీ-సుశ్రీ	MR-MS

विशेषण		విశేషణము		ADJECTIVE
लाल कलम	एर्रनि कलमु	**ఎర్రని** కలము	లాల్ కలమ్	**RED** PEN
सफेद घोड़ा	तेल्लनि गुर्रमु	**తెల్లని** గుర్రము	సఫేద్ ఘోడా	**WHITE** HORSE
वह लड़का	आ बालुडु	**ఆ** బాలుడు	వహ్ లడక	**THAT** BOY
ये लोग	आ मनुष्युलु	**ఆ** మనుష్యులు	యే లోగ్	**THOSE** PEOPLE
दूसरा बच्चा	रेंडवा पिल्लावाडु	**రెండవ** పిల్లవాడు	దూస్‌రా బచ్చా	**SECOND** CHILD
बहुत आदमी	एक्कुवा मंदि	ఎక్కువమంది	బహుత్ ఆద్మీ	**MANY** PEOPLE
प्रत्येक पुस्तक	प्रत्येकमैना पुस्तकमु	**ప్రత్యేకమైన** పుస్తకము	ప్రత్యేక్ పుస్తక్	**EVERY** BOOK
पांच दिन	ऐदु रोजुलु	**ఐదు** రోజులు	పాంచ్ దిన్	**FIVE** DAYS
चार मीटर	नालुगु मीटर्लु	**నాలుగు** మీటర్లు	చార్ మీటర్	**FOUR** METERS
पाव भर दूध	पावु लीटरु पालु	**పావు లీటరు** పాలు	పావ్ బర్ దూద్	**ONE QUARTER** MILK
पेट भर भोजन	कडुपु निंडा भोजनमु	**కడుపు నిండా** భోజనము	పేట్ బర్ భోజన్	**STOMACH FUL** FOOD
थोड़ा पानी	कोंचेमु नीरु	**కొంచెము** నీరు	థోడా పానీ	**LITTLE** WATER

क्रिया ‌ ‌ క్రియలు ‌ ‌ VERBS

खाना	तिनड़म	తినడం	ఖానా	TO EAT
जीना	जिविंचटम	జీవించటం	జీనా	TO LIVE
सोना	निद्रींचटम्	నిద్రించటం	సోనా	TO SLEEP
रोना	एडवटम्	ఏడవటం	రోనా	TO CRY
उठना	लेवटम्	లేవటం	వుఠ్‌నా	TO GET UP
उड़ना	एगरडम्	ఎగరడం	ఉడ్‌నా	TO FLY
काटना	कत्तीरिंचटम्	కత్తిరించటం	కాట్‌నా	TO CUT
करना	चेइडम्	చేయడం	కర్‌నా	TO DO
खींचना	लागडम्	లాగడం	ఖీంచ్‌నా	TO PULL
खिलना	विकसिंचटम्	వికసించటం	ఖిల్‌నా	TO BLOSSOM
खेलना	आडटम्	ఆడటం	ఖేల్‌నా	TO PLAY
गिरना	पड़ीपोवडम्	పడిపోవడం	గిర్‌నా	TO FALL
घूमना	तिरगडम	తిరగడం	ఘూమ్‌నా	TO ROAM
चढ़ना	एक्कडम्	ఎక్కడం	చఢ్‌నా	TO CLIMB
चलना	नडमटम्	నడవటం	చల్‌నా	TO WALK
चुनना	एरडम्	ఏరడం	చున్‌నా	TO PICK
छिपना	दाचीपेट्टडम्	దాచిపెట్టటం	ఛిప్‌నా	TO HIDE
जगना	मेलुकोवटम्	మేలుకోవటం	జగ్‌నా	TO WAKEUP
झुकना	वंगटम्	వంగటం	ఝుక్‌నా	TO BEND
डरना	भयपडवटम्	భయపడపడం	డర్‌నా	TO FEAR
टूटना	विरगटम्	విరగటం	టూట్‌నా	TO BREAK
तैरना	इदडम्	ఈదడం	తైర్‌నా	TO SWIM
नाचना	नृत्यं चेइटम्	నృత్యంచేయటం	నాచ్‌నా	TO DANCE
पकाना	वंडटम्	వండటం	పకానా	TO COOK
पीटना	कोट्टडम्	కొట్టటం	పీట్‌నా	TO BEAT
पालना	पेंचटम्	పెంచటం	పాల్‌నా	TO BRINGUP
पीसना	रूब्बटम्	రుబ్బటం	పీస్‌నా	TO GRIND
बनाना	तैयारचइटम्	తయారుచేయటం	బనానా	TO MAKE
भागना	पारीपोटम्	పారిపోవటం	భాగ్‌నా	TO RUN
मिटाना	चेरिपेइटम्	చెరిపేయటం	మిటానా	TO WIPE

मरना	चनिपोवडम्	చనిపోవటం	మర్‌నా	TO DIE
मिलना	कलवटम्	కలవటం	మిల్‌నా	TO MEET
रोना	एड़वटम्	ఏడవటం	రోనా	TO CRY
लड़ना	पोटलाडटम्	పోట్లాడటం	లడ్‌నా	TO FIGHT
सुखाना	एंड़ापोइडम्	ఎండపోయటం	సుఖానా	TO DRY
हँसना	नव्वटम्	నవ్వటం	హస్‌నా	TO LAUGH
हिलना	कदलटम्	కదలటం	హిల్‌నా	TO MOVE
बैठना	कूर्चोवटम्	కూర్చోవటం	బైఠ్‌నా	TO SIT
फैलना	व्यापिंचटम्	వ్యాపించటం	ఫైల్‌నా	TO SPREAD
छिपना	दायटम्	దాయటం	ఛిపానా	TO HIDE
सोना	पड़ुकोवटम्	పడుకోవటం	సోనా	TO SLEEP
धोना	कड़गटम्	కడగటం	ధోనా	TO WASH
फेंकना	विसरटम ्	విసరటం	ఫేంక్‌నా	TO THROW
कूदना	दुकटम्	దూకటం	కూద్‌నా	TO JUMP
ढ़केलना	तोयटम्	తోయటం	ధకేల్‌నా	TO PUSH
गाना	पाडटम्	పాడటం	గానా	TO SING
खोलना	तेरवटम्	తెరవటం	ఖోల్‌నా	TO OPEN
बंदकरना	मूयटम्	మూయటం	బంద్‌కర్‌నా	TO CLOSE
चबाना	नमलटम्	నమలటం	చబానా	TO CHEW
काटना	कोरकटम्	కొరకటం	కాట్‌నా	TO BITE
खोना	पोगोट्टुकोवटम्	పోగొట్టుకోవటం	ఖోనా	TO LOSE
काँपना	वणकटम्	వణకటం	కాంప్‌నా	TO SHAKE
बचाना	रक्षिंचटम्	రక్షించటం	బచానా	TO SAVE
बहना	प्रवहिंचटम्	ప్రవహించటం	బహ్‌నా	TO FLOW
बेचना	अम्मटम्	అమ్మటం	బేచ్‌నా	TO SELL
खरीदना	कोनटम्	కొనటం	ఖరీద్‌నా	TO BUY
छूना	ताकटम्	తాకటం	ఛూనా	TO TOUCH
छोड़ना	विडवटम ्	విడవటం	ఛోడ్‌నా	TO LEAVE
छापना	मुद्रिचटम्	ముద్రించటం	ఛాప్‌నా	TO PRINT
जाँचना	परीक्षिंचुटम्	పరీక్షించటం	జాంచ్‌నా	TO TEST
पकड़ना	पट्टुकोवटम्	పట్టుకోవటం	పకడ్‌నా	TO HOLD
चखना	रूचिचूड़टम्	రుచిచూడటం	చఖ్‌నా	TO TASTE
सीखना	नेर्चुकोंवटम्	నేర్చుకోవటం	సీఖ్‌నా	TO LEARN
सुनना	वीनटम्	వినటం	సున్‌నా	TO LISTEN
गारना	पिंडटम्	పిండటం	గార్‌నా	TO SQUEEZE

तोड़ना	विरवटम्	విరవటం	తోడ్‌నా	TO BREAK
रोकना	आपटम्	ఆపటం	రోక్‌నా	TO STOP
नहाना	स्नानमचेयटम्	స్నానంచేయటం	నహానా	TO BATH
पीना	त्रागटम्	త్రాగటం	పీనా	TO DRINK
पुकारना	पिलवटम्	పిలవటం	పుకార్‌నా	TO CALL
पहनना	धरिंचटम्	ధరించటం	పహననా	TO WEAR
उबालना	उडिंकिंचटम्	ఉడికించటం	ఉబాల్‌నా	TO BOIL
गिनना	लेकिंचटम्	లెక్కించటం	గిన్‌నా	TO COUNT
बातकरना	माटलाड़टम्	మాట్లాడటం	బాత్‌కర్‌నా	TO TALK
भूलना	मरवटम	మరవటం	భూల్‌నా	TO FORGET
बाँटना	पंचटम	పంచటం	బాంట్‌నా	TO DISTRIBUTE
चुराना	दोंगिलिंचुटम	దొంగిలించటం	చురానా	TO STEAL
कहना	चेप्पटम	చెప్పటం	కహ్‌నా	TO TELL

क्रिया रूप(क्रियानुसार)

तू	तुम	आप	YOU
नीवु	नीवु	मीरु	
నీవు	నీవు	మీరు	
తూ	తుమ్	ఆప్	
आ	आओ	आइये	COME
रा	रा	रंडि	
రా	రా	రండి	
ఆ	ఆవో	ఆయియే	
जा	जाओ	जाइये	GO
वेल्लु	वेल्लु	वेल्लंडि	
వెళ్లు	వెళ్లు	వెళ్లండి	
జా	జావో	జాయియే	
खा	खाओ	खाइए	EAT
तिनु	तिनु	तिनंडि	
తిను	తిను	తినండి	
ఖా	ఖావో	ఖాయియే	
सो	सोओ	सोइए	SLEEP
पडुको	पडुको	पडुकोंडि	
పడుకో	పడుకో	పడుకోండి	
సో	సోఒ	సోయియే	

बोल	बोलो	बोलिए	TELL
माट्लाडु	माट्लाडु	माट्लाडंडि	
మాట్లాడు	మాట్లాడు	మాట్లాడండి	
బోల్	బోలో	బోలిఏ	

ले	लेलो	लिजिए	TAKE
तीसुको	तीसुको	तीसुकोंडि	
తీసుకో	తీసుకో	తీసుకోండి	
లే	లేలో	లిజిఏ	

दो	देदो	दीजिए	GIVE
इव्वु	इव्वु	इव्वंडि	
ఇవ్వు	ఇవ్వు	ఇవ్వండి	
దో	దేదో	దీజిఏ	

क्रिया रूप(कालानुसार)

1) खाता	खाया	खारहा	खाएगा
तिनुनु	तिनेनु	तिंटुनाडु	तिंटाडु-तिनुनु
తినును	తినెను	తింటున్నాడు	తింటాడు–తినును
ఖాతా	ఖాయా	ఖారహ	ఖాఎగా
EATS	EATEN	EATING	WILL EAT
2) सोता	सोया	सो रहा	सोएगा
पडुकोनुनु	पडुकोनेनु	पडुकुंटुन्नारु	पडुकोनुनु
పడుకొనును	పడుకొనెను	పడుకుంటున్నారు	పడుకొనును
సోతా	సోయా	సోరహ	సోఎగా
SLEEPS	SLEPT	SLEEPING	WILL SLEEP
3) बैठता	बैठा	बैठरहा	बैठेगा
कूर्चोनुनु	कूर्चोनेनु	कूर्चोन्टून्नारु	कूर्चोनुनु
కూర్చొనును	కూర్చొనెను	కూర్చొంటున్నారు	కూర్చొనును
బైఠ్‌తా	బైఠా	బైఠ్‌రహ	బైఠేగా
SITS	SAT	SITTING	WILL SIT
4) जाता	गया	जारहा	जाएगा
वेलताडु	वेल्लाडु	वेलतुन्नाडु	वेलताडु
వెళతాడు	వెళ్ళాడు	వెళుతున్నాడు	వెళతాడు
జాతా	గయా	జారహ	జాయేగా
GOES	GONE	GOINING	WILL GO
5) रहता है	रहता था	रह रहा है	रहेगा
उंटुन्नाडु	उंडेवाडु	उंटू उन्नाडु	उंटाडु
రహ్‌తా హై	రహ్‌తా	రహ్ రహా హై	రహేగా
ఉంటున్నాడు	ఉండేవాడు	ఉంటూ ఉన్నాడు	ఉంటాడు
LIVES	LIVED	LIVING	WILL LIVE

वाक्यांश పదబంధాలు PHRASES

ईश्वर का धन्यावाद	देवुनिदया	దేవునిదయ	ఈశ్వర్ కా ధన్యీవాద్	THANK GOD
शाबाश	शबाष	శభాష్	శాభాష్	WELL DONE
बहुत बढ़िया	चालाबागुंदि	చాలాబాగుంది	బహుత్‌బఢియా	EXCELLENT
सच में/सचमुच	निजंगा	నిజంగా	సచ్ మే/సచ్‌ముచ్	REALLY
हे भगवान	वोरि देवुडा	ఓరి దేవుడా	హే భగవాన్	OH GOD
तुम्हारी इतनी हिम्मत	एंता धैर्यमू नीकु	ఎంతధైర్యంనీకు	తుమ్హారీ ఇతనీ హిమ్మత్	HOW DARE YOU
कितना सुन्दर	एंता बावुंदि	ఎంత బావుంది	కిత్‌నా సుందర్	HOW LOVELY
जल्दी करो	त्वरगा चेयि	త్వరగా చేయి	జల్దీకరో	HURRY UP
सुनो/सुनिये	विनु/विनंडि	విను/వినండి	సునో/సునియా	LISTEN
ओह!क्या होगया	अय्यो पापम्	అయ్యోపాపం	వోహ్!క్యా హోగయా	WHAT A PITY
शांत रहो	निश्शब्दम्गाउंडु	నిశ్శబ్దంగావుండు	ఛుప్‌రహో	KEEP QUIET
बधाई	शुभाकांक्षलु	శుభాకాంక్షలు	బధాఈ	CONGRATULATIONS
कितनी शर्म की बात है	एंता सिग्गुचेटु	ఎంతసిగ్గుచేటు	కిత్‌నీ శర్మ్‌కీ బాత్ హై	WHAT A SHAME
कितनी दु:खद बात है	एंता बाधाकरम्	ఎంతబాధాకరం	కిత్‌నీ దు:ఖద్ బాత్‌హై	HOW TRAGIC
छि!छि!	छि:छि:	ఛీ!ఛీ	ఛీ!ఛీ!	HOW DISGUSTING
कहीं नजर ना लगे	दिष्टि तगुलुतुंदि	దిష్టితగులుతుంది	కహీనజర్‌నలగే	TOUCH WOOD
अब चाहे जोहो	एमैते अदवनी	ఏమైతేఅదవనీ	అబ్‌చాహేజోహో	COME WHAT MAY
कितनी बढिया सूझ है	एंता मंचि आलोचना	మంచి ఆలోచన	కిత్‌నీ బఢియా సూజ్‌హై	WHAT AN IDEA
मुझे पता है	नाकु तेलुसु	నాకు తెలుసు	ముఝేపతాహై	I KNOW
बेशक	तप्पाकुंडा	తప్పకుండా	బేశక్	SURE
कल मिलेंगे	रेपु कलुद्दामु	రేపుకలుద్దాము	కల్‌మిలేంగే	WE WILL MEET TOMORROW
एक मिनट	वोक्का निमिषम्	ఒక్కనిమిషం	ఏక్‌మినట్	JUST A MINUTE
संभालकर	जाग्रत्ता	జాగ్రత్త	సంభాల్‌కర్	BE CAREFULL
चिंता मत करो	विचारिंचकु	విచారించకు	చింతామత్‌కర్	DONOT WORRY

काल कాలాలు TENSE

वर्तमान काल ***వర్తమానకాలము*** ***PRESENT TENSE***

<u>सामान्य वर्तमान</u>

मैं पढ़ता हूँ।
नेनु चदुवुतुन्नानु ।
నేను చదువుతున్నాను.
మై పఢ్‌తా హూ.
I READ

वह पढ़ता है।
अतडु चदुवुचुन्नाडु ।
అతడు చదువుతున్నాడు.
వహ్ పఢ్‌తా హై.
HE READS

तुम पढ़ते हो।
नीवु चदुवुतुन्नावु ।
నీవు చదువుతున్నావు.
తుమ్ పఢ్‌తే హో.
YOU READ

मैं खाती हूँ।
नेनु तिनुचुन्नानु ।
నేను తినుచున్నాను.
మై ఖాతీ హూ.
I EAT

वह खाती है।
आमे तिनुचुन्नदि ।

ఆమె తినుచున్నది.
వహ్ ఖాతీ హై.
SHE EATS

तुम खाती हो ।
नीवु तिनुचुन्नावु ।
నీవు తినుచున్నావు.
తుమ్ ఖాతీ హో.
YOU EAT

तात्कलिक वर्तमान काल PRESENT-CONTINUOUS TENSE

मैं पढ़ रहा हूँ ।
नेनु चदुवुतू वुन्नानु ।
నేను చదువుతూ వున్నాను.
మై పడ్ రహా హూ.
I AM READING

वह पढ़ रहा है ।
अतडु चदुवुतू वुन्नाडु ।
అతడు చదువుతూ వున్నాడు.
వహ్ పడ్ రహా హై.
HE IS READING

तुम पढ़ रहे हो ।
नीवु चदुवुतू वुन्नावु ।
నీవు చదువుతూ వున్నావు.
తుమ్ పడ్ రహే హో.
YOU ARE READING

मैं सो रही हूँ ।
नेनु निद्रपोतू उन्नानु ।
నేను నిద్రపోతూవున్నాను.
మై సో రహీ హూ.
I AM SLEEPING

वह सो रहा है ।
अतडु निद्रपोतू उन्नाडु !
అతడు నిద్ర పోతూ వున్నాడు.
వహ్ సో రహా హై.
HE IS SLEEPING

तुम सो रही हो ।
नीवु निद्रपोतू वुन्नावु ।
నీవు నిద్ర పోతూవున్నావు.
తుమ్ సో రహీ హో.
YOU ARE SLEEPING

संदिग्ध वर्तमान **PRESENT INDEFINITE TENSE**

సందిగ్ధ వర్తమానకాలము

1) मैं पढ़ता हूँगा ।
नेनु चदुवुतुन्नानेमो ।
నేను చదువుతున్నానేమో.
మై పడ్‌తా హూంగా.
I MIGHT BE READING

2) वह पढ़ता होगा ।
अतडु चदुवुतुन्नाडेमो ।
అతడు చదువుతున్నాడేమో.
వహ్ పడ్‌తా హోగా.
HE MIGHT BE READING

3) तुम पढ़ते होगे ।
नीवु तदुवुतुन्नावेमो ।
నీవు చదువుతున్నావేమో.
తుమ్ పఢ్‌తే హోగే.
YOU MIGHT BE READING

4) मैं देख रही हूँगी ।
नेनु चुस्तुन्नानेमो ।
నేను చూస్తున్నానేమో.
మై దేఖ్ రహీ హూంగీ.
I MIGHT BE LOOKING.

5) सीता देख रही होगी ।
सीता चुस्तू वुंदेमो ।
సీత చూస్తూ వుందేమో.
సీతా దేఖ్ రహీ హోగీ.
SITA MIGHT BE LOOKING.

6) तुम देख रही होगी ।
नीवु चुस्तुन्नावेमो ।
నీవు చూస్తున్నావేమో.
తుమ్ దేఖ్ రహీ హోగీ.
YOU MIGHT BE LOOKING.

सामान्य

1) मैं ने खाया ।
नेनु तिन्नानु ।
నేను తిన్నాను.
మై నే ఖాయా.
I ATE

2) उसने खाया ।
अतडु तिन्नाडु ।
అతడు తిన్నాడు.
ఉస్‌నే ఖాయా.
HE ATE

3) तुमने खाया ।
नीवु तिन्नावु ।
నీవు తిన్నావు.
తుమ్‌నే ఖాయా.
YOU ATE

4) मैं सोयी ।
नेनु निद्रपोयानु ।
నేను నిద్రపోయాను.
మై సోయీ.
I SLEPT

5) वह सोयी ।

आमे निद्रपोइंदि ।
ఆమె నిద్రపోయింది.
వహ్ సోయి.
SHE SLEPT

6) तुम सोयी ।
नीवु निद्रपोयावु ।
నీవు నిద్రపోయావు.
తుమ్ సోయీ.
YOU SLEPT

7) हमने सिनेमा देखा ।
मेमु सिनिमा चूसामु ।
మేము సినిమా చూసాము.
హమ్‌నే సినిమా దేఖా.
WE WATCHED A MOIVE

8) वे लोग सिनेमा देखे ।
वारु सिनिमा चुसारु ।
వారు సినిమా చూసారు.
వే లోగ్ సినేమా దేఖే.
THEY WATCHED A MOVIE

9) मैं ने चाय पी ली है ।
नेनु टी तागेसानु ।
నేను టీ తాగేసాను.
మై నే ఛాయ్ పీ లీ హై.
I HAD MY TEA.

10) उसने चाय पी ली है ।
आमे टी तागेसिंदि ।
ఆమె టీ తాగేసింది.
వుస్‌నే చాయ్ పీ లీ హై.
SHE HAD TEA

11) तुमने चाय पी ली है ।

नीवु टी तागेसावु ।
నీవు టీ తాగేసావు.
తుమ్‌నే చాయ్ పీ లీ హై.
YOU HAD TEA

पूर्ण भूतकाल **PAST TENSE** పూర్ణభూతకాలము

1) मैं खाता था ।
नेनु तिनेवाडिनि .
నేను తినేవాడిని.
మై ఖాతా థా.
I USED TO EAT

2) तुम खाते थे ।
नीवु तिनेवाडिवि ।
నీవు తినేవాడివి.
తుమ్ ఖాతే థే.
YOU USED TO EAT

3) वे खाते थे ।
वारु तिनेवारु ।
వారు తినేవారు.
వే ఖాతే థే.
THEY USED TO EAT

4) मैं नाचती थी ।
नेनु नाट्यमू चेस्तुंडेदानिनि ।
నేను నాట్యం చేస్తుండేదానిని.
మై నాచ్‌తీ థీ.
I USED TO DANCE

5) वह नाचती थी ।
आमे नाट्यमू चेस्तुंडेदि ।

ఆమె నాట్యం చేస్తుండేది.
వహ్ నాచ్‌తీ థీ.
SHE USED TO DANCE

6) तुम नाचती थी ।
नीवु नाट्यमू चेस्तुंडेदानिवि ।
నీవు నాట్యం చేస్తుండేదానివి.
తుమ్ నాచ్‌తీ థీ.
YOU USED TO DANCE

संदिग्ध भूतकाल | PAST INDEFINITE TENSE | సందిగ్ధ భూతకాలము

1) मैं ने खाया होगा ।
नेनु तिने उंटानु ।
నేను తినే వుంటాను.
మైనే ఖాయా హోగా.
I MUST HAVE EATEN

2) तुमने खाया होगा ।
नीवु तिने वुंटावु ।
నీవు తినే వుంటావు.
తుమ్‌నే ఖాయా హోగా.
YOU MUST HAVE EATEN

3) उसने खाया होगा ।
अतडु तिने उंटाडु ।
అతడు తినే వుంటాడు.
ఉస్‌నే ఖాయా హోగా.
HE MUST HAVE EATEN

4) मैंने लिखी होगी ।
नेनु व्रासी वुंटानु ।
నేను వ్రాసి వుంటాను.
మైనే లిఖీ హోగీ.

I MUST HAVE WRITTEN

5) तुम लिखी होगी ।
नीवु व्रासी वुंटावु ।
నీవు వ్రాసి వుంటావు.
తుమ్ లిఖీ హోగీ.

YOU MUST HAVE WRITTEN
6) उसने लिखा होगा ।
अतडु व्रासी वुंटाडु ।
అతడు వ్రాసి వుంటాడు.
ఉస్‌నే లిఖీ హోగా.
HE MUST HAVE WRITTEN

भविष्यत काल భవిష్యత్‌కాలము FUTURE TENSE

1) मैं आऊँगा ।
नेनु वस्तानु ।
నేను వస్తాను.
మై ఆవూంగా.
I WILL COME

2) तुम आओगे ?
नुव्वु वस्तावा ?
నువ్వు వస్తావా?
తుమ్ ఆవోగే?
WILL YOU COME?
3) वह आएगा ।
अतडु वस्ताडु ।
అతడు వస్తాడు.
వహ్ ఆయేగా.
HE WILL COME

4) मैं जाऊँगी ।
नेनु वेलतानु ।
నేను వెళతాను.
మై జావూంగీ.
I WILL GO

5) वह जाएगी ।
आमे वेलुतुंदि ।
ఆమె వెళుతుంది.
వహ్ జాయేగీ.
SHE WILL GO

6) तुम जाओगी ।
नीवु वेलतावु ।
నీవు వెళతావు.
తుమ్ జావోగీ.
YOU WILL GO

7) मैं सिनेमा देखुंगी ।
नेनु सिनिमा चूस्तानु ।
నేను సినిమా చూస్తాను.
మై సినేమా దేఖూంగీ.
I WILL WATCH MOVIE

8) वे सिनेमा देखेंगे ।
वारु सिनिमा चूस्तारु ।
వారు సినిమా చూస్తారు.
వే సినేమా దేఖేంగే.
THEY WILL WATCH MOVIE

विभक्ति

कर्त्ता-ने

1) राम ने फल खाया ।
रामु फलमुनु तिन्नाडु ।
రాము ఫలమును తిన్నాడు.
రామ్ నే ఫల్ ఖాయా.
RAM ATE A FRUIT.

2) सीता ने रोटी खायी ।
सीता रोट्टेनु तिन्नदि ।
సీత రొట్టెను తిన్నది.
సీత నే రోటీ ఖాయి.
SITA ATE ROTI.

3) उन्होंने पत्र लिखा ।
वारु उत्तरमु व्रासारु ।
వారు ఉత్తరము వ్రాసారు.
ఉన్హోనే పత్ర్ లిఖా.
THEY WROTE A LETTER.

कर्म-को

1) राम ने रावण को मारा ।
रामुडु रावणुनि चंपेनु ।
రాముడు రావణుని చంపెను.
రామ్ నే రావణ్ కో మారా.
RAM KILLED RAVAN.

2) सीता ने गीता को चिढ़ाया ।
सीता गीतनु वेलाकोलमु चेसेनु ।
సీత గీతను వేళాకోళము చేసెను.
సీత నే గీత కో చిఢాయా.
SITA TEASED GITA.

3) उन्होंने सबको डंडे मारा।
वारु अंदरिनि कर्रातो कोट्टारु !
వారు అందరిని కఱ్ఱతో కొట్టారు.
ఉన్హోనే సబ్‌కో డండా సే మారా.
THEY BEAT EVERYONE WITH STICK.

करण-से

1) चोर को डंडे से मारा ।
दोंगनु कर्रातो कोट्टारू ।
దొంగను కఱ్ఱతో కొట్టారు.
చోర్ కో డండే సే మారా.
THE THEIF WAS BEATEN WITH A STICK.

2) सीता चाकू से फल काटी ।
सीता कत्तितो फलमुनु कोसेनु ।
సీత కత్తితో ఫలమును కోసెను.
సీత చాకూ సే ఫల్ కాటీ.
SITA HAS CUT THE FRUIT WITH A KNIFE.

3) मोहन कलम से लिखता है ।
मोहन कलमुतो व्रास्ताडु ।
మోహన్ కలముతో వ్రాస్తాడు.
మోహన్ కలమ్ సే లిఖ్‌తా హై.
MOHAN WRITES WITH PEN.

संबंध-का-के-की

1) राम श्याम का मित्र है ।
रामु श्याम योक्का मित्रुडु ।
రాము శ్యామ్ యొక్క మిత్రుడు.
రామ్ శ్యమ్ కా మిత్ర్ హై.
RAM IS A FRIEND OF SHAYAM.

2) बाहर गीता की कार खड़ी है ।
गीता योक्का कारु बयटा निलिचि उन्नदि ।
గీత యొక్క కారు బయట నిలిచివున్నది.
బాహర్ గీత కీ కార్ ఖడీ హై.
GITA'S CAR IS PARKED OUTSIDE.

3) राम के घर में कुत्ता है ।
रामुनि इंटिलो कुक्का उन्नदि ।
రాముని ఇంటిలో కుక్క ఉన్నది.
రామ్ కే ఘర్ మే కుత్తా హై.
THERE IS A DOG IN RAM'S HOUSE.

संबंध -रा-रे-री

1) मेरा भाई पुलिस वाला है ।
ना सोदरुडु पोलिसु ।
నా సోదరుడు పోలీసు.
మేరా భాయీ పులీస్ వాలా హై.
MY BROTHER IS A POLICEMAN.

2) मेरी बहन अच्छा गाती है ।
ना सोदरि बागा पाडुतुंदि ।
నా సోదరి బాగా పాడుతుంది.
మేరీ బహన్ అచ్ఛా గాతీ హై.
MY SISTER SINGS WELL.

3) आज मेरे यार की शादी है ।
ई रोजु ना मित्रुनि विवाहमु ।
ఈ రోజు నా మిత్రుని వివాహము.
ఆజ్ మేరే యార్ కీ షాతీ హై.
TODAY IS MY FRIEND'S MARRIAGE.

संप्रदान-को-के लिए

1) राम मेरे लिए उपहार लाया ।
रामु ना कोसमु बहुमति तेच्चाडु ।
రాము నా కోసము బహుమతి తెచ్చాడు.
రామ్ మేరే లియే వుపహార్ లాయా.
RAM BROUGHT A GIFT FOR ME.

2) राम ने सीता को फूल दिया ।
रामु सीताकु पूवुलनिच्चाडु ।
రాము సీతకు పూవుల నిచ్చాడు.
రామ్ నే సీత కో ఫూల్ దియా.
RAM GAVE FLOWERS TO SEETA.

3) माहात्मा गाँधी ने जनता को संदेश दिया ।
माहात्मा गाँधी प्रजलकु संदेशमिच्चेनु ।
మహాత్మగాంధీ ప్రజలకు సందేశమిచ్చెను.
మహాత్మగాంధీ నే జనతా కో సందేశ్ దియా.
MAHATMA GANDHI GAVE A MESSAGE TO THE PEOPLE.

अपादान -से

1) बच्चे स्कूल से घर आ गये ।
पिल्ललु स्कूलु नुंचि इंटिकि वच्चारु ।
పిల్లలు స్కూలు నుంచి ఇంటికి వచ్చారు.
బచ్చే స్కూల్ సే ఘర్ ఆ గయే.
CHILDREN ARE BACK HOME FROM SCHOOL.

2) किताब से पन्ने फाड़ दिये ।
पुस्तकमु नुंचि पेजीलु चिंचिवेसारु ।
పుస్తకము నుంచి పేజీలు చించివేసారు.
కితాబ్ సే పన్నే ఫాడ్ దియే.
THE PAGES FROM BOOK HAVE BEEN TORN.

अधिकरण - मे , पर

1) छत पर दो कबूतर हैं ।

मेड़ा मीदा रेंडु पावुरालु उन्नायि ।
మేడ మీద రెండు పావురాలు ఉన్నాయి.
ఛత్ పర్ దో కబూతర్ హై.
THERE ARE TWO PEGIONS ON THE TERRACE.

2) किताबों में अच्छी बातें लिखी होती है ।
पुस्तकाल्लो मंचि विषयालु व्रासि उंटायि ।
పుస్తకాల్లో మంచి విషయాలు వ్రాసి ఉంటాయి
కితాబో మే అచ్చి బాతే లిఖీ హోతీ హై.
GOOD SAYINGS ARE WRITTEN IN THE BOOKS.

संबोधन -हे-अरे

1) हे भगवान । ये क्या हो गया ?
भगवंतुड़ा । इदि एमि जरिगिंदि ।
భగవంతుడా ! ఇది ఏమిజరిగింది.
హే భగవాన్ ! యే క్యా హోగయా.
OH GOD ! WHAT HAS HAPPEND ?

2) अरे बच्चे ! सभी इधर आओ ।
ओ पिल्ललु ! अंदरू इला रंडि ।
ఓ పిల్లలూ ! అందరూ ఇలారండి.
అరే బచ్చే ! సభీ ఇధర్ ఆవో.
HEY KIDS ! COME HERE.

अभ्यास   అభ్యాసం   ***PRACTICE***

1) आपने क्या कहा ?
मीरु एमि चेप्परु ?
మీరు ఏమి చెప్పారు?
ఆప్‌నే క్యా కహా?
WHAT DID YOU SAY ?

2) बच्चे को दूध पिलाओ ।
पिल्ललकु पालु त्रागिंचु ।
పిల్లలకు పాలు త్రాగించు.
బచ్చే కో దూద్ పిలావో.
MAKE THE CHILDREN DRINK MILK.

3) राम के लिए खाना दो ।
रामु कु भोजनम् इव्वु ।
రాముకు భోజనం ఇవ్వు.
రామ్ కే లియే ఖానా దో.
GIVE FOOD FOR RAM.

4) आप कहाँ से आए हैं ?
मीरु एक्कडि नुंचि वच्चारु ।
మీరు ఎక్కడి నుంచి వచ్చారు.
ఆప్ కహా సే ఆయే హై.
WHERE HAVE YOU COME FROM ?

5) मेरी बहन ने मुझे राखी बांधी ।
ना सोदरि नाकु राखी कट्टिंदि ।
నా సోదరి నాకు రాఖీ కట్టింది.
మేరీ బహన్ నే ముఝే రాఖీ బాంధీ.
MY SISTER TIED A RAKHI TO ME.

6) कबूतर छत पर गूटरगूं कर रहा है ।
पावुरमु मेडा मीदा शब्दमु चेस्तुंदि ।
పావురము మేడ మీద శబ్ధము చేస్తుంది.
కబుతర్ ఛత్ పర్ గుట్‌రగూ కర్ రహా హై.
PIGEON IS MAKING NOISE UPSTAIRS.

7) हम लोग हवाई जहाज से जाएंगे ।
मेमु विमानमुलो वेलतामु ।
మేము విమానములో వెళతాము.
హమ్ లోగ్ హవాయి జహాజ్ సే జాయేంగే.
WE WILL GO BY AEROPLANE.

8) सीता राम की पत्नी है ।
सीता रामुनि भार्य ।
సీత రాముని భార్య.
సీత రామ్ కీ పత్నీ హై.
SITA IS RAM'S WIFE.

9) राम ने रावण को तीर से मारा ।
रामुडु रावणुनि बाणमुतो चंपेनु ।
రాముడు రావణుని బాణముతో చంపెను.
రామ్ నే రావణ్ కో తీర్ సే మారా.
RAM KILLED RAVANA WITH AN ARROW.

10) पुलिस ने चोर को डंडे से मारा ।
पोलिसुलु दोंगनु कर्रा तो कोट्टिनारु ।
పోలిసులు దొంగను కఱ్ఱతో కొట్టినారు.
పులీస్ నే చోర్ కో డండే సే మారా.
POLICE BEAT THE THIEF WITH A STICK.

अभ्यास (कालनुसार) భూత, వర్తమాన, భవిష్యత్‌కాలాలు

PAST, PRESENT, FUTURE TENSE

1) राम आम खाता है ।
रामु मामिडिपंड्डु तिंटुन्नाडु ।
రాము మామిడిపండు తింటున్నాడు.
రామ్ ఆమ్ ఖాతా హై.
RAM EATS A MANGO.

2) राम आम खा रहा है ।
रामु मामिडिपंड्डु तिंटू वुन्नाडु ।
రాము మామిడిపండు తింటూ వున్నాడు
రామ్ ఆమ్ ఖా రహా హై.
RAM IS EATING A MANGO.

3) राम आम खाता होगा ।
रामु मामिडिपंड्डु तिंटू वुंटाडु ।
రాము మామిడిపండు తింటూ వుంటాడు.
రామ్ ఆమ్ ఖాతా హోగా.
RAM MIGHT EAT A MANGO.

4) राम ने आम खाया ।
रामु मामिडिपंड्डु तिंन्नाडु ।
రాము మామిడిపండు తిన్నాడు.
రామ్ నే ఆమ్ ఖాయా.
RAM HAS EATEN A MANGO.

5) राम आम खाया था ।
रामु मामिडिपंड तिनेसाडु ।
రాము మామిడిపండు తినేసాడు.
రామ్ ఆమ్ ఖాయా థా.
RAM HAD EATEN A MANGO.

6) राम आम खाता था ।
रामु मामिडिपंडु तिनेवाडु ।
రాము మామిడిపండు తినేవాడు.
రామ్ ఆమ్ ఖాతా థా.
RAM USED TO EAT MANGO.

7) राम आम खाता रहा था ।
रामु मामिडिपंडु तिंटु उंडेवाडु ।
రాము మామిడిపండు తింటూ వుండేవాడు.
రామ్ ఆమ్ ఖాతా రహా థా.
RAM HAD BEEN EATING A MANGO.

8) राम आम खाएगा।
रामु मामिडिपंडु तिंटाडु ।
రాము మామిడిపండు తింటాడు.
రామ్ ఆమ్ ఖాయేగా.
RAM WILL EAT A MANGO.

9) राम आम खाता रहा होगा ।
रामु मामिडिपंडु तिंटु वुंडि वुंटाडु ।
రాము మామిడిపండు తింటూ వుండి వుంటాడు.
రామ్ ఆమ్ ఖాతా రహా హోగా.
RAM MIGHT HAVE BEEN EATING A MANGO.

10) सीता रोटी खाती है ।
सीता रोट्टे तिंटुंदि ।
సీత రొట్టె తింటుంది.
సీత రోటీ ఖాతీ హై.
SITA EATS ROTI.

11) सीता रोटी खा रही है ।
सीता रोट्टे तिंटू वुंदि ।
సీత రొట్టె తింటూ వుంది.
సీత రోటీ ఖా రహీ హై.
SITA IS EATING ROTI.
12) सीता रोटी खाती होगी ।

सीता रोट्टे तिंटू वुंडि वुंटुंदि ।
సీత రొట్టె తింటూ వుండి వుంటుంది.
సీత రోటీ ఖాతీ హోగీ.
SITA MIGHT BE EATING A ROTI.

13) सीता ने रोटी खायी ।
सीता रोट्टे तिन्नदि ।
సీత రొట్టె తిన్నది.
సీతా రోటీ ఖాయి.
SITA ATE ROTI.

14) सीता ने रोटी खायी थी ।
सीता रोट्टे तिन्नदि ।
సీత రొట్టె తిన్నది.
సీత రోటీ ఖాయి థీ.
SITA HAD EATEN A ROTI.

15) सीता रोटी खाती थी ।
सीता रोट्टे तिनेदि ।
సీత రొట్టె తినేది.
సీత రోటీ ఖాతీ థీ.
SITA USED TO EAT ROTI.

16) सीता रोटी खाती रही थी ।
सीता रोट्टे तिंटू वुन्नदि ।
సీత రొట్టె తింటూ వున్నది.
సీత రోటీ ఖాతీ థీ.
SITA HAD BEEN EATING ROTI.

17) सीता रोटी खएगी।
सीता रोट्टे तिंटुंदि ।
సీత రొట్టె తింటుంది.
సీత రోటీ ఖాయేగీ.
SITA WILL EAT ROTI.

18) सीता रोटी खाती रही होगी ।

सीता रोट्टे तिंटू उंडि उंटुंदि।
సీత రొట్టె తింటూగి. వుండి వుంటుంది.
సీత రోటీ ఖాతీ రహీ హో
SITA MIGHT HAVE BEEN EATING A ROTI.

19) सीता रोटीयाँ खायी।
सीता रोट्टेलु तिन्नदि ।
సీత రొట్టెలు తిన్నది.
సీత రోటీయా ఖాయి.
SITA ATE ROTIS.

अभ्यास छोटे वाक्य చిన్న వాక్యాల అభ్యాసం PRACTICING SMALL SENTENCE

1) मैं टीवी देखता हूँ ।
नेनु टी वी चूस्तुन्नानु ।
నేను టీవీ చూస్తున్నాను.
మై టీవీ దేఖ్‌తా హూ.
I WATCH T.V.

2) हम स्कूल जाते हैं ।
मेमु स्कूलुकु वेलुतुन्नामु ।
మేము స్కూలుకు వెళుతున్నాము.
హమ్ స్కూల్ జాతే హై.
WE GO TO SCHOOL.

3) लड़कियाँ नाचती हैं ।
अम्माइलु नाट्यमू चेस्तुन्नारु ।
అమ్మాయిలు నాట్యం చేస్తున్నారు.
లడ్‌కియా నాచ్‌తీ హై.
THE GIRLS ARE DANCING.

4) श्याम दिल्ली मे रहता है ।
श्याम दिल्लीलो निवशिस्तुन्नाडु ।
శ్యామ్ ఢిల్లీలో నివసిస్తున్నాడు.
శ్యామ్ ఢిల్లీ మే రహ్‌తా హై.
SHYAM LIVES IN DELHI.

5) बच्चे गेंद खेल रहे हैं ।
पिल्ललु बंताटा आडुतुन्नारु ।
పిల్లలు బంతాట ఆడుతున్నారు.
బచ్చే గేంద్ ఖేల్ రహే హై.
THE CHILDREN ARE PLAYING WITH THE BALL.

6) तू यह काम कर ।
नीवु ई पनि चयि।
నీవు ఈ పని చేయి.
తూ యహ్ కామ్ కర్.
YOU DO THIS WORK.

7) उसे मत मारो ।
अतनिनि कोट्टवद्दु ।
అతనిని కొట్టవద్దు.
ఉసే మత్ మారో.
DO NOT BEAT HIM.

8) तुम छोड़ दो ।
नुव्वु वदिलेयि ।
నువ్వు వదిలేయి.
తుమ్ ఛోడ్ దో.
YOU LEAVE IT.

9) तू वहाँ बैठ ।
नीवु अक्कड कूर्चो ।
నీవు అక్కడ కూర్చో.
తూ వహా బైఠ్.
YOU SIT THERE.

10) तुम वहाँ बैठो ।
नीवु अक्कडा कूर्चो ।
నీవు అక్కడ కూర్చో.
తుమ్ వహా బైఠో.
YOU SIT THERE.

11) आप वहाँ बैठिए ।
मीरु अक्कड कूर्चोंडि ।
మీరు అక్కడ కూర్చోండి
ఆప్ వహాం బైఠియే.
YOU SIT THERE.

12) लालकिला दिल्ली में है ।
लालकिला दिल्ली लो उंदि ।
లాల్‌కిలా ఢిల్లీలో వుంది.
లాల్‌కాలా దిల్లీ మే హై.
REDFORT IS IN DELHI.

13) पानी ठंडा है ।
नीरु चल्लगा उंदि ।
నీరు చల్లగా వుంది.
పానీ ఠండా హై.
WATER IS COOL.

14) धूप तेज है ।
एंडा तीव्रंगा उंदि ।
ఎండ తీవ్రంగా వుంది.
ధూప్ తేజ్ హై.
IT IS SUNNY.

15) बाल काले हैं ।
जुट्टु नल्लगा उंदि ।
జుట్టు నల్లగా ఉంది.
బాల్ కాలే హై.
HAIR IS BLACK.

16) उसका रंग गोरा है ।
अतडु तेल्लगा उंटाडु ।
అతడు తెల్లగా వుంటాడు.
ఉస్‌కా రంగ్ గోరా హై.
HE IS FAIR IN COLOUR.

17) गाय घास खाती है ।

आवु गड्डि तिंटुंदि ।
ఆవు గడ్డి తింటుంది.
గాయ్ ఘాస్ ఖాతీ హై.
COW EATS GRASS.

स्वपरिचय   స్వపరిచయం   SELF INTRODUCTION

1) मैं राजू हूँ / मेरा नाम राजू है ।
नेनु राजुनि / ना पेरु राजु ।
నేను రాజుని/నా పేరు రాజు.
మై రాజూ హూ/ మేరా నామ్ రాజూ హై.
I AM RAJU/MY NAME IS RAJU.

2) मैं विद्यार्थी हूँ ।
नेनु विद्यार्थीनि ।
నేను విద్యార్థిని.
మై విద్యార్థి హూ.
I AM A STUDENT.

3) मैं पांचवी कक्षा मे पढ़ रहा हूँ ।
नेनु ऐदवा तरगति चदुवुतुन्नानु ।
నేను ఐయిదవ తరగతి చదువుతున్నాను.
మై పాంచ్వి క్లాస్ మే పఢ్ రహా హూ.
I AM STUDYING IN 5TH CLASS.

4) मैं खुशी हूँ ।
नेनु खुशीनि ।
నేను ఖుషీని.
మై ఖుషీ హూ.
I AM KHUSHI.

5)मैं महाविद्यालय मे पढ़ रही हूँ ।
नेनु महाविद्यालयमु लो चदुवुतुन्नानु ।
నేను మహావిద్యాలయంలో చదువుతున్నాను.
మై మహావిద్యాలయ్ మే పఢ్ రహీ హూ.
I AM STUDYING IN COLLEGE.

6) मुझे क्रिकेट बहुत पसंद है ।
नाकु क्रिकेट चाला इष्ट्म् ।
నాకు క్రికెట్ చాలా ఇష్టం.
ముఝే క్రికెట్ బహుత్ పసంద్ హై.
I LOVE CRICKET.

7) मैं किताबें पढ़ना पसंद करती हूँ ।
नेनु पुस्तकालु चदवटान्नि इष्टपडतानु ।
నేను పుస్తకాలు చదవటాన్ని ఇష్టపడతాను.
మై కితాబే పఢ్నా పసంద్ కరతీ హూ.
I LOVE TO READ BOOKS.

8) मेरी सहेली का नाम पलक है ।
ना स्नेहितुरालि पेरु पलक ।
నా స్నేహితురాలి పేరు పలక్
మేరీ సహేలీ కా నామ్ పలక్ హై.
MY FRIEND'S NAME IS PALAK.

9) मेरे दोस्त का नाम अमित है ।
ना स्नेहितुनि पेरु अमित ।
నా స్నేహితుని పేరు అమిత్.
మేరే దోస్త్ కా నామ్ అమిత్ హై.
MY FRIEND'S NAME IS AMIT.

10) मुझे मैगी खाना पसंद है ।
नाकु मेगी तिनटम् इष्टम् ।
నాకు మేగీ తినడం ఇష్టం.
ముఝే మేగీ ఖానా పసంద్ హై.
I LIKE TO EAT MAGGI.

11) मैं दोसा खाना पसंद करता हूँ ।
नेनु दोसा तिनटम् इष्टपडतानु ।
మై దోసా ఖానా పసంద్ కర్తా హూ.
నేను దోశ తినటం ఇష్టపడతాను.
I LIKE TO EAT DOSA.

12) हम दोनो एक ही कोलोनी मे रहते है ।
मेमिद्दरम ओके कोलोनी लो उंटामु ।
హమ్ దోనో ఏక్‌హీ కొలనీ మే రహ్‌తే హై.
మేమిద్దరం ఒకే కొలనీ లో వుంటాము.
WE BOTH LIVE IN THE SAME COLONY.

13) मुझे संगीत सुनना पसंद है ।
नाकु संगीतमु विनटम इष्टम ।
నాకు సంగీతము వినటం ఇష్టం.
ముఝే సంగీత్ సున్‌నా పసంద్ హై.
I LIKE TO HEAR MUSIC.

14) मेरे दो भाई एक बहन है ।
नाकु इद्दरु सोदरुडु ओका सोदरि उन्नारु ।
నాకు ఇద్దరు సోదరులు,ఒక సోదరి వున్నారు.
మేరే దో భాయీ ఎక్ బహన్ హై.
I HAVE TWO BROTHERS AND A SISTER.

15) मेरे पिता इंजीनियर है ।
मा नान्नगारु इंजनीयरु ।
మా నాన్నగారు ఇంజనీయరు.
మేరే పితా ఇంజనీయర్ హై.
MY FATHER IS AN ENGINEER.

16) मेरी मां गृहिणी है ।
ना तल्लि गृहिणि ।
మేరీ మా గృహిణి హై.
నా తల్లి గృహిణి.
MY MOTHER IS A HOMEMAKER.

सामान्य वार्तालाप సంభాషణ NORMAL CONVERSATION

1) आप कैसे है ?
मीरेला वुन्नारु ?
మీరెలా వున్నారు ?
ఆప్ కైసే హై ?
HOW ARE YOU ?

2) मैं ठीक हूँ ।
नेनु बागाने उन्नानु ।
నేను బాగానే ఉన్నాను.
మై ఠీక్ హూ.
I AM FINE.

3) आप क्या करते है ?
मीरु एमि चेस्तुंटारु ?
మీరు ఏమి చేస్తుంటారు ?
ఆప్ క్యా కర్‌తే హై ?
WHAT DO YOU DO ?

4) मैं इंजीनियरिंग कर रहा हूँ ।
नेनु इंजीनियरिंगु चेस्तुन्नानु ।
నేను ఇంజనీరింగు చేస్తున్నాను.
మై ఇంజనీరింగ్ కర్ రహా హూ.
I AM DOING ENGINEERING.

5) और आप ?
मरि मीरु ?
మరి మీరు ?
అవుర్ ఆప్ ?
WHAT ABOUT YOU ?

6)मैं एम.एस.सी.कर रहा हूँ ।
नेनु एम.एस.सी.चेस्तुन्नानु ।

నేను ఎమ్.ఎస్.సి చేస్తున్నాను.
మై ఎమ్.ఎస్.సి కర్ రహా హూ.
I AM DOING M.SC.

7) और आगे क्या करने का इरादा है ?
मरि तरुवाता एम चेध्दामनुकुंटुंन्नारु ?
మరి తరువాత ఏం చేద్దామనుకుంటున్నారు ?
అవుర్ ఆగే క్యా కర్‌నే కా ఇరాదా హై ?
WHAT DO YOU WANT TO DO AFTER THIS ?

8) पढ़ाई पूरी करके प्रतियोगी परीक्षा की तैयारी करूंगा ।
चदुवु पूर्ति चेसि पोटी परीक्षलकु तयारवुतानु ।
చదువు పూర్తి చేసి పోటీ పరీక్షలకు తయారవుతాను.
పఢాయి పూర్తీ కర్‌కే ప్రతియోగీ పరీక్షా కీ తైయారీ కరూంగా.
AFTER FINISHING STUDIES, I WANT TO PREPARE FOR COMPETITIVE EXAMS.

9) चलिए चाय पीते है ।
पदंडि,टी तागुदामु ।
పదండి, టీ తాగుదాము.
చలియే, ఛాయ్ పీతే హై.
COME, LET US HAVE TEA.

10) मैं चाय नहीं पीता ।
नेनु टी तागनु ।
నేను టీ తాగను.
మై చాయ్ నహీ పీతా.
I DON'T DRINK TEA.

11) कोई बात नहीं तुम दूध ले लेना ।
फरवालेदु नुव्वु पालु तीसुको ।
ఫరవాలేదు నువ్వు పాలు తీసుకో.
కోయీ బాత్ నహీ తుమ్ దూద్ లే లేనా.
IT IS OK. HAVE MILK

12) ठीक है ।
सरे अयिते ।
సరే అయితే.
ఠీక్ హై.
OK.

13) तुम रखो पैसे मैं दे देता हूँ ।
नुव्वु उंडु, डब्बुलु नेनिस्तानु ।
నువ్వు వుండు డబ్బులు నేనిస్తాను.
తుమ్ రఖో పైసే మై దే దేతా హూ.
LEAVE IT. I WILL PAY.

14) मेरे पास खुले पैसे है ।
ना दग्गरा चिल्लरा डब्बुलुन्नाइ ।
నా దగ్గర చిల్లర డబ్బులు వున్నాయి.
మేరే పాస్ ఖులే పైసే హై.
I HAVE CHANGE.

15) कोई बात नहीं तुम रखो ।
फरवालेदु नुव्वु उंचुको ।
ఫరవాలేదు నువ్వు వుంచుకో.
కోయీ బాత్ నహీ తుమ్ రఖో.
IT IS OK. YOU KEEP IT.

16) इंजीनियरिंग के बाद क्या इरादा है ।
इंजीनियरिंगु तरुवाता एम चेध्दमनुकुंटुंन्नावु ।
ఇంజనీరింగు తరువాత ఏం చేద్దామనుకుంటున్నావు ?
ఇంజనీరింగ్ కే బాద్ క్యా ఇరాదా హై ?
WHAT DO YOU PLAN TO DO AFTER ENGINEERING ?

17) गेट परीक्षा की तैयारी करूंगा ।
गेट परीक्षकु तयारवुतुन्नानु ।
గేట్ పరీక్ష కు తయారవుతున్నాను.
గేట్ పరీక్షా కీ తైయారి కరూంగా.
I WILL PREPARE FOR GATE EXAMINATION.

18) आप से मिलकर बहुत अच्छा लगा ।

मिम्मलनि कलवटम बागा अनिपिंचिंदि ।
మిమ్మల్ని కలవటం బాగా అనిపించింది.
ఆప్ సే మిల్‌కర్ బహుత్ అచ్చా లగా.
IT IS A PLEASURE TO MEET YOU.

विनती　　అభ్యర్థన　　REQUEST

1)कृपया मेरी बातें सुनिए ।
दयचेसि ना माटा विनंडि ।
దయచేసి నా మాట వినండి.
కృపయా మేరీ బాతే సునియే.
KINDLY LISTEN TO ME.

2)थोड़ी देर वहाँ बैठीए ।
कासेपु अक्कड़ा कूर्चोंडि ।
కాసేపు అక్కడ కూర్చోండి.
థోడీ దేర్ వహా బైఠియే.
SIT THERE FOR A WHILE.

3)क्या आपने खाना खाया ?
मीरु भोजनम् चेसारा ?
మీరు భోజనం చేసారా ?
క్యా ఆప్‌నే ఖానా ఖాయా ?
DID YOU HAVE YOUR MEALS ?

4)मुझे वह किताब चाहिए ।
नाकु आ पुस्तकमु कावालि ।
నాకు ఆ పుస్తకము కావాలి.
ముఝే వహ్ కితాబ్ చాహియే.
I WANT THAT BOOK.

5)मैं फिर आपसे मिलता हूँ ।
नेनु मिम्मालिनि तरुवाता कलुस्तानु ।
నేను మిమ్మల్ని తరువాత కలుస్తాను.
మై ఫిర్ ఆప్‌సే మిల్‌తా హూ.
I WILL MEET YOU AFTERWARDS.

6)क्या आप थोड़ा सरकेंगे ?
मीरु कास्ता जरुगुतारा ?
మీరు కాస్త జరుగుతారా ?
క్యా ఆప్ థోడా సర్కేంగే ?
WILL YOU MOVE A LITTLE?

7)कृपया अपनी कलम दीजिए ।
दयाचेसि मी पेन्नु इव्वंडि ।
దయచేసి మీ పెన్ను ఇవ్వండి.
కృపయా అప్నీ కలమ్ దీజియే .
KINDLY GIVE YOUR PEN.

8)क्या आप मेरे लिए भी पानी ले आएंगे ?
मीरु नाक्कूड़ा नीरु तेस्तारा ?
మీరు నాక్కూడా నీరు తెస్తారా ?
క్యా ఆప్ మేరే లియే భీ పానీ లే ఆయేంగే ?
CAN YOU FETCH WATER FOR ME TOO?

9)मदद करने से हमें खुशी मिलती है ।
सहायम चेस्ते मनकि आनंदं लभिस्तुंदि ।
సహాయం చేస్తే మనకి ఆనందం లభిస్తుంది.
మదద్ కర్నే సే హమే ఖుషీ మిల్తీ హై.
WE FIND HAPPINESS BY HELPING OTHERS.

10)बाजार से चावल ले आइए ।
बजारु नुंचि बिय्यम तीसुकुरंडि ।
బజారు నుంచి బియ్యం తీసుకురండి.
బాజార్ సే చావల్ లే ఆయియే.
BRING RICE FROM MARKET.

11)एक बार देखिए,बहुत अच्छा लगेगा ।
ओकसारि चूडंडि । चाला बावुंटुंदि ।
ఒక్కసారి చూడండి. చాలా బావుంటుంది.
ఏక్ బార్ దేఖిఏ. బహుత్ అచ్ఛా లగేగా.
LOOK AT IT ONCE. IT WILL BE GOOD.

12)इस प्रकार के कटु शब्दों का प्रयोग मत कीजिए ।
इटुवंटि कटुवैना पदालु वाड़ावद्दु ।
ఇటువంటి కటువైన పదాలు వాడవద్దు.
ఇస్‌ప్రకార్ కే కటు శబ్ద్ కా ప్రయోగ్ మత్ కీజాఎ.
DON'T USE SUCH HARSH WORDS.

13)ये सभी में बाँट दो ।
इदि अंदरिकी पंचु ।
ఇది అందరికి పంచు.
యే సభీ మే బాంట్ దో.
DISTRIBUTE THIS AMONG EVERYONE.

आज्ञाकारी वाक्य ఆజ్ఞాపూర్వక వాక్యములు ORDERING SENTENCES

1) वहाँ बैठो ।
अक्कड़ा कूर्चो ।
అక్కడ కూర్చో.
వహా బైఠో.
SIT OVER THERE.

2) चुप रहो ।
निशब्दमुगा वुंडु ।
నిశ్శబ్ధంగా వుండు.
చుప్ రహో.
KEEP QUIET.

3) बातें मत करो ।
माट्लाडवद्दु।
మాట్లాడవద్దు.
బాతే మత్ కరో.
STOP TALKING.

4) जल्दी उठो ।
त्वरगा ले ।
త్వరగా లే.
జల్ది ఉటో.
GET UP FAST.

5) इस सब पर ध्यान मत दो ।
वीटन्निटि मीद ध्यासा पेट्टोद्दु ।
వీటన్నిటి మీద ధ్యాస పెట్టొద్దు.
ఇస్ సబ్ పర్ ధ్యాన్ మత్ దో.
DONT TAKE CARE OF ALL THESE THINGS.

6) मत जाओ ।
वेल्लोद्दु ।
వెళ్ళొద్దు.
మత్ జావో.
DONT GO.

7) मत बैठो ।
कूर्चो वद्दु ।
కూర్చో వద్దు.
మత్ బైఠో.
DO NOT SIT.

8) खड़े रहो ।
निलबडि वुंडु ।
ఖడే రహో.
నిలబడి వుండు.
KEEP STANDING.

9) मेरी बात सुनो ।
ना माटा विनु ।
మేరీ బాత్ సునో.
నా మాట విను.
LISTEN TO ME.

10) गाना मत गाओ ।
पाटा पाडवद्दु ।
గానా మత్ గావో.
పాట పాడవద్దు.
DO NOT SING A SONG.

11) वहाँ मत जाओ ।
अक्कडकु वेल्लोद्दु ।
వహా మత్ జావో.
అక్కడకు వెళ్ళొద్దు.
DO NOT GO THERE.

12) जल्दी दौड़कर जाओ ।
त्वरगा परिगेत्तुकुनि वेल्लु ।
జల్ది దౌడ్ కర్ జావో.
త్వరగా పరిగెత్తుకుని వెళ్లు.
GO RUNNING FAST.

13) मेरे पास मत आओ ।
ना दग्गरकु रावोद्दु ।
మేరే పాస్ మత్ ఆవో.
నా దగ్గరకు రావొద్దు.
DONT COME NEAR ME.

14) ये मत खाओ ।
इदि तिनवद्दु ।
యే మత్ ఖావో.
ఇది తినవద్దు.
DONT EAT THIS.

15) सच-सच बताओ ।
निजम चेप्पु ।
సచ్ సచ్ బతావో.
నిజం చెప్పు.
TELL THE TRUTH.

16) झूठ मत बोलो ।
अबध्दमाडवद्दु।
ఝూట్ మత్ బోలో.
అబద్ధమాడవద్దు.
DONT LIE.

17) वो लेकर आओ ।
अवि तीसुकुनि रा ।
వో లేకర్ ఆవో.
అవి తీసుకుని రా.
BRING THOSE/FETCH THAT.

18) जल्दी करो समय नहीं है ।
त्वरगा चेयि, समयम् लेदु ।
జల్ది కరో సమయ్ నహీ హై.
త్వరగా చేయి సమయం లేదు.
DO FAST, WE DONT HAVE TIME.

19) पहले सोओ ।
मुंदु पडुको ।
పహలే సోఓ.
ముందు పడుకో.
SLEEP FIRST.

20) स्कूल जाओ ।
स्कूलुकु वेल्लु ।
స్కూల్ జావో.
స్కూలుకు వెళ్లు.
GO TO SCHOOL.

21) ध्यान से करो ।
श्रध्दगा चेयि ।
ధ్యాన్ సే కరో.
శ్రద్ధగా చేయి.
DO YOUR WORK WITH CONCENTRATION.

22) भूलना मत ।
मरचि पोवध्दु ।
మరచి పోవద్దు.
భూల్‌నా మత్.
DONT FORGET.

23) नम्रता से पेश आओ ।
विनया विधेयतलतो प्रवर्तिंचु ।
వినయ విధేయతలతో ప్రవర్తించు.
నమ్రతా సే పేష్ ఆవో.
BE POLITE.

24) मधुर वाणी बोलो ।

तीयगा माट्लाड्डु ।
తీయగా మాట్లాడు.
మధుర్ వాణీ బోలో.
TALK SWEETLY.

25) मेरे पीछे आओ ।
ना वेनाकाले रा ।
నా వెనకాలే రా.
మేరే పీచే ఆఒ.
COME AFTER ME.

26) जल्दी आओ ।
त्वरगा रा ।
త్వరగా రా.
జల్ది ఆవో.
COME FAST.

27) ऊपर जाइये ।
पैकि वेक्लंडि ।
పైకి వెళ్ళండి.
ఊపర్ జాయియే.
GO UP.

28) रुकिये ।
आगंडि ।
ఆగండి.
రుకియే.
STOP.

29) धीरे-धीरे जाइए ।
नेम्मादिगा वेक्लंडि ।
నెమ్మదిగా వెళ్ళండి.
ధీరే ధీరే జాయియే.
WALK SLOWLY.

30) सावधान रहिए ।
जाग्रत्तगा वुंडंडि ।

జాగ్రత్తగా వుండండి.
సావాధాన్ రహియే.
BE CAREFULL/STAY ALERT.

31) चलो । हटो
वेळ्ळंडि,तप्पुकोंडि ।
వెళ్ళండి,తప్పుకోండి.
చలో హటో.
GIVE WAY.

32) जोर से बोलो ।
गट्टिगा चेप्पु ।
గట్టిగా చెప్పు.
జోర్ సే బోలో.
SAY IN LOUD VOICE.

33) फिर कोशिश करो ।
मळ्ळी प्रयतिंचु ।
మళ్లీ ప్రయత్నించు.
ఫిర్ కోషిష్ కరో.
TRY AGAIN.

34) मुझे परेशान मत करो ।
नन्नु इब्बंदि पेट्टावद्दु ।
నన్ను ఇబ్బంది పెట్టవద్దు.
ముఝే పరేషాన్ మత్ కరో.
DONT TROUBLE ME.

35) उसे देखने दो ।
दानिनि चूडानिव्वु ।
దానిని చూడనివ్వు.
ఉసే దేఖ్ నే దో.
LET ME SEE THAT.
36) आगे देखिए ।
मुंदुकु चुडंडि ।
ఆగే దేఖియే.

ముందుకు చూడండి.

LOOK FRONT.

37) करो या मरो ।

चेय्यु लेकापोते चावु ।

కరో యా మరో.

చెయ్యి లేకపోతే చావు.

DO OR DIE.

IMPLEMENTING QUESTION WORDS

कब	एप्पुडु	ఎప్పుడు	కబ్	WHEN ?
कहाँ	एक्कड़ा	ఎక్కడ	కహాం	WHERE ?
कौन	एवरु	ఎవరు	కౌన్	WHO ?
किसका	एवरियोक्का	ఎవరియొక్క	కిస్‌కా	WHOSE ?
किधर	एक्कड़ा	ఎక్కడ	కిధర్	WHERE ?
किसलिए	एंदुचेता	ఎందుచేత	కిస్‌లిఏ	FOR WHAT ?
क्यों	एंदुकु	ఎందుకు	క్యూం	WHY ?
कितना	एंता	ఎంత	కితనా	HOW MUCH ?
कितने	एन्नि	ఎన్ని	కితనె	HOW MANY ?
क्या	एमिटि	ఏమిటి	క్యా	WHAT ?
काहे	एंदुकु	ఎందుకు	కాహె	WHY ?
कौन सा	एदि	ఏది	కౌన్‌సా	WHICH ONE ?
कैसा	एला	ఎలా	కైసా	HOW ?

1) कब ? **ఎప్పుడు ?** WHEN ?

तुम कब आओगे?
नीवु एप्पुडु वस्तावु?
నీవు ఎప్పుడు వస్తావు ?
తుమ్ కబ్ ఆవోగే ?
WHEN WILL YOU COME ?

2) कहां? **ఎక్కడ ?** **WHERE ?**

तुम कहाँ रहते हो?
नीवु एक्कडा उंटावु?
నీవు ఎక్కడ ఉంటావు ?
తుమ్ కహా రహ్తే హో ?
WHERE DO YOU LIVE ?

3) कौन? **ఎవరు ?** **WHO ?**

दरवाजे पर कौन खड़ा है?
तलुपु दग्गरा एवरु निलचुनिवुन्नारु?
తలుపు దగ్గర ఎవరు నిలుచునివున్నారు ?
దర్వాజే పర్ కౌన్ ఖడా హై ?
WHO IS STANDING AT THE DOOR ?

4) किसका? **ఎవరియొక్క ?** **WHOSE ?**

यह घर किसका है?
ई इल्लु एवरिदि?
ఈ ఇల్లు ఎవరిది ?

యహ్ ఘర్ కిస్‌కా హై ?
WHOSE HOUSE IS THIS ?

5) किधर? **ఎక్కడ ?** **WHERE ?**

मुझे किधर ले जा रहे हो?
नन्नु एक्कडकु तीसुकुवेलतुन्नावु?
నన్ను ఎక్కడికి తీసుకువెళ్తున్నావు ?
ముఝే కిధర్ లే జా రహే హో ?
WHERE ARE YOU TAKING ME ?

6) किसलिए? **ఎందుచేత ?** **FOR WHAT ?**

तुम यहाँ किसलिए आए हो?
नीवु इक्कडिकि एंदुकु वच्चावु?
నీవు ఇక్కడికి ఎందుకు వచ్చావు ?
తుమ్ యహాం కిస్‌లియే ఆయే హో ?
WHY DID YOU COME HERE ?

7) क्यों? **ఎందుకు ?** **WHY ?**

इतनी जल्दी क्यों जा रहे हो?
इंता त्वरगा एंदुकु वेलतुन्नावु?
ఇంత త్వరగా ఎందుకు వెళుతున్నావు ?
ఇతని జల్దీ క్యోం జా రహే హో ?
WHY ARE YOU LEAVING SO EARLY ?

8) कितना? **ఎంత ?** **HOW MANY ?**

दिल्ली से मुंबई का भाड़ा कितना है?
दिल्ली नुन्चि मुंबई वरकु प्रयाणपु खर्चु एंता?
ఢిల్లీ నుంచి ముంబాయి వరకు ప్రయాణము ఖర్చు ఎంత ?
ఢిల్లీ సే ముంబాయి కా భాడా కితనా హై ?
WHAT IS THE FARE BETWEEN MUMBAI AND DELHI ?

9) कितने? **ఎన్ని ?** **HOW MUCH ?**

और कितने लोग बचे हैं?
इंका एंतामन्दि उन्नारु?
ఇంకా ఎంతమంది ఉన్నారు ?
ఔర్ కితనే లోగ్ బచే హై ?
HOW MANY PEOPLE ARE LEFT ?

10) क्या? **ఏమిటి ?** **WHAT ?**

तुम्हे उनसे क्या काम है ?
नीकु वारितो एमि पनि ?
నీకు వారితో ఏమి పని ?
తుమ్హే ఉన్సే క్యా కామ్ హై ?
WHAT DO YOU WANT FROM THEM ?

11) काहे? **ఎందుకు ?** **WHY ?**

हमें काहे नही बताए?
मातो एंदुकु चेप्पलेदु?
మాతో ఎందుకు చెప్పలేదు ?
హమే కాహే నహీ బతాయే ?
WHY DIDN'T YOU TELL US ?

12) कौन सी? **ఏది ?** **WHICH ONE ?**

तुम्हे कौन सी साड़ी पसंद हैं?
नीकु ए चीरा इष्टमु ?
నీకు ఏ చీర ఇష్టము ?
తుమ్హే కౌన్ సీ సాఢీ పసంద్ హై ?
WHICH SAREE DO YOU LIKE ?

13) कैसी? **ఎలా ?** **HOW ?**

अभी आपकी तबीयत कैसी है?
इप्पुडु मी आरोग्यमु एला उन्दि?
ఇప్పుడు మీ ఆరోగ్యము ఎలా ఉంది ?
అభీ ఆప్‌కీ తబీయత్ కైసీ హై ?
HOW IS YOUR HEALTH NOW ?

प्रश्नवाचक वाक्य ప్రశ్నార్థక వాక్యములు QUESTION SENTENCES

1) माँ, आज क्या बनायी?
अम्मा इरोजु एम चेसावु/वंडावु?
అమ్మ ఈరోజు ఏం చేసావు/వండావు ?
మా ఆజ్ క్యా బనాయి ?
MOM, WHAT DID YOU PREPARE TODAY?

2) तुम क्यों सोई हो?
नुव्वु एंदुकु पडुकुन्नावु ?
నువ్వు ఎందుకు పడుకున్నావు ?
తుమ్ క్యోం సోయీ హో ?
WHY ARE YOU ASLEEP ?

3) जल्दी उठो स्कूल जाना है ।
वेगंगा ले स्कूल कि वेल्लालि कदा ।
వేగంగా లే స్కూలుకి వెళ్ళాలి కదా.
జల్దీ ఉఠో స్కూల్ జానా హై.
GET UP FAST. YOU HAVE TO GO TO SCHOOL.

4) आज टिफिन मे क्या ले जाओगे ?
ईरोजु टिफिन एम तिसु केल्ताउ ?
ఈరోజు టిఫిన్ ఏం తీసుకెళ్తావు ?
ఆజ్ టిఫిన్ మే క్యా లే జావోగే ?
WHAT WILL YOU TAKE IN TIFFIN TODAY ?

5) होमवर्क किया?
होमवर्कु चेसावा?
హోమ్‌వర్కు చేసావా ?
హోమ్‌వర్క్ కియా ?
DID YOU FINISH YOUR HOMEWORK ?

6) क्या खाओगे? क्या बनाऊ?
एम तिंटावु? एम चेयनु?
ఏం తింటావు ? ఏం తయారు చేయను ?
క్యా ఖావోగే ? క్యా బనాఊం ?
WHAT WILL YOU EAT ? WHAT SHALL I MAKE ?

7) आज का दिन कैसा रहा?
ईरोजु एला जरिगिंदि?
ఈరోజు ఎలా జరిగింది ?
ఆజ్ కా దిన్ కైసా రహా ?
HOW WAS YOUR DAY ?

8) तुम क्या कर रहे हो ?
नीवु एमि चेस्तुन्नावु ?
నీవు ఏమి చేస్తున్నావు ?
తుమ్ క్యా కర్ రహే హో ?
WHAT ARE YOU DOING ?

9) तुम कहाँ जाओगे ?
नीवु एक्कडिकि वेल्तावु ?
నీవు ఎక్కడికి వెళ్తావు ?
తుమ్ కహా జావోగే ?
WHERE WILL YOU GO ?

10) तुम्हारा नाम क्या है ?
नी पेरेमिटि ?
నీ పేరేమిటి ?
తుమ్‌హరా నామ్ క్యా హై ?
WHAT IS YOUR NAME ?

11) राम क्या काम करता है ?
रामु एमि पनि चेस्तुन्नाडु ?
రాము ఏమి పని చేస్తున్నాడు ?
రాము క్యా కామ్ కర్తా హై ?
WHAT WORK DOES RAM DO ?

12) राम की मां कैसी है ?
रामुनि तल्लि एला वुंदि ?
రాముని తల్లి ఎలా వుంది ?
రామ్ కీ మా కైసీ హై ?
HOW IS RAM'S MOTHER ?

13) उसने ऐसा क्यों किया ?
अतडु अला एंदुकु चेसाडु ?
అతడు అలా ఎందుకు చేసాడు ?
వుస్‌నే ఐసా క్యోం కియా ?
WHY DID HE DO LIKE THIS ?

14) सोहन कैसा पढ़ता है ?
सोहन एला चदुवुतुन्नाडु ?
సోహన్ ఎలా చదువుతున్నాడు ?
సోహన్ కైసా పఢ్‌తా హై ?
HOW DOES SOHAN STUDY ?

15) क्या गीता ठीक है ?
गीता बागाने उन्नदा ?
గీత బాగానే వున్నదా ?
క్యా గీతా ఠీక్ హై ?
IS GITA FINE ?

16) उसको क्या चाहिए ?
अतडिकि एमि कावालि ?
అతడికి ఏమి కావాలి ?
వుస్‌కో క్యా చాహియే ?
WHAT DOES HE WANT?

17) क्या तुझे जाना चाहिए ?
एमिटि नुव्वु वेल्लालसि उंदा ?
ఏమిటి నువ్వు వెళ్లాల్సి వుందా ?
క్యా తుఝే జానా చాహియే ?
ARE YOU SUPPOSED TO GO THERE ?
18) क्या तुम उससे प्यार करते हो ?

एमिटि नुव्वतडिनि प्रेमिस्तुन्नावा ?
ఏమిటి నువ్వతడిని ప్రేమిస్తున్నావా ?
క్యా తుమ్ వుసే ప్యార్ కర్‌తే హో ?
DO YOU LOVE HIM ?

19) क्या वह तुम्हे भी प्यार करती है ?
आमे कूड़ा निन्नु प्रेमिस्तुंदा ?
ఆమె కూడా నిన్ను ప్రేమిస్తుందా ?
క్యా వహ్ తుమ్‌హే భి ప్యార్ కర్‌తీ హై ?
DOES SHE LOVE YOU TOO ?

20) ये किसकी बेटी है ?
ईमे एवरी कूतुरु ?
ఈమె ఎవరి కూతురు ?
యే కిస్‌కీ బేటీ హై ?
WHOSE DAUGHTER IS SHE ?

21) इसके माता-पिता कौन है ?
ईमे तल्लिदंड्रुलु एवरु ?
ఈమె తల్లిదండ్రులు ఎవరు ?
ఇస్‌కే మాతా–పితా కౌన్ హై ?
WHO ARE HER PARENTS ?

22) मैं क्या करू ?
नेनु एमि चेयनु?
నేను ఏమి చేయను ?
మై క్యా కరూ?
WHAT DO I DO ?

23)क्या आप भी समोसे खाएंगे ?
मीरु कूड़ा समोसालु तिंटारा ?
మీరు కూడా సమోసాలు తింటారా ?
క్యా ఆప్ భీ సమోసే ఖాయేంగే ?
WOULD YOU ALSO EAT SAMOSAS ?
24) मांने तुमसे क्या कहा ?
अम्म नीतो एमि अन्नारु ?

అమ్మ నీతో ఏమి అన్నారు ?
మా నే తుమ్‌సే క్యా కహా ?
WHAT DID MOM TELL YOU ?

25) क्यों देर हो गई ?
एंदुकु आलस्यम अइंदि ?
ఎందుకు ఆలస్యం అయింది ?
క్యోం దేర్ హోగయీ ?
WHY WAS THERE A DELAY ?

26) वह कौन है ?
अतडु एवरु ?
అతడు ఎవరు ?
వహ్ కౌన్ హై ?
WHO IS HE ?

27) आप कहाँ गये थे ?
मीरु एक्कडिकि वेल्लारु ?
మీరు ఎక్కడికి వెళ్లారు ?
ఆప్ కహా గయే థే ?
WHERE DID YOU GO ?

28) आप कहाँ रहते है ?
मीरु एक्कड़ा उंटारु ?
మీరు ఎక్కడ వుంటారు ?
ఆప్ కహా రహతే హై ?
WHERE DO YOU STAY ?

29) आपकी क्या राय है ?
मी अभिप्रायमू एमिटि ?
మీ అభిప్రాయం ఏమిటి ?
ఆప్ కీ క్యా రాయ్ హై ?
WHAT IS YOUR OPINION ?

नहीं/मत లేదు/కాదు NO-DON'T

1) ऐसा मत कहो ।
अला अनावद्दु ।
అలా అనవద్దు.
ఐసా మత్ కహో.
DON'T SAY THIS.

2) झूठ मत बोलो ।
अबध्दम चेप्पवद्दु ।
అబద్ధం చెప్పవద్దు.
ఝూట్ మత్ బోలో.
DON'T LIE.

3)मेरे पास नहीं है ।
ना दग्गरा लेदु ।
నా దగ్గర లేదు.
మేరే పాస్ నహీ హై.
I DON'T HAVE IT.

4) आज की रात मत जाओ ।
इवाला रात्रि वेळ्ळावद्दु ।
ఇవాళ రాత్రి వెళ్ళవద్దు.
ఆజ్ కీ రాత్ మత్ జావో.
DON'T GO TONIGHT.

5) मैं ने नहीं कहा ।
नेनु अनलेदु ।
నేను అనలేదు.
మైనే నహీ కహా.
I DIDN'T SAY.

6) मुझे नहीं चाहिए ।
नाकु वद्दु ।
నాకు వద్దు.
ముఝే నహీ చాహియే.
I DON'T WANT.

7) नहीं रे, वह यहाँ नहीं है ।
लेदुरा अतनु इक्कड़ा लेडु ।
లేదురా అతను ఇక్కడ లేడు.
నహీ రే వహ్ యహా నహీ హై.
NO DUDE, HE IS NOT HERE.

8) यहाँ मत ढूँढ़ो,यहाँ नहीं है ।
इक्कडा वेतकवद्दु,इक्कड़ा लेडु ।
ఇక్కడ వెతకవద్దు. ఇక్కడ లేడు.
యహా మత్ ఢూంఢో, యహా నహీ హై.
DON'T SEARCH HERE, HE IS NOT HERE .

वाला/वाली शब्द का प्रायोग వాలా/వాలీ ప్రయోగము WALA/LI USAGE

1) वह मेरी घरवाली है ।
आमे न इंटि इल्लालु ।
ఆమె నా ఇంటి ఇల్లాలు.
వహ్ మేరీ ఘర్‌వాలీ హై.
SHE IS MY WIFE.

2) वह मेरा घरवाला है ।
अतडु ना भर्ता ।
అతడు నా భర్త.
వహ్ మేరా ఘర్‌వాలా హై.
HE IS MY HUSBAND.

3) ये चाभी रिंग १०० रूपये वाली है ।
ई तालम गुत्ति वंद रुपायलदि ।
ఈ తాళం గుత్తి వంద రుపాయలది.
యే చాభీ రింగ్ సౌ రుపయే వాలీ హై.
THIS KEY RING IS OF 100 RUPEES.

4) मेरी रेल आनेवाली है ।
ना रैलु राबोतुंदि ।
నా రైలు రాబోతుంది.
మేరీ రైల్ ఆనేవాలీ హై.
MY TRAIN IS ABOUT TO ARRIVE.

5) यहाँ से कोई जानेवाला नहीं है ।
इक्कडनुंचि एव्वरु वेल्लेला लेरु ।
ఇక్కడి నుంచి ఎవ్వరూ వెళ్ళేలా లేరు.
యహాం సే కోయీ జానేవాలా నహీ హై.
NOBODY WILL BE LEAVING FROM HERE

संबंधार्थक शब्द व उसके प्रयोग

जब-तब	एप्पुडु-अप्पुडु	ఎప్పుడు-అప్పుడు	జబ్-తక్	WHEN-THEN
जहाँ-वहाँ	एक्काडा-अक्काडा	ఎక్కడ-అక్కడ	జహాం-వహాం	HERE-THERE
जो	एदैते	ఏదైతే	జో	WHATEVER
जैसे-वैसे	एलागैते-अलागे	ఎలాగైతే-అలాగే	జైసే-	BY THE WAY NAMELY
जिसमे	एंदुलो	ఎందులో	జిస్‌మే	IN WHICH
जिनकी	एवरियोक्का	ఎవరియొక్క	జిన్‌కీ	WHOSE
जिनसे	एवरिचेता	ఎవరిచేత	జిన్‌సే	FROM WHOM
जितने	एन्नयिते	ఎన్నయితే	జిత్‌నే	AS MANY AS
ऐसा ही	अलागे	అలాగే	ఏసాహీ	LIKE THAT

जब-तब

1)मैं जब जाता हूँ तब वह चला जाता है ।
नेनु एप्पुडु वेलतानो अप्पुडु अतडु वेलताडु ।
నేను ఎప్పుడు వెళతానో అప్పుడు అతడు వెళతాడు.
మై జబ్ జాతా హూం తబ్ వహ్ చలా జాతా హై.
WHENEVER I GO HE LEAVES.

2)जहाँ-वहाँ

तुम जहाँ जाओगे मुझे वहाँ पाओगे ।
नुव्वेक्कडिकेल्ते अक्काडा नेनुंटानु ।
నువ్వెక్కడికెళ్తే అక్కడ నేనుంటాను.
తుమ్ జహా జావోగే ముఝె వహాం పావోగే.
YOU WILL FIND ME WHEREVER YOU GO.

3)जो

तुम्हारे पास जो भी है दे दो ।
नी दग्गरा उन्नदंता इच्चेयि ।
నీ దగ్గర ఉన్నదంతా ఇచ్చేయి.
తుమ్‌హారే పాస్ జోభీహైదేదో.
GIVEME WHATEVER YOU HAVE

4)जैसे-वैसे

राम जैसे निकला वैसे ही बारिस शुरू हुई ।

रामु इला बयटकु वच्चिना वेंटने अला वर्षम मोदलैंदि ।

రాము ఇలా బయటకు వచ్చిన వెంటనే వర్షం మొదలైంది.

రామ్ జైసే నిక్‌లా వైసే హీ బారిష్ షురూ హుయీ.

AS SOON AS RAM CAMEOUT, THE RAIN STARTED FALLING.

5)ज्यों-त्यों

ज्यों ही बिजली कड़की,त्यों ही बिजली चली गई ।

इला वुरुमुलु मेरुपुलु मोदलवागाने अला विद्युत/विद्युत सराफरा निलिचिपोयिंदि ।

ఇలా ఉరుములు మెరుపులు మొదలవగానే అలా విద్యుత్ సరఫరా నిలిచిపోయింది.

జ్యోం హీ బిజలీ కడకీ త్యోం హీ బిజలీ చలీ గయి.

AS SOON AS THE THUNDRING, LIGHTING STARTED, THE ELECTRICAL SUPPLY STOPPED.

6)जिसमे

जिसमे हिम्मत हो बाहर आकर बातें करो ।

एवरिकैना दम्मुंटे बयटकु वच्चि माट्लाडंडि ।

ఎవరికైన దమ్ముంటే బయటకు వచ్చి మాట్లాడండి.

జిస్‌మే హిమ్మత్ హో బాహర్ ఆకర్ బాతే కరో.

WHOEVER HAS THE GUTS, COMEOUT AND TALK.

7)जिनकी

यह चाबी जिनकी है वो ले लो ।

इवि एवरि तालामो वारु तीसुकोंडि ।

ఇది ఎవరి తాళమో వారు తీసుకోండి.

యహ్ చాబీ జిన్‌కీ హై వో లేలో.

WHOSEVER KEYS ARE THESE, TAKE THEM.

8)जिनसे

जिनसे नहीं बनता वे छोड़ दें ।

एवरु चेयलेरो वारु वदिलेयंडि ।

ఎవరు చేయలేరో వారు వదిలేయండి.

జిన్‌సే నహీ బన్‌తా వే ఛోడ్ దే.

THOSE WHO ARE NOT ABLE TO DO IT, LEAVE IT.

9)जितने

तुम्हे जितने चाहिए ले जाओ ।

नीकेंता कावालो अंता तीसुको ।

నీకెంతా కావాలో అంతా తీసుకో.

తుమ్‌హే జితనే చాహియే లే జాఒ.

TAKE AS MUCH AS YOU WANT.

10)ऐसा ही **అలాంటి** TO SAME

मुझे ऐसा ही रुमाल चाहिए ।

नाकु अलांटि रुमाले कावालि ।

నాకు అలాంటి రుమాలే కావాలి.

ముఝె ఐసా హీ రుమాల్ చాహిఎ.

I WANT THE SAME TYPE OF HANDKERCHIEF.

संबंध बोधक वाक्य   విభక్తిప్రత్యయాలు   PREPOSITIONS

1) **के पास**   **దగ్గర**   TO NEAR

मेरा घर चौक के पास है ।
ना इल्लु कूड़लि दग्गरा उन्नदि ।
నా ఇల్లు కూడలి దగ్గర ఉన్నది.
మేరా ఘర్ చౌక్ కే పాస్ హై.
MY HOUSE IS NEAR THE JUNCTION.

तुम्हारी कलम नीलम के पास है ।
नी कलमु नीलम दग्गरा उन्नदि ।
నీ కలము నీలమ్ దగ్గర వున్నది.
తుమ్హారీ కలమ్ నీలమ్ కే పాస్ హై.
YOUR PEN IS WITH NEELAM.

2) **की तरह**   **లాగే**   LIKE

शाहरुख खान अमिताभ बच्चन की तरह अभिनय करता है ।
शाहरुख खान अमिताभ बच्चन ला नटिस्ताडु ।
షాహరుఖాన్ అమితాబ్ బచ్చన్ లా నటిస్తాడు.
షాహరుఖాన్ అమితాబ్ బచ్చన్ కీ తరహ్ అబినయ్ కర్తా హై.
SHAHRUKH KHAN ACTS LIKE AMITABH BACHAN.

हमें माहात्मा गाँधी की तरह सोचना चाहिए ।
मनमु माहात्मा गाँधी गारिला आलोचिंचालि ।
మనము మహాత్మాగాంధీ గారిలా ఆలోచించాలి.
హమే మహాత్మాగాంధీ కీ తరహ్ సోచనా చాహిఎ.
WE SHOULD THINK LIKE MAHATMA GANDHI.

3) **के कारण** **వలన** ***AS/SINCE***

परीक्षा समाप्त होने के कारण आज मै नही पढ़ूंगी ।
परीक्षलु पूर्ति अयिनंदुवलना नेनीरोजु चदवनु ।
పరీక్షలు పూర్తి అయినందువలన నేనీరోజు చదవను.
పరీక్ష సమాప్త్ హోనే కే కారణ్ ఆజ్ మై నహీ పఢూంగీ.
AS MY EXAMS HAVE FINISHED I WON'T STUDY TODAY.

बारिश होने के कारण मैं भीग गयी ।
वर्षम वच्चिनंदुवलना नेनु तडिचिपोयानु ।
వర్షం వచ్చినందువలన నేను తడిచిపోయాను.
బారిష్ హోనే కే కారణ్ మై భీగ్ గయీ.
SINCE IT WAS RAINING, I GOT WET.

4) **की तरफ** **వైపు** ON BEHALF OF

मैं अपनी स्कूल की तरफ से खेलने गई ।
नेनु ना स्कूलु तरुपुना आडटानिकि वेल्लानु ।
మై అపనీ స్కూల్ కీ తరఫ్ సే ఖేల్‌నే గయీ.
నేను నా స్కూలు తరుపున ఆడటానికి వెళ్ళాను.
I WENT TO PLAY ON BEHALF OF MY SCHOOL.

मेरा घर तरणताल की तरफ है ।
ना इल्लु ईताकोलनु वैपु उंदि ।
నా ఇల్లు ఈతకొలను వైపు ఉంది.
మేరా ఘర్ తరణ్‌తాల్ కీ తరఫ్ హై.
MY HOME IS TOWARDS THE SWIMMING POOL.

5) **के समान** **సమానము** SIMILAR

श्याम का कुत्ता राम के समान है ।
श्याम चोक्का राम लांटिदि ।
శ్యామ్ చొక్కా రామ్ లాంటిది.
శ్యామ్ కా కుర్తా రామ్ కే సమాన్ హై.

SHYAM'S SHIRT IS SIMILAR TO RAM'S SHIRT.

विधि के समक्ष सभी एक समान है ।
विधि मुन्दु अन्ता समानमु ।
విధి ముందు అంతా సమానము.
విధి కే సమక్ష్ సభీ ఎక్ సమాన్ హై.
ALL ARE EQUAL BEFORE THE DESTINY.

6) **के व्दारा** **ద్వారా** THROUGH

पत्र के द्वारा मुझे पता चला ।
उत्तरमु द्वारा नाकु तेलिसिंदि ।
ఉత్తరము ద్వారా నాకు తెలిసింది.
పత్ర్ కే ద్వారా ముఝే పతా చలా.
I CAME TO KNOW THAT THROUGH THE LETTER.

सारा घर ईंट के द्वारा बनाया गया है ।
इल्लु मोत्तमू इटुकलातो तयारैंदि ।
ఇల్లు మొత్తం ఇటుకలతో తయారయ్యింది.
సారా ఘర్ ఈఁట్ కే ద్వారా బనాయా గయా హై.
THE WHOLE HOUSE IS MADE UP OF BRICKS.

7) **के पहले** **ముందు** **BEFORE**

सोमवार मंगलवार के पहले आता है ।
सोमवारमु मंगलवारम् मुंदु वस्तुंदि ।
సోమవారము మంగళవారం ముందు వస్తుంది.
సోమవార్ మంగళవార్ కే పహలే ఆతా హై.
MONDAY COMES BEFORE TUESDAY.

श्रेया श्रेष्ठा के पहले बैठती है ।
श्रेया श्रेष्ठा कु मुंदु कूर्चुटुंदि ।
శ్రేయ శ్రేష్ఠ కు ముందు కూర్చుంటుంది.
శ్రేయ శ్రేష్ఠ కే పహలే బైఠతీ హై.
SHREYA SITS I FRONT SHRESTA.

8) के पीछे   వెనుక   BEHIND

श्रेया के घर के पीछे पहाड़ है ।
श्रेया इंटि वेनुका कोंडा वुन्दि ।
శ్రేయ ఇంటి వెనుక కొండ వుంది.
శ్రేయ కే ఘర్ కే పీచే పహాడ్ హై.
THERE IS A HILL BEHIND SHREYA'S HOUSE .

बिल्ली चूहे के पीछे दौड़ती है ।
पिल्लि एलुका वेनुका परिगेड्डुतुन्दि ।
పిల్లి ఎలుక వెనుక పరిగెడుతుంది.
బిల్లీ చూహే కే పీచే దౌడ్తీ హై.
THE CAT RUNS BEHIND THE RAT.

9) के आगे   ముందు   IN FRONT OF

डर के आगे जीत है ।
भयानिकि मुंदु जयमु उन्टुंदि ।
భయానికి ముందు జయం ఉంటుంది.
డర్ కే ఆగే జీత్ హై.
VICTORY, LIES BEYOND FEAR

भैया के घर के आगे मिठाई की दुकान है ।
अन्नय्या वाल्ला इंटि मुंदु मिठाई दुकाणम् उंदि ।
అన్నయ్య వాళ్ల ఇంటి ముందు మిఠాయి దుకాణం వుంది.
భైయా కే ఘర్ కే ఆగే మిఠాఈ కీ దుకాన్ హై.
THERE IS A SWEET SHOP IN FRONT OF BHAYA'S HOUSE.

10) के सामने   ఎదురుగా   IN FRONT OF

मंदिर के सामने तालाब है ।
गुडि एदुरुगा कोलनु उन्दि ।
గుడి ఎదురుగా కొలను ఉంది.
మందిర్ కే సామ్నే తాలాబ్ హై.

THERE IS A POND IN FRONT OF THE TEMPLE.

मेरे घर के सामने बच्चे खेलते है ।
ना इंटि एदुरुगा पिल्ललु आडुकुंटारु ।
నా ఇంటి ఎదురుగా పిల్లలు ఆడుకుంటారు.
మేరే ఘర్ కే సామ్‌నే బచ్చే ఖేల్‌తే హై.
THE CHILDREN PLAY IN FRONT OF MY HOUSE.

11) **के ऊपर** **మీద** ON

हिमालय के ऊपर बर्फ है ।
हिमालयाला मीदा मन्चु उंदि ।
హిమాలయాల మీద మంచు ఉంది.
హిమాలయ్ కే ఊపర్ బర్ఫ్ హై.
THERE IS SNOW ON THE HIMALAYAS.

मेज के ऊपर किताबें है ।
मेजाबल्ला मीदा पुस्तकालु उन्नवि ।
మేజాబల్ల మీద పుస్తకాలు వున్నవి.
మేజ్ కే ఊపర్ కితాబే హై.
THERE ARE BOOKS ON THE TABLE

.

12) **के नीचे** **క్రింద** **UNDER**

मेज के नीचे बिल्ली है ।
मेजाबल्ला क्रिंदा पिल्ली उंदि ।
మేజాబల్ల క్రింద పిల్లి ఉంది.
మేజ్ కే నీచే బిల్లీ హై.
THERE IS A CAT UNDER THE TABLE.

पेड़ के नीचे चिड़ियाँ दाना चुग रहीं है ।
चेट्टु क्रिंदा पक्षुलु गिंजलु तिंटुन्नाइ ।
చెట్టు క్రింద పక్షులు గింజలు తింటున్నాయి.
పేడ్ కే నీచే చిడియాం దానా చుగ్ రహిం హై.
BIRDS ARE EATING SEEDS UNDER THE TREE.

13) **के भीतर** **లోపల** **INSIDE**

मेरे थैले के भीतर किताबें है ।
ना संचि लोपला पुस्तकमुलु वुन्नवि ।
నా సంచి లోపల పుస్తకములు వున్నవి.
మేరే థైలే కే భీతర్ కితాబే హై.
THERE ARE BOOKS IN MY BAG.

आजकल बच्चे घर के भीतर ही खेलते है ।
ई रोजुल्लो पिल्ललु इंटि लोपले आडुकुंटुन्नारु ।
ఈ రోజుల్లో పిల్లలు ఇంటి లోపలే ఆడుకుంటున్నారు.
ఆజ్‌కల్ బచ్చే ఘర్ కే భీతర్ హీ ఖేల్‌తే హై.
NOWADAYS, CHILDREN PLAY IN THEIR HOMES.

14) **के बाहर** **బయట** **OUTSIDE**

शाम को घर के बाहर खेलना चाहिए ।
सायंत्रम् इंटि बयटा आडुकोवाली ।
సాయంత్రం ఇంటి బయట ఆడుకోవాలి.
షామ్ కో ఘర్ కే బాహర్ ఖేల్‌నా చాహియే.
WE SHOULD PLAY OUTSIDE IN THE EVENING .

कछुआ तालाब के बाहर आ गया ।
ताबेलु कोलनु बयटकु वच्चिंदि ।
తాబేలు కొలను బయటికు వచ్చింది.
కచువా తాలాబ్ కే బాహర్ ఆగయా.
THE TORTOISE CAME OUT OF THE POND.

15) **के मध्य/के बीच मे** **మధ్యలో** **BETWEEN**

आठ और दस के बीच मे नौ आता है ।
एनिमिदि मरियु पदि मध्यलो तोम्मिदि वस्तुन्दि ।
ఎనిమిది మరియు పది మధ్యలో తొమ్మిది వస్తుంది.
ఆఠ ఔర్ దస్ కే బీచ్ మే నౌ ఆతా హై.
NINE COMES BETWEEN EIGHT AND TEN.

बिहार और उड़ीसा के मध्य झारखंड है ।
बीहारु मरियु ओडिसा मध्या लो झारखंड उन्नदि ।
బీహారు మరియు ఒడిశా మధ్యలో ఝార్ఖండ్ వున్నది.
బిహార్ ఔర్ ఒడిసా కే మద్య ఝార్ఖండ్ హై.
JHARKHAND IS BETWEEN BIHAR AND ODISHA.

अच्छे आचरण सభ్యత-సంస్కారము GOOD MANNERS

1) कृपया मुझे अपनी कलम देंगें?
दयाचेसि मी कलमु नाकु इस्तारा ?
దయచేసి మీ కలము నాకు ఇస్తారా ?
కృపయా ముఝే అప్నీ కలమ్ దేంగే ?
CAN YOU GIVE YOUR PEN TO ME PLEASE.

2) क्या मैं कुछ अर्ज कर सकता हूँ?
नेनु कोंचेंम माटलाडवच्चा?
నేను కొంచెం మాట్లాడవచ్చా?
క్యా మై కుఛ్ అర్జ్ కర్ సక్‌తా హూ ?
CAN I SAY SOMETHING?

3) क्षमा करें, मेरी बात सुनिये.
दयचेसि नेनु चेप्पेदि विनंडि
దయచేసి నేను చెప్పేది వినండి.
క్షమా కరే, మేరి బాత్ సునియే
KINDLY LISTEN TO ME.

4) माफ कीजिए ऐसा नही है
क्षमिंचंडि अट्ला कादु
క్షమించండి అట్లాకాదు.
మాఫ్ కీజియే యైసా నహీ హై.
PARDON ME. IT IS NOT LIKE THAT.

5) बहुत बहुत धन्यावाद ।
धन्यवादमुलु ।
ధన్యవాదములు.
బహుత్ బహుత్ ధన్యవాద్.
THANK YOU VERY MUCH.

6) क्या मुझे यह मिल सकता है ?
दयचेसी नाकु अदि इस्तारा ?
దయచేసి నాకు అది ఇస్తారా ?
క్యా ముఝే యహ్ మిల్ సక్‌తా హై ?
CAN I HAVE IT KINDLY CAN YOU GIVE IT TO ME.

१)नीचे-ऊपर **క్రింద-మీద** **UP-DOWN**

आलामारी में कपडा कहाँ रखे हो.नीचे रेक मे या ऊपर?
अलमारालो बट्टलु एकड़ा पेट्टावु,क्रिदा अरा लोना लेका मीदा अरा लोना?
అలమారా లో బట్టలు ఎక్కడ పెట్టావు.క్రింద అర లోనా లేక మీద అర లోనా?
అల్‌మారీ మే కపడా కహాం రఖే హో.నీచే రేక్ మే యా ఊపర్?
WHERE DID YOU KEEP THE CLOTHES IN THE ALMRAH? ON THE UPPER RACK OR THE LOWER?

२)बाहर-अंदर **బయట-లోపల** **OUTSIDE-INSIDE**

बाहर धूप बहुत है,अंदर आओ.
बयटा एंडगा उंदि लोपलिकि रा.
బయట ఎండగా వుంది లోపలికి రా.
బాహర్ దూప్ బహుత్ హై.అందర్ ఆవో.
IT IS VERY HOT OUTSIDE, COME INSIDE.

३)ठंडा-गरम **చల్లగా-వేడిగా** **COLD-HOT**

चाय तो ठंडी हो गई,मुझे तो गरम पसंद है.
टी चल्लगा अयिपोइंदि,नाकु वेडिगा इष्म.
టీ చల్లగా అయిపోయింది, నాకు వేడిగా ఇష్టం.
ఛాయ్ తో ఠండీ హోగయి, ముఝేతో గరమ్ పసంద్ హై.
THE TEA HAS BECOME COLD. I LIKE IT HOT

४)हल्का-भारी **తేలిక-బరువు** **LIGHT-HEAVY**

वो हल्का वाला बैग तुम लेलो, यह भारी वाली पेटी मैं लेकर आता हूँ.
आ तेलिका बेग नुव्वु पटुको, इ बरुवैना पेट्टे नेनु तीसुकु वस्तानु.
ఆ తేలిక బేగ్ నువ్వు పట్టుకో, ఈ బరువైన పెట్టె నేను తీసుకు వస్తాను.
వో హల్కావాలా బేగ్ తుమ్ లేలో, యహ్ భారీవాలీ పేటీ మై లేకర్ ఆతాహుం.

YOU TAKE THIS LIGHTER BAG. I WILL TAKE THE HEAVIER ONE

५)**हराभरा-ठूंठ** **పచ్చగా–మోడు** **GREEN-DRY**

कल ही तो ये पेड़ हराभरा था,आज ठूंठ कैसा हो गया?

इ चेट्टू निन्ने पच्चागाने उंडेदी,इ रोजु मोडू एला आइ पोइंदि ?

ఈ చెట్టు నిన్న పచ్చగానే ఉండేది, ఈ రోజు మోడు ఎలా అయిపోయింది?

కల్ హీ తో యే పేడ్ హరాబరా థా, ఆజ్ ఠూంఠ్ కైసే హోగయా?

THIS TREE WAS GREEN YESTERDAY, HOW IS IT DRIED TODAY?

६)**खाली-भरा** **ఖాళీ–నిండుగా** **EMPTY-FULL**

सभी घड़े खाली हो गए,पानी भर दो ।

अन्नि बिन्देलु खाली अयिपोयायि नील्लु निंपु ।

అన్ని బిందెలు ఖాళీ అయిపోయాయి నీళ్లు నింపు.

సభీ ఘడే ఖాళీ హోగయే, పానీ బర్‌దో.

ALL THE PITCHERS ARE EMPTY, FILL WATER.

७)**सफेद-काला** **తెలుపు–నలుపు** **WHITE-BLACK**

जेब्रा की सफेद व काली धारी बहुत अच्छी लगती है.

जीब्रा ओटि मीदा तेलुपु नलुपु चारलु चाला बावुंन्नायि.

జీబ్రా ఒంటి మీద తెలుపు నలుపు చారలు చాలా బావున్నాయి.

జీబ్ర కీ సఫేద్ వ కాలీ ధారీ బహుత్ అచ్ఛా లగ్‌తీ హై.

THE WHITE AND BLACK STRIPES OF THE ZEBRA LOOKS GOOD.

८)**दिन-रात** **పగలు–రాత్రి** **DAY-NIGHT**

मुझे दिन-रात तेरा ख्याल आता है।

नाकु पगलु रात्री नी ध्यासे ।

నాకు పగలు రాత్రి నీ ధ్యాసే.

ముఝే దిన్ రాత్ తేరా ఖ్యాల్ ఆతా హై.

YOUR THOUGHTS COME TO ME DAY AND NIGHT.

९)सुबह-शाम **ఉదయం-సాయంత్రం** **MORNING-EVENING**

मेरी सास सुबह शाम मंदिर जाती है ।
मा आत्तागारु उदायम्-सायंत्रम् गुडिकी वेलतारु ।
మా అత్తగారు ఉదయం-సాయంత్రం గుడికి వెళ్తారు.
మేరి సాస్ సుబహ్ షామ్ మందిర్ జాతీ హై.
MY MOTHER IN LAW GOES TO THE TEMPLE IN THE MORNING AND IN THE EVENING.

१०)चहलपहल-शांत **గోలగోలగా-ప్రశాంతంగా** **NOISY-QUITE**

बच्चे से पार्क चहलपहल रहता है नहीं तो शांत रहता है ।
पिल्लल वल्लने पार्क गोलागोलागा उंटाई लेकपोते प्रशांतंगा उंटाई ।
పిల్లల వల్లనే పార్క్ గోలాగోలగా ఉంటాయి లేకపోతే ప్రశాంతంగా ఉంటాయి.
బచ్చే సే పార్క్ చహల్‌పహల్ రహ్‌తా హై నహి తో శాంత్ రహ్‌తా హై.
IT IS NOISY IN THE PARK WHEN THERE ARE KIDS, OTHERWISE IT IS PEACEFUL.

११)सीधा-उल्टा **తిన్నగా-వంకరగా** **STRAIGHT-INVERTED**

उस तस्वीर को सीधा रखो उल्टा नहीं ।
आ फोटोनि तिन्नागा पेट्टु वंकरगा कादू ।
ఆ ఫోటోని తిన్నగా పెట్టు వంకరగా కాదు.
ఉస్ తస్వీర్ కో సీధా రఖో ఉల్టా నహీ.
PUT THE PHOTO STRAIGHT NOT CROOKED.

१२)लंबा-नाटा **పొడుగు-పొట్టి** **TALL-SHORT**

मेरा बेटा मुझसे लंबा है पर मेरी बेटी मुझसे नाटी है ।
मा अब्बाई ना कंटे पेड्डुगु कानी मा अम्माई नाकंटे पोट्टी ।
మా అబ్బాయి నాకంటే పొడుగు కాని మా అమ్మాయి నాకంటే పొట్టి.
మేరా బేటా ముఝ్‌సే లంబా హై పర్ బేటీ ముఝ్‌సే నాటీ హై.
MY SON IS TALLER THAN ME BUT DAUGHTER IS SHORTER THAN ME.

१३)गोरी-काली **తెల్లగా-నల్లగా** **FAIR-DARK**

सीता गोरी है लेकिन गीता काली है ।
सीता तेल्लगा उंटुंदि कानी गीता नल्लगा उंटुंदि ।
సీత తెల్లగా ఉంటుంది కాని గీత నల్లగా ఉంటుంది
సీత గోరి హై లేకిన్ గీత కాలీ హై.
SITA IS FAIR BUT GITA IS DARK.

१४)**आगे-पीछे** **ముందు-వెనుక** **FRONT-BACK**

मेरे आगे पीछे मत चलो ।
ना छुट्टु प्रक्कला तिरगकु ।
నా చుట్టు ప్రక్కల తిరగకు.
మేరే ఆగే పీఛే మత్ చలో.
DO NOT LOITER AROUND ME.

१५)**सोना - जागना** **నిద్రపోవటం-మెల్కొను** **WAKING-SLEEPING**

तुम अब सो जाओ ।
नुव्वु निद्रापो ।
నువ్వు నిద్రపో.
తుమ్ అబ్ సో జావో.
YOU GO TO SLEEP NOW.

जागो, स्कूल जाना है ।
निद्रा ले, स्कूलकि वेल्लालि ।
నిద్ర లే, స్కూల్‌కి వెళ్లాలి.
జాగో స్కూల్ జానా హై.
WAKE UP YOU HAVE TO GO TO SCHOOL.

वो रोज छः बजे उठता है ।
अतडु उदयान्ने आरु गंटलकि मेलकुंटाडु ।
అతడు ఉదయాన్నే ఆరు గంటలకి మేల్కుకుంటాడు.
వో రోజ్ ఛా బజే ఉఠ్‌తా హై.
HE WAKESUP AT SIX O' CLOCK IN THE MORNING EVERYDAY.

१६) **धूप - छॉव** **ఎండ-నీడ** **SUN-SHADE**

धूप में मत जाओ ।
एंडलो वेल्लोद्दु ।
ఎండలో వెళ్ళొద్దు.
దూప్ మే మత్ జావో.
DO NOT GO OUT IN THE SUN

धूप में सुखा दो ।
एंडलो आरवेय्यि ।
ఎండలో ఆరవెయ్యి.
ధూప్ మే సుఖా దో.
DRY IT IN THE SUN.

मैंने सुखा ली ।
नेनु आरवेसानु ।
నేను ఆరవేసాను.
మైనే సుఖా లీ.
I ALREADY DRIED IT.

छॉव में सुखा दो ।
नीड़लो आरवेय्यि ।
నీడలో ఆరవెయ్యి.
ఛావ్ మే సుఖా దో.
DRY IT IN THE SHADE.

१७)**उठना-बैठना** **నిలబడు-కూర్చోను** **STANDING-SITTING**

आप उठीए उनको बैठने दीजिए ।
मीरु निलबड़ि आमेनु कूर्चोनिव्वंडी ।
మీరు నిలబడి ఆమెను కూర్చోనివ్వండి.
ఆప్ ఉఠిఏ ఉన్‌కో బైఠ్‌నే దీజిఏ.
YOU STAND AND LET HER SIT.

१८)**अच्छा-बुरा** **మంచి-చెడు** **GOOD-BAD**

राम अच्छा लड़का है उसमे कोई बुराई नहीं हैं ।
रामुडु मंचि बालुडु अतनिलो एमि चेडुगुणालु लेवु ।
రాముడు మంచి బాలుడు అతనిలో ఏమి చెడుగుణాలు లేవు.
రామ్ అచ్చా లడకా హై ఉస్‌మే కోయీ బురాయీ నహీ హై.
RAM IS A GOOD BOY, HE DOESN'T HAVE ANY BAD CHARACTERISTICS.

बुरी बात मुँह से मत निकालो ।
चेडु माटलु नोटितो उच्चरिंचवद्दु ।
చెడు మాటలు నోటితో ఉచ్చరించవద్దు.
బురి బాత్ ముహ్‌సే మత్ నికాలో.
DO NOT MOUTH BAD WORDS

1)माँ कहाँ है ?
अम्मा एक्कड़ा उंदि ?
అమ్మ ఎక్కడ ఉంది ?
మా కహా హై ?
WHERE IS MOTHER ?

2)आपसे कोई मिलने आया है ।
मिम्मलनि कलवडानिकि एवरो वच्चारु ।
మిమ్మల్ని కలవడానికి ఎవరో వచ్చారు.
ఆప్ సే కోయీ మిల్నే ఆయా హై.
SOME ONE CAME TO MEET YOU.

3)देखो, बाहर कौन है ?
चूड्डु, बयटा एवरोच्चारो ?
చూడు బయట ఎవరొచ్చారో ?
దేఖో బాహర్ కౌన్ హై ?
LOOK, WHO IS OUTSIDE ?

4)मैं तो पूछना ही भूल गया ।
नेनु अडगटमे मरिचि पोयानु ।
నేను అడగటమే మరిచి పోయాను.
మై తో పూచ్నా హీ భూల్ గయా.
I FORGOT TO ASK.

5)तुमने खाना खा लिया ?
नीवु भोजनम् चेसावा ?
నీవు భోజనం చేసావా ?
తుమ్నే ఖానా ఖా లియా ?
DID YOU HAVE YOUR MEALS ?

6)अब चलो सब सो जाओ ।
पदंडि अंदरू निद्रपोंडि ।
పదండి అందరూ నిద్రపోండి.
అబ్ ఛలో సబ్ సో జావో.
NOW LET US ALL SLEEP.

7)आओ सभी पहले नाश्ता कर ले ।
अंदरू रंडि मुंदु टिफिन चेयंडि ।
అందరూ రండి ముందు టిఫిన్ చేయండి.
ఆవో సభీ పహలే నాస్తా కర్ లే.
ALL OF YOU COME. HAVE BREAKFAST FIRST.

8)मेरी कमीज मे इस्त्री नहीं है ।
ना चोक्का इस्त्री चेसिलेदु ।
నా చొక్కా ఇస్త్రీ చేసిలేదు.
మేరి కమీజ్ మే ఇస్త్రీ నహీ హై.
MY SHIRT IS NOT IRONED.

9)सभी बाहर गये है ।
अंदरू बयटकेल्लारु ।
అందరూ బయటకెళ్ళారు.
సభీ బాహర్ గయే హై.
EVERYONE WENT OUT.

10)मुझे अभी भूख नहीं है ।
नाकिप्पुडु आकलिगा लेदु ।
నాకిప్పుడు ఆకలిగా లేదు.
ముఝె అభీ భూక్ నహీ హై.
IAM NOT HUNGRY NOW.

11)मुझे नींद नहीं आ रही है ।
नाकु निद्रा रावटमु लेदु ।
నాకు నిద్ర రావటం లేదు.
ముఝె నీంద్ నహీ ఆ రహీ హై.
IAM NOT SLEEPY.

12)अंधेरे में टीवी मत देखो ।
चिकटलो टीवी चुड़वद्दु ।
చీకట్లో టీవీ చూడవద్దు.
అంధేరే మే టీవీ మత్ దేఖో.
DON'T WATCH TV IN THE DARK.

13)जल्दी सोवोगे तब तो जल्दी उठोगे ।
त्वरगा पडुकुंटे त्वरगा निद्रा लेस्तावु ।
త్వరగా పడుకుంటే త్వరగా నిద్ర లేస్తావు.
జల్దీ సోవోగే తబ్ తో జల్దీ వుటోగే.
IF YOU SLEEP EARLY ONLY THEN YOU CAN WAKE UP EARLY.

14)आज मेहमान घर आ रहे हैं मिठाइयाँ लेते आइएगा ।
इवाला इंटिकि आतिधुलु वस्तुन्नारु मिठाइलु तिसुकुनि रंडि ।
ఇవాళ ఇంటికి అతిధులు వస్తున్నారు మిఠాయిలు తీసుకుని రండి.
ఆజ్ మెహ్మాన్ ఘర్ ఆ రహే హై మిఠాయియా లేతే ఆయియేగా.
TODAY SOME GUESTS ARE VISITING OUR PLACE. BRING SWEETS.

15)सब्जी में नमक ज्यादा हो गया है ।
कूरलो उप्पु एक्कुवयिंदि ।
కూరలో ఉప్పు ఎక్కువయింది.
సబ్జీ మే నమక్ జ్యాదా హో గయా హై.
THE CURRY HAS MORE SALT.

16)मुझे सोनेदो ।
नन्नु निद्रपोनिव्वु ।
నన్ను పడుకోనివ్వు.
ముఝే సోనే దో.
LET ME SLEEP.

17)टीवी की आवाज धीमी करो ।
टीवी शब्दमु तग्गिंचु ।
టీవీ శబ్ధము తగ్గించు.
టీవీ కీ ఆవాజ్ ధీమీ కరో.
REDUCE THE TV VOLUME.
18)मेरा चश्मा कहाँ है ?

ना कल्लाजोड्डु एक्कड़ा उंदि ?
నా కళ్ళ జోడు ఎక్కడ వుంది ?
మేరా ఛష్మా కహా హై ?
WHERE ARE MY SPECTACLES?

19)मृदुल कहाँ गया है ?
मृदुल एक्कडकि वेह्लाडु ?
మృదుల్ ఎక్కడికి వెళ్ళాడు ?
మృదుల్ కహా గయా హై ?
WHERE HAS MRUDUL GONE?

20)पहले दूध पीओ फिर बात करते है ।
मुंदु पालु तागु तरुवाता माट्लाडदामु ।
ముందు పాలు తాగు తరువాత మాట్లాడదాము.
పహలే దూద్ పీఓ ఫిర్ బాత్ కర్‌తే హై .
HAVE MILK FIRST. WE WILL TALK AFTERWARDS.

21)गृहकार्य पूरा कर लिया ना ?
इंटि पनि पूर्ति चेसेसावु कदा ?
ఇంటి పని పూర్తి చేసేసావు కదా ?
గృహకార్య్ పూరా కర్ లియా నా ?
DID YOU COMPLETE THE HOMEWORK?

शरीर संबंधी बातें శరీర భాగముల గురించి సంభాషణ

CONVERSATION ABOUT BODY PARTS

1) तुम्हारे बाल बहुत सुन्दर हैं।
मी जुत्तु चाला बागुंदि।
మీ జుట్టు చాలా బాగుంది.
తుమ్‌హారే బాల్ బహుత్ సుందర్ హై.
YOUR HAIR IS BEAUTIFUL.

2) मेरे बाल बहुत झड़ रहे हैं।
ना जुट्टु एक्कुवगा ऊडिपोतुंदि।
నా జుట్టు ఎక్కువగా ఊడిపోతుంది.
మేరే బాల్ బహుత్ ఝడ్ రహే హై.
MY HAIR FALLS HEAVILY.

3) मेरा सिर दर्द कर रहा हैं।
नाकु तलानोप्पिगा उंदि।
నాకు తలనొప్పిగా ఉంది.
మేరా సిర్ దర్ద్ కర్ రహా హై.
MY HEAD IS ACHING.

4) सीता की आँखे बहुत सुंदर हैं।
सीता कल्लु चाला बागुन्नायि।
సీత కళ్ళు చాలా బాగున్నాయి.
సీతా కీ ఆంఖే బహుత్ సుందర్ హై.
SITA HAS BEAUTIFUL EYES.

5) उसका नाक बहुत बड़ा हैं।
आमे मुक्कु चाला पेद्दि।
ఆమె ముక్కు చాలా పెద్దది.
ఉస్‌కీ నాక్ బహుత్ బడా హై.
SHE HAS A VERY BIG NOSE

6) राम का कान छोटा हैं।
रामुडि चेवुलु चिन्नवि।
రాముడి చెవులు చిన్నవి.
రామ్ కా కాన్ ఛోటా హై.
RAM HAS SMALL EARS.

7) पहले अपना मुँह बंद करो।
मुंदु नुव्वु नोरु मूसुको।
ముందు నువ్వు నోరు మూసుకో.
పహలే అప్‌నా మూంహ్ బంద్ కరో.
FIRST OF ALL, KEEP YOUR MOUTH SHUT.

8) मेरा गला सुख रहा है।
ना गोंतु एंडिपोतुंदि।
నా గొంతు ఎండిపోతుంది.
మేరా గలా సూఖ్ రహా హై.
MY THROAT IS DRYING.

9) मेरे हाथ मे कुछ नहीं हैं।
ना चेतुल्लो एमी लेदु।
నా చేతుల్లో ఏమీ లేదు.
మేరే హాథ్ మే కుఛ్ నహీ హై.
THERE IS NOTHING IN MY HANDS.

10) मेरा नाखून टूट गया ।
ना गोल्लु विरिगिपोयायि ।
నా గోళ్లు విరిగిపోయాయి.
మేరా నాఖూన్ టూట్ గయా.
MY NAILS ARE BROKEN.

11) मेरे कमर में दर्द हैं ।
नाकु नडुंमुनोप्पिगा उंदि ।
నాకు నడుము నొప్పిగా ఉంది.
మేరే కమర్ మే దర్ద్ హై.
I HAVE PAIN IN MY WAIST.

12) तुम्हारा पेट बहुत निकल गया है ।
नी पोट्टा पेरिगिंदि ।
నీ పొట్ట పెరిగింది.
తుమ్హారా పేట్ బహుత్ నికల్ గయా హై.
YOUR STOMACH GAS GROWN BIGGER.

13) मेरे पेट मे दर्द हैं ।
नाकु कडुपु नोप्पिगा उंदि ।
నాకు కడుపు నొప్పిగా ఉంది.
మేరే పేట్ మే దర్ద్ హై.
MY STOMACH IS ACHING.

14) मेरा पैर दुखने लगा ।
ना काल्लु नोप्पिगा उन्नायि ।
నా కాళ్లు నొప్పిగా ఉన్నాయి.
మేరా పైర్ దుఖ్‌నే లగా.
MY LEGS ARE ACHING.

15) छोटी बच्ची के गाल फूले-फूले हैं ।
चिन्ना पापा बुग्गलु बूरे बुग्गलु ।
చిన్నపాప బుగ్గలు బూరె బుగ్గలు.
ఛోటీ బచ్చీ కే గాల్ ఫులే-ఫులే హై.
THE LITTLE GIRL HAS CHUBBY CHEEKS.

16) तुम्हारे दाँत चमकदार हैं ।
नी पल्लु मेरुस्तू उंटायि ।
నీ పళ్లు మెరుస్తూ ఉంటాయి.
తుమ్హారే దాంత్ చమకదార్ హై.
YOUR TEETH ARE SPARKLING.

17) पानी पीलो,तुम्हारे होंठ सूंख रहे हैं ।
नील्लु तागु नी पेदालु एंडिपोतुन्नायि ।
నీళ్లు తాగు నీ పెదాలు ఎండిపోతున్నాయి.
పానీ పీలో, తుమ్హారే హోంఠ్ సూఖ్ రహే హై.
HAVE WATER. YOUR LIPS ARE DRYING.

डॉक्टर से बातें   దాక్టరుతో సంభాషణ   CONVERSATION WITH A DOCTOR

1) डॉक्टर साहब । मेरी तबीयत ठीक नहीं लग रही है ।

डॉक्टर गारु । नाकु ओंट्लो बागोलेदन्डि ।

దాక్టరు గారు ! నాకు ఒంట్లో బాగోలేదండి.

దాక్టర్ సాహబ్ ! మేరీ తబీయత్ ఠీక్ నహీ లగ్ రహీ హై.

DOCTOR ! I AM NOT FEELING WELL.

2) क्या हुआ ?

एमैंदि ?

ఏమైంది ?

క్యా హువా ?

WHAT HAPPENED?

3) मेरे सिर मे दर्द है ।

नाकु तलानोप्पिगा उंदि ।

నాకు తలనొప్పిగా ఉంది.

మేరే సిర్ మే దర్ద్ హై.

I HAVE HEADACHE.

4) मुझे रात से पेट में दर्द है ।

रात्रि नुंचि नाकु कडुपु नोप्पिगा उंदि ।

రాత్రి నుంచి నాకు కడుపు నొప్పిగా ఉంది.

ముఝే రాత్ సే పేట్ మే దర్ద్ హై.

I HAVE BEEN HAVING STOMACH ACHE SINCE LAST NIGHT.

5) मुझे बुखार है ।

नाकु ज्वरंगा उंदि।

నాకు జ్వరంగా ఉంది.

ముఝే బుఖార్ హై.

I HAVE FEVER.

6) मुझे भूख नही लगती है ।

नाकु आकलि वेयटम लेदु ।
ముఝే భూఖ్ నహీ లగ్‌తీ హై.
నాకు ఆకలి వేయటం లేదు.
I DO NOT FEEL HUNGRY.

7) मुझे कभी-कभी चक्कर आता है ।
नाकु अप्पुडप्पुडु तला तिरुगुतुंदि ।
ముఝే కభీ-కభీ చక్కర్ ఆతా హై.
నాకు అప్పుడప్పుడు తల తిరుగుతుంది.
MY HEAD REELS SOMETIMES.

8) आपकी उम्र क्या है ?
मी वयसेंता ?
ఆప్‌కీ ఉమ్ర్ క్యా హై ?
మీ వయసెంతా ?
HOW OLD ARE YOU?

9) आप जरा आराम करने की कोशिश कीजिए ।
मीरु कोंचेम विश्रांन्ति तीसुकोवटानिकि प्रयन्तिंचंडि ।
ఆప్ జరా ఆరామ్ కర్‌నే కీ కోషిష్ కీజియే.
మీరు కొంచెము విశ్రాంతి తీసుకోవటానికి ప్రయత్నించండి.
YOU TRY TO TAKE SOME REST.

10) अभी कुछ गोलियाँ देता हूँ ,पाँच दिन बाद फिर मिलिए ।
इप्पुडु कोन्नि मात्रलु इस्तानु,ऐदु रोजुला तरुवाता कलवंड़ि ।
అభీ కుఛ్ గోలియా దేతా హూం పాంచ్ దిన్ బాద్ ఫిర్ మిలిఏ.
ఇప్పుడు కొన్ని మాత్రలు ఇస్తాను, ఐదు రోజుల తరువాత కలవండి.
I'LL GIVE YOU SOME TABLETS NOW. VISIT ME AFTER 5 DAYS.

11) रात मे जल्दी सोइए ।
रात्रि त्वरगा पडुकोंड़ि ।
రాత్ మే జల్దీ సోయిఏ.
రాత్రి త్వరగా పడుకోండి.
SLEEP EARLY AT NIGHT.

12) क्या मै कुछ भी खा सकता हूँ?
नेनु अन्नी तिनोच्चा?

మై కుఛ్ భీ ఖా సక్‌తా హూం ?
నేను అన్నీ తినోచ్చా ?
CAN I EAT ANYTHING ?

13) हाँ कोई भी हल्की चीज खा सकते है ।
सरे एदैना तेलिकैना आहारमु तिनवच्चु ।
సరే ఏదైనా తేలికైన ఆహారము తినవచ్చు.
హాం కోయీ భీ హల్కీ చీజ్ ఖా సక్‌తే హై.
YES, YOU CAN EAT EASILY DIGESTIBLE FOOD ITEMS.

14) पैर में दर्द है ।
काल्लु नोप्पिगा उन्नाई ।
కాళ్ళు నొప్పిగా ఉన్నాయి.
పైర్ మే దర్ద్ హై.
THERE IS PAIN IN MY LEGS.

15) भूख लगती है ?
आकलि वेस्तुंदा ?
ఆకలి వేస్తుందా ?
భూఖ్ లగ్‌తీ హై ?
DO YOU FEEL HUNGRY ?

16) आपकी उम्र क्या है ?
मी वयसेंता ?
మీ వయసెంత ?
ఆప్‌కీ ఉమ్ర్ క్యా హై ?
HOW OLD ARE YOU ?

17) उल्टी जैसा लगता है ।
वांति वस्तुनट्टु अनिपिस्तुंदि ।
వాంతి వస్తున్నట్టు అనిపిస్తుంది.
ఉల్టి జైసా లగ్‌తా హై.
I FEEL LIKE VOMIT.

18) पचास वर्ष हो गये ।
याभै संवस्तारालु ।
యాభై సంవత్సరాలు.

పఛాస్ వర్ష్ హో గయే.
I AM 50 YRS OLD.

19) क्या सुबह घूमने जाते है ?
उदयमू वाकिंगुकु वेलतारा ?
ఉదయం వాకింగుకు వెళతారా ?
క్యా సుభహ్ ఘుమ్‌నే జాతే హే ?
DO YOU GO FOR A WALK IN THE MORNING ?

20) रात मे कितने बजे सोते है ?
रात्रि एन्नि गंटलकु पडुकुंटारु ?
రాత్రి ఎన్ని గంటలకు పడుకుంటారు ?
రాత్ మే కిత్‌నే బజే సోతే హై ?
AT WHAT TIME DO YOU SLEEP AT NIGHT ?

21) रात को जल्दी ही सो जाता हूँ कभी-कभी देर होती है ।
रात्रि त्वरगाने पडुकुंटानु अप्पुडप्पुडु आलस्यमवुतुंदि ।
రాత్రి త్వరగానే పడుకుంటాను అప్పుడప్పుడు ఆలస్యమవుతుంది.
రాత్ కో జల్దీ హీ సో జాతా హూం కభీ-కభీ దేర్ హోతీ హై.
GENERALLY I SLEEP EARLY, BUT IT GETS LATE SOMETIMES.

22) नियमित रूप से नहीं घूम पाता ।
क्रममु तप्पकुंडा नडव लेकापोतुन्नानु ।
క్రమము తప్పకుండా నడవ లేక పోతున్నాను.
నియమిత్ రూప్ సే నహీ ఘూమ్ పాతా.
I AM UNABLE TO GO FOR WALK REGULARLY.

23) नियमित रूप से योगाभ्यास कीजिए ।
क्रममु तप्पकुंडा योगाभ्यासमु चेयंडि ।
క్రమము తప్పకుండా యోగ్యాభ్యాసము చేయండి.
నియమిత్ రూప్ సే యోగాభ్యాస్ కీజియే.
DO YOGA REGULARLY.
24) कम से कम तीन मील पैदल जरूर चलिए ।
कनीसम् मूडु मैल्लु तप्पकुंडा नडवालि ।
కనీసం మూడు మైళ్లు తప్పకుండా నడవాలి.
కమ్ సే కమ్ తీన్ మీల్ పైదల్ జరూర్ చలియే.

WALK FOR AT LEAST 3 MILES.

25) कुछ दवाएं देता हूँ। नियमित रूप से लिजिए।
कोन्नि मंदुलु इस्तानु। क्रममु तप्पकुंडा तीसुकोंडि।
కొన్ని మందులు ఇస్తాను. క్రమము తప్పకుండా తీసుకోండి.
కుచ్ దవాయే దేతా హూ. నియమిత్ రూప్ సే లీజియే.
I WILL GIVE YOU SOME MEDICINES. TAKE THEM REGULARLY.

26) पांच दिन बाद फिर मिलिए।
ऐदु रोजुला तरुवाता मळ्ळी कलवंडि।
ఐదు రోజుల తరువాత మళ్ళీ కలవండి.
పాంచ్ దిన్ బాద్ ఫిర్ మిలియే.
MEET ME AGAIN AFTER 5 DAYS.

27) मैं खाने में क्या ले सकता हूँ ?
नेनु भोजनमु लोकि एमि तीसुकोवच्चु ?
నేను భోజనములోకి ఏమి తీసుకోవచ్చు ?
మై ఖానే మే క్యా లే సక్తా హూ ?
WHAT ALL CAN I TAKE IN THE MEALS ?

28) कुछ भी खा सकते है। पर अभी कुछ दिन हल्का ही लिजिए।
एमैना तीसुकोवच्चु, कोन्नि रोजुलु तेलिकपाटि आहारम तीसुकोंडि।
ఏమైనా తీసుకోవచ్చు.కాని కొన్ని రోజులు తేలికపాటి ఆహారం తీసుకోండి.
కుచ్ భీ ఖా సక్తే హై.పర్ కుచ్ దిన్ హల్కా హీ లీజియే.
YOU CAN EAT EVERYTHING. BUT HAVE EASILY DIGESTIBLE FOOD FOR SOMEDAYS.

29) फल के रस का नियमित सेवन कीजिए।
पळ्ळारसमु क्रममु तप्पकुंडा तीसुकोंडि।
పళ్ల రసము క్రమము తప్పకుండా తీసుకోండి.
ఫల్ కే రస్ కా నియమిత్ సేవన్ కీజియే.
DRINK FRUIT JUICES REGULARY.

30) माँस-मदिरा से परहेज कीजिए।
मांसमु,मत्तु पदार्दाला नुंचि दूरंगा उंडंडि।
మాంసము,మత్తుపదార్థాల నుంచి దూరంగా ఉండండి.
మాంస్-మదీరా సే పర్హేజ్ కీజియే.
ABSTAIN FROM MEAT AND ALCOHOL.

बच्चों से बातें   పిల్లలతో సంభాషణ

CONVERSATION WITH CHILDREN

1) उठो छः बज गये।
ले आरु गंटलयि पोइंदि ।
లే ఆరుగంటలయిపోయింది.
ఉఠో ఛే బజ్ గయే.
GET UP, IT IS ALREADY 6'O CLOCK.

2) जल्दी स्नान कर लो,नाश्ता तैयार है।
त्वरगा स्नानमु चेय्यि,टिफिन तैयारुगा उंदि ।
త్వరగా స్నానము చెయ్యి, టిఫిన్ తయారుగా ఉంది.
జల్దీ స్నాన్ కర్ లో, నాస్తా తైయార్ హై.
TAKE BATH QUICKLY BREAK FAST IS REDAY.

3) अभी तक क्यों सोए हो,तबीयत ठीक नही है क्या?
इपट्टि वरकु एंदुकु पडुकुन्नावु,आरोग्यम बागालेदा?
ఇప్పటి వరకు ఎందుకు పడుకున్నావు, ఆరోగ్యం బాగాలేదా ?
అభీతక్, క్యోం సోయే హో, తబీయత్ ఠీక్ నహీ హై క్యా ?
WHY ARE YOU STILL ASLEEP, IS YOUR HEALTH NOT GOOD ?

4) बाहर देखो तुम्हारा दोस्त मिलने आया है ।
चूडु बयटा नी स्नेहितुडु निन्नु कलवडानिकि वच्चाडु ।
చూడు బయట నీ స్నేహితుడు నిన్ను కలవడానికి వచ్చాడు.
బాహర్ దేఖో తుమ్‌హారా దోస్త్ మిల్‌నే ఆయా హై.
LOOK OUTSIDE. YOUR FRIEND HAS COME TO MEET YOU.

5) जाओ, बाहर जाकर खेलो ।
वेल्लु, बयटकेल्लि आडुको ।
వెళ్లు, బయటికెళ్లి ఆడుకో.
జావో, బాహర్ జాకర్ ఖేలో.
GO PLAY OUTSIDE

6) दिन भर विडियो गेम मत खेलो ।
रोजंता विडियो गेमलु आडवद्दु ।
రోజంతా విడియోగేమ్‌లు ఆడవద్దు.
దిన్ భర్ విడియోగేమ్ మత్ ఖేలో.
DO NOT PLAY VIDEO GAMES WHOLE DAY.

7) मुझे परेशान मत करो,मुझे सोने दो ।
नन्नु इब्बन्दि पेट्टकु,नन्नु पडुकोनी ।
నన్ను ఇబ్బంది పెట్టకు, నన్ను పడుకోనీ.
ముఝే పరేషాన్ మత్ కరో, ముఝే సోనే దో.
DO NOT TROUBLE ME. LET ME SLEEP.

8) दरवाजा बंद कर दिया ना ?
तलुपुलु वेशावा ?
తలుపులు వేశావా ?
దర్వాజా బంద్ కర్ దియానా ?
DID YOU CLOSE THE DOORS ?

9) एक और रोटी लो ।
इंको रोट्टि वेसुको ।
ఇంకో రొట్టి వేసుకో.
ఏక్ ఔర్ రోటీ లో.
TAKE ONE MORE ROTI.

10) जल्दी सोओ तब तो जल्दी उठोगे ।
तोंदरगा पडुकुंटे तोंदरगा लेस्तावु ।
తొందరగా పడుకుంటే తొందరగా లేస్తావు.
జల్దీ సోవో తబ్ తో జల్దీ ఉఠోగే.
SLEEP EARLY, ONLY THEN YOU CAN WAKE UP EARLY.

11) तुम किससे मिलने जा रहे हो?
नीवु येवरिनि कलवडानिकि वेल्तुन्नावु?
నీవు ఎవరిని కలవడానికి వెళ్తున్నావు ?
తుమ్ కిస్‌సే మిల్‌నే జా రహే హో ?
WHO ARE YOU GOING TO MEET ?

12) काम समाप्त कर जल्दी आना ।

पनि पुर्ति चेसुकोनि तोंदरगा रा ।

పని పూర్తి చేసుకోని తొందరగా రా.

కామ్ సమాప్త్ కర్ జల్దీ ఆనా.

FINISH YOUR WORK AND COME FAST.

13) बहुत थके लग रहे हो, चाय पीलो ।

चाला अलिसिपोयिनट्टुन्नवु, टी तागु ।

చాలా అలిసిపోయినట్టున్నావు, టీ తాగు.

బహుత్ థకే లగ్ రహే హో చాయ్ పీలో.

YOU LOOK TIRED. HAVE TEA.

14) आज मेरा दिन बहुत अच्छा रहा ।

ईरोजु अंता बागुंदि ।

ఈరోజు అంతా బాగుంది.

ఆజ్ మేరా దిన్ బహుత్ అచ్ఛా రహా.

I HAD A VERY GOOD DAY.

15) आज मै थका हूँ, दिनभर काम करता रहा ।

ई रोजु चाला अलसटगा उंदि, रोजंता पनि चेस्तू उन्नानु ।

ఈరోజు చాలా అలసటగా ఉంది, రోజంతా పని చేస్తూ వున్నాను.

ఆజ్ మై థకా హూ, దిన్‌భర్ కామ్ కర్‌తా రహా.

I AM VERY TIRED TODAY. I HAVE BEEN WORKING ALL DAY.

16) जल्दी खाना दो बहुत भुख लगी है ।

त्वरगा भोजनमु पेट्टु चाला आकलिगा उंदि ।

త్వరగా భోజనము పెట్టు చాలా ఆకలిగా ఉంది.

జల్దీ ఖానా దో బహుత్ భూఖ్ లగీ హై.

GIVE ME FOOD QUICKLY. I AM VERY HUNGRY.

17) आज मै रात भर टीवी देखूंगी ।

ई रोजु रात्रंता टीवी चूस्तानु ।

ఆజ్ మై రాత్ భర్ టీవీ దేఖూంగీ.

ఈరోజు నేను రాత్రంతా టీవీ చూస్తాను.

I WILL WATCH TV ALL NIGHT.

18) मुझे सुबह मत उठाना ।

नन्नु प्रोद्दुने लेपवद्दु ।

ముఝే సుబహ్ మత్ ఉఠానా.
నన్ను ప్రొద్దున్నే లేపవద్దు.
DO NOT WAKE ME UP IN THE MORNING.

संबंधी బంధుత్వాలు RELATIONS

१)मेरे बच्चे हर साल गर्मी की छुट्टी मे नाना-नानी के घर जाते है ।
मा पिल्ललु प्रति वेसवि सेलवुल्लो वाल्ल आम्मम-तातय्या गारिंटिकि वेल्तारु ।
మా పిల్లలు ప్రతి వేసవి సెలవుల్లో వాళ్ల అమ్మమ్మ-తాతయ్య గారింటికి వెళ్తారు.
మేరే బచ్చే హర్ సాల్ గర్‌మీ కీ ఛుట్టీ మే నానా-నానీ కే ఘర్ జాతే హై.
MY CHILDREN GO TO THEIR GRAND PARENTS PLACE EVERY SUMMER HOLIDAYS.

२)ये मेरे बड़े भाई है ।
ईयना मा अन्नय्या ।
ఈయన మా అన్నయ్య.
యే మేరే బడే భాయీ హై.
HE IS MY ELDER BROTHER.

३)यह छत्तीसगढ़ मे डाक्टर है ।
अतडु छत्तीसगढ़ लो डाक्टरु ।
అతడు ఛత్తీస్‌గఢ్ లో డాక్టరు.
యహ్ ఛత్తీస్‌గఢ్ మే డాక్టర్ హై.
HE IS A DOCTOR IN CHATTISGARH.

४) ये मेरी बहन है ।
ईमे मा सोदरि ।
ఈమె మా సోదరి.
యే మేరీ బహన్ హై.
SHE IS MY SISTER.

५) ये मगध विश्वविद्यालय मे प्रोफेसर है ।
आयना/आमे मगध विश्वविद्यालयम लो प्रोफेसरु ।
ఆయన/ఆమె మగధ విశ్వవిద్యాలయంలో ప్రొఫేసరు.
యే మగధ్ విశ్వవిధ్యాలయ్ మే ప్రొఫేసర్ హై.
HE/SHE IS A PROFESSOR IN MAGADH UNIVERCITY.

६) ये मेरी मां हैं,यह गृहिणी है ।
इमें मा अम्मा, तनु गृहिणि ।
ఈమె మా అమ్మ, తను గృహిణి.
యే మేరీ మా హై, యహ్ గృహిణీ హై.
SHE IS MY MOTHER. SHE IS A HOMEMAKER.

७) वहाँ जो नीले कमीज पहना है मेरे मामा का बेटा है ।
आक्कडा नीलम चोक्का वेसुकुन्नातनु मा मामय्या कोडुकु ।
అక్కడ నీలం చొక్కా వేసుకున్నతను మా మామయ్య కొడుకు.
వహాం జో నీలే కమీజ్ పహనా హై మేరే మామా కా బేటా హై.
THE PERSON THERE WHO IS WEARING BLUE SHIRT IS MY UNCLE'S SON

८) वो जिसके लम्बे-लम्बे बाल है वो मेरी ननद है ।
आ पोडवाटि जुट्टु उन्ना अम्माइ मा आडपडुचु ।
ఆ పోడవాటి జుట్టు ఉన్న అమ్మాయి మా ఆడపడుచు.
వో జిస్‌కే లంబే-లంబే బాల్ హై వో మేరీ ననద్ హై.
THE GIRL OVER THERE WITH A LONG PLAIT IS MY SISTER IN LAW.

९) ये मेरे पिताजी हैं ।
इयना मा नान्नगारू ।
ఈయన మా నాన్నగారు.
యే మేరే పితాజీ హై.
HE IS MY FATHER.

१०) जिसने अभी गाना गाया वो मेरा बड़ा बेटा है ।
इपुडु पाटा पाड़िनतनु मा पेद्दब्बायि ।
ఇప్పుడు పాట పాడినతను మా పెద్దబ్బాయి.
జిస్‌నే అబీ గానా గాయా వో మేరా బడా బేటా హై.
THE ONE WHO JUST SANG IS MY ELDER SON.

११) जो गिटार बजा रहा था वो मेरा छोटा बेटा है ।

आ गिटारु वाइंचिनतनु मा चिन्नब्बायि ।

ఆ గిటారు వాయించినతను మా చిన్నబ్బాయి.

జో గిటార్ బజా రహా థా వో మేరా ఛోటా బేటా హై.

THE ONE WHO WAS PLAYING GUITARE IS MY YOUNGER SON.

१२) ये मेरे पति है,स्टील प्लांट मे इंजीनियर है ।

ईयना मा श्री वारु, स्टील प्लंट लो इंजीनीयरु ।

ఈయన మా ఆయన/శ్రీవారు స్టీల్‌ప్లాంట్ లో ఇంజీనియర్.

యే మేరే పతీ హై, స్టీల్‌ప్లాంట్ మే ఇంజీనియర్ హై.

THIS IS MY HUSBAND. HE IS AN ENGINEER IN STEEL PLANT.

१३) ये मेरे देवर है, आज ही अमेरिका से आये हैं ।

इतनु मा मरिदी, अमेरिका नुंचि इवाले वच्चारु ।

ఇతను మా మరిది, అమెరికా నుంచి ఇవాళే వచ్చారు.

యే మేరే దేవర్ హై, ఆజ్ హీ అమెరికా సే ఆయా హై.

THIS IS MY BROTHER-IN-LAW. HE HAS JUST ARRIVED FROM USA.

१४) ये सुंदर लड़की मेरी देवरानी की बेटी है ।

ई अंदमयिना अम्मायि मा तोटिकोड़लि कुतुरु ।

ఈ అందమైనా చిన్న పాప మా తీటికోడలి కూతురు.

యే సుందర్ లఢకీ మేరీ దేవ్‌రానీ కీ బేటీ హై.

THIS BEAUTIFUL GIRL IS MY CO- SISTER'S DAUGHTERS.

१५) मेरी सास-ससुर मंदिर गए है,वे अभी आ जायेंगें ।

मा अत्तागारु-मामागारु गुडिकि वेल्लारु,इप्पुडे वच्चेस्तारु ।

మా అత్తగారు-మామగారు గుడికి వెళ్లారు, ఇప్పుడే వచ్చేస్తారు.

మేరీ సాస్-ససుర్ మందిర్ గయేం హై, అబీ ఆజాయేంగే.

MY MOTHER-IN-LAW AND FATHER-IN-LAW WENT TO TEMPLE. THEY'LLRETURN ANYTIME NOW.

डाँटने वाले वाक्यांश దండన/దూషణ పదములు SCOLDING PHRASES

१) बकवास बंद करो ।
पिच्चि-पिच्चिगा माट्लाडवद्दु ।
పిచ్చి-పిచ్చిగా మాట్లాడవద్దు.
బక్‌వాస్ బంద్ కరో.
DO NOT TALK RUBBISH.

२) अपना मुंह बंद रखो ।
नोर मुसुको ।
నోర్ మూసుకో.
అప్‌నా మూంహ్ బంద్ రఖో.
SHUT YOUR MOUTH.

३) ज्यादा मत बोलो ।
एक्कुआ माट्लाडकु ।
ఎక్కువ మాట్లాడకు.
జ్యాదా మత్ బోలో.
DO NOT TALK MUCH.

४) मेरा दिमाग मत खाओ ।
ना बुर्रा तिनकु ।
నా బుర్ర తినకు.
మేరా దిమాగ్ మత్ ఖావో.
DO NOT EAT MY BRAIN.

५) भागो नही तो खींच के मारूंगा ।
वेल्लकपोते लागी पेट्टि कोडतानु ।
వెళ్ళకపోతే లాగిపెట్టి కొడతాను.
భాగో నహీ తో ఖీంచ్ కే మారూంగా.
GO AWAY ELSE I'LL GIVE YOU A SLAP.

६) चलो भागो यहाँ से ।
इक्कड़ि निंचि वेल्लिपो ।
ఇక్కడి నించి వెళ్లిపో.
చలో భాగో యహాంసే.
GO AWAY FROM HERE.

७) गधा कहीं का ।
बुर्रालेनि गाड़िदा ।
బుర్రలేని గాడిదా.
గధా కహీంకా.
BRAINLESS ASS.

८) आलसी कहीं का ।
बद्धकिष्टी ।
బద్దకిష్టీ
ఆలసీ కహీంకా.
LAZY FELLOW.

९) तुम्हें समझ नहीं आता क्या?
नीकु अर्थम अव्वटम् लेदा ?
నీకు అర్థం అవ్వటం లేదా ?
తుమ్హే సమజ్ నహీ ఆతా క్యా ?
DON'T YOU UNDERSTAND?

१०) क्या दिमाग मे भूसा भरा है ?
नीदि मट्टि बुर्रा ?
నీది మట్టి బుర్రా ?
క్యా దిమాగ్ మే భుసా భరా హై ?
ARE YOU A DUMBHEAD.

११) अक्कल नहीं है क्या?
बुर्रा लेदा?
బుర్ర లేదా ?
అక్కల్ నహీం హై క్యా ?
DON'T YOU HAVE ANY SENSE?

१२) दिमाग कम है क्या?

तेलिवि तक्कुवा वेधवा?

తెలివి తక్కువ వెధవా ?

దిమాగ్ కమ్ హై క్యా ?

ARE YOU AN IDIOT?

१३) ऐसा करो नही तो मार खाओ ।

अला चेय्यकपोते तन्नुलु तिंटाऊ ।

అలా చెయ్యకపోతే తన్నులు తింటావు.

యైసా కరో నహీతో మార్ ఖావోగే.

YOU WILL BE SEVERELY BEATEN IF YOU DON'T DO LIKE THAT.

१४) मैं जैसे कहती हूँ वैसा करो नहीं तो मार खाओगे ।

नेनु चेप्पिनट्टु चेय्यु लेका पोते तन्नुलु तिंटावु ।

నేను చెప్పినట్టు చెయ్యి లేకాపోతే తన్నులు తింటావు.

మై జైసే కహ్‌తీ హూ వైసా కరో నహీతో మార్ ఖావోగే.

YOU WILL BE BEATEN IF YOU DO NOT DO AS I SAY.

१५) क्या दिमाग काम नहीं कर रहा है?

नी बुर्रा पनि चेयटम लेदा?

నీ బుర్ర పని చేయటం లేదా.

క్యా దిమాగ్ కామ్ నహీ కర్ రహా హై.

HAS YOUR BRAIN STOPPED WORKING?

पडोसियों से ఇరుగుపొరుగు వాళ్ళతో WITH NEIGHBOURS

1)क्या आपके घर में लाइट है ?
मी इंट्लो लैट उंदा/करंटु वुंदा ?
మీ ఇంట్లో లైటు ఉందా/ కరెంటు వుందా?
క్యా ఆప్‌కే ఘర్ మే లైట్ హై ?
DO YOU HAVE ELECTRIC SUPPLY WORKING IN YOUR HOUSE?

2)क्या, भाई साहब आफिस से आ गये ?
अन्नय्या गारू आफिसु नुंचि वच्चेसारा ?
అన్నయ్యగారు ఆఫీసు నుంచి వచ్చేసారా ?
క్యా భాఈ సాహబ్ ఆఫీస్ సే ఆ గయే ?
DID YOUR HUSBAND RETURN FROM OFFICE?

3) क्या आपके घर में चायपत्ति है ?
मी इंट्लो टी पोडि उंदा ?
మీ ఇంట్లో టీ పొడి ఉందా ?
క్యా ఆప్‌కే ఘర్ మే ఛాయ్ పత్తి హై ?
DO YOU HAVE TEA LEAVES IN YOUR HOUSE?

4)ये चाबी मेरे बेटे को दे दीजिए ।
ई तालालु मा अब्बायिकि इव्वंडि ।
ఈ తాళము మా అబ్బాయికి ఇవ్వండి.
యే ఛాబి మేరే బేటే కో దీజిఏ.
GIVE THESE KEYS TO MY SON.

5)मेरा कोई पत्र आपके घर आया क्या ?
ना उत्तरम् एदैना मी इंटिकि वच्चिंदा ?
నా ఉత్తరంఏదైనా మీ ఇంటికి వచ్చిందా ?
మేరా కోయీ పత్ర్ ఆప్‌కే ఘర్ ఆయా క్యా ?
HAS ANY OF MY LETTERS REACHED YOUR HOUSE?

6)मैं बाहर जा रहा हूँ, मेरा कोरियर ले लिजिएगा ।
नेनु बैटकु वेलुतुन्नानु, ना कोरियर तीसुकोंडि ।
నేను బయటకు వెళ్తున్నాను, నా కొరియర్ తీసుకోండి.
మై బాహర్ జా రహా హూ, మేరా కొరియర్ లే లీజియెగ.
I AM GOING OUT. TAKE MY COURIER.

7)मै ने पनीर की सब्जी बनायी है, क्या आप टे्स्ट करेंगे ?
नेनु पनीर कूरा चेसानु, मीरू रूचि चूस्तारा ?
నేను పనీర్ కూర చేసాను, మీరు రుచి చూస్తారా ?
మై నే పనీర్ కీ సబ్జీ బనాయి హై, క్యా ఆప్ టేస్ట్ కరేంగే ?
I HAVE MADE PANEER CURRY. WILL YOU TASTE IT?

8) आप निश्चिंत रहिए । मै सब देख लूँगी ।
मीरू निश्चिंतगा उंडंडि । नेनु मोत्तम चूसुकुंटानु ।
మీరు నిశ్చితంగా వుడండి, నేను మొత్తం చూసుకుంటాను.
ఆప్ నిశ్చింత్ రహియే, మై సబ్ దేఖ్ లుంగి.
YOU DONT WORRY. I WILL TAKE CARE OF EVERYTHING.

9) मेरा मिक्सी काम नहीं कर रहा ।
ना मिक्सी पनि चेयटम् लेदु ।
నా మిక్సి పని చేయటం లేదు.
మేరా మిక్సి కామ్ నహి కర్ రహా.
MY GRINDER IS NOT WORKING.

10)क्या आप चौक के तरफ ही जा रहे है ?
मीरु चौक वैपे वेल्तुन्नारा ?
మీరు జంక్షను వైపే వెళుతున్నారా ?
క్యా ఆప్ చౌక్ కే తరఫ్ హీ జా రహే హై ?
ARE YOU GOING TOWARDS THE JUNCTION?

11)मेरे लिए भी बाजार से फल ले आइए ।
बजारु नुंडि नाकोसमु कूड़ा पल्लु तीसुकु रंडि ।
బజారు నుండి నాకోసము కూడా పళ్లు తీసుకు రండి.
మేరే లియె భీ బాజార్ సే ఫల్ లే ఆయియే.
BRING FRUITS FROM THE MARKET FOR ME TO

12)आपकी साड़ी बहुत सुंदर है, कहाँ से ली ?
मी चीरा चाला बागुंदि, एक्कडा तीसुकुन्नारू ?
మీ చీర చాలా బాగుంది, ఎక్కడ తీసుకున్నారు ?
ఆప్‌కీ సాఢీ బహుత్ సుందర్ హై, కహా సే లీ ?
YOUR SAREE IS NICE. WHERE DID YOU BUY IT FROM?

13)कल फिर बाजार चलें क्या ?
रेपु बजारुकु मळ्ळी वेलदामा ?
రేపు బజారుకు మళ్ళీ వెళదామా ?
కల్ ఫిర్ బాజార్ చలే క్యా ?
SHALL WE GO TO THE MARKET AGAIN TOMORROW?

14)आपकी कामवाली आई क्या ?
मी पनिमनिषि वच्चिंदा ?
మీ పనిమనిషి వచ్చిందా ?
ఆప్‌కీ కామ్‌వాలీ ఆయీ క్యా ?
HAS YOUR SERVANT MAID ARRIVED ?

15) मेरी कामवाली काम करके चली गई ।
मा पनिमनिषि पनि चेसि वेळ्ळिपोइंदि ।
మా పనిమనిషి పని చేసి వెళ్ళిపోయింది.
మేరీ కామ్‌వాలీ కామ్ కర్‌కే చలీ గయీ.
MY MAID FINISHED HER WORK AND LEFT.

16) आपका घर चमक रहा है कौन काम करती है ?
मी इल्लु मेरुस्तुंदि । एवरू पनि चेस्तारू ?
మీ ఇల్లు మెరుస్తుంది ! ఎవరు పని చేస్తారు ?
ఆప్‌కా ఘర్ ఛమక్ రహా హై కౌన్ కామ్ కర్‌తీ హై ?
YOUR HOUSE IS SPARKLING. WHO WORKS HERE?

17) आप कामवाली को कितना देती है ?

मीरु पनिमनिषिकि एंता इस्तारु ?
మీరు పనిమనిషికి ఎంత ఇస్తారు ?
ఆప్ కామ్‌వాలీ కో కిత్‌నా దేతీ హై ?
HOW MUCH DO YOU PAY YOUR MAID ?

18) क्या दही के लिए थोड़ा जोरन दीजिएगा ?
पेरूगु कोसमू कोंचेम तोडु इस्तारा ?
పెరుగు కోసము కొంచెము తోడు ఇస్తారా ?
క్యా దహి కే లియే థోడా జోరన్ దీజియేగ ?
CAN YOU GIVE SOME CURD TO SET OURS?

19) हरीमिर्ची का अचार तो बहुत बढ़िया है । कैसे बनाया ?
पच्चिमिर्च पच्चडि चाला बागुंदि एला चेसारू ?
పచ్చిమిర్చి పచ్చడి చాలా బాగుంది. ఎలా చేసారు ?
మిర్చి కా ఆచార్ తో బహుత్ బఢియా హై. కైసే బనాయా ?
GREEN CHILLIES PICKLE IS VERY GOOD. HOW DID YOU MAKE IT?

1) आपसे मिलकर बहुत खुशी हुई ।
मिम्मल्नि कलिसिनंदुकु चाला संतोषंमुगा उंदि ।
మిమ్మల్ని కలిసినందుకు చాలా సంతోషంగా వుంది.
ఆప్ సే మిల్‌కర్ బహుత్ ఖుషీ హుయీ.
VERY HAPPY TO MEET YOU.

2) आपका सफ़र कैसा रहा ।
मी प्रयाणमु एला जरिगिंदि ।
మీ ప్రయాణము ఎలా జరిగింది.
ఆప్‌కా సఫర్ కైసా రహా.
HOW DID YOUR JOURNEY GO ?

3) सफ़र काफी खुशगवार(अच्छा) रहा ।
प्रयानमु बागा जरिगिंदि ।
ప్రయాణము బాగా జరిగింది.
సఫర్ ఖాఫీ ఖుష్‌గవార్(అచ్చా) రహా.
JOURNEY WAS GOOD.

4) रेल में ज्यादा भीड़ तो नहीं थी न ?
रैलु लो रद्दी एक्कुवगा लेदु कदा ?
రైలు లో రద్దీ ఎక్కువగా లేదుకదా ?
రైల్ మే జ్యాదా భీడ్ తో నహీ థీ నా ?
WAS THE TRAIN OVER CROWDED ?

5) भीड़ तो थी पर आरक्षण के कारण दिक्कत नहीं हुई ।
रद्दीगाने उंदि कानि रिजर्वेशनु उंडाटम वलना कष्टमनिपिंचलेदु ।
రద్దీగానే వుంది కాని రిజర్వేషను వుండటము వలన కష్టమనిపించలేదు.
భీడ్ తో థీ పర్ ఆరక్షణ్ కే కారణ్ ధిక్కత్ నహీ హుయి.
IT WAS CROWDED, HOWEVER IT WASN'T OF MUCH TROUBLE BECAUSE OF RESERVATION.

6) आप पहले स्नान करेंगे या चाय कॉफी लेंगे ?
मीरु मुंदु स्नानमू चेस्तारा लेका टी-कॉफी लेमैना तिसुकुंटारा ?
మీరు ముందు స్నానము చేస్తారా లేక టీ కాఫీలేమైనా తీసుకుంటారా ?
ఆప్ పహలే స్నాన్ కరేంగే యా ఛాయ్ కాఫీ లేంగే ?
WILL YOU TAKE BATH OR HAVE TEA OR COFFEE FIRST ?

7) चाय पीकर स्नान करुंगा ।
टी तिसुकुन्नाका स्नानम चेस्तानु ।
టీ తీసుకున్నాక స్నానం చేస్తాను.
ఛాయ్ పీకర్ స్తాన్ కరుంగా.
I WILL TAKE BATH AFTER HAVING TEA.

8) नाश्ते में क्या लेना पसंद करेंगे ?
फलहारमु लो एमि तिनटानिकि इष्टपडतारु ?
ఫలహారము లో ఏమి తినటానికి ఇష్టపడతారు ?
నాష్తే మే క్యా లేనా పసంద్ కరేంగే ?
WHAT WOULD YOU LIKE TO HAVE FOR BREAKFAST ?

9) कुछ हल्का ही लुंगा । रास्ते भर कुछ न कुछ खाता ही रहा ।
एदैना तेलिकपाटि आहारमु तीसूकुंटानु । दारिलो एदो वकटि तिंटूने उन्नानु ।
ఏదైనా తేలికపాటి ఆహారము తీసుకుంటాను ! దారిలో ఏదో ఒకటి తింటూనే వున్నాను.
కుచ్ హల్కా హి లుంగా ! రాస్తే భర్ కుచ్ న కుచ్ ఖాతా హి రహా.
I WILL TAKE SOMETHING LIGHT. I WAS EATING SOMETHING OR OTHER ON THE WAY.

10) ठीक है इडली ठीक रहेगा हल्का भी स्वादिष्ट भी ।
सरे । इड्ली बागाने उंटुंदि. तेलिकगानु उंटुंदि आरोग्याकरमु कूड़ा ।
సరే ! ఇడ్లి బాగానే ఉంటుంది.తేలికగాను ఉంటుంది ఆరోగ్యకరము కూడా.
ఠీక్ హై ఇడ్లి ఠీక్ రహేగా హల్కా భీ స్వాదిష్ట్ భీ.
OK. IDLY WOULD BE GOOD. EASY TO DIGEST AND DELICIOUS TOO.

11) आज आपका क्या कार्यक्रम है ?
इवाला मि कार्यक्रममु एमिटि ?
ఇవాళ మీ కార్యక్రమము ఏమిటి ?
ఆజ్ ఆప్‌కా క్యా కార్య్రకమ్ హై ?
WHAT IS YOUR PROGRAM TODAY ?

12) दफ्तर में कुछ अधिकारियों से मिलना है ।
कार्यलयमुलो कोंतामंदि अधिकारूलनु कलवालि ।
కార్యాలయంలో కొంతమంది అధికారులను కలవాలి.
దఫ్తర్ మే కుచ్ అధికారియోంసే మిల్నా హై.
I HAVE GO TO MEET SOME OFFICIALS IN THE OFFICE.

13) चलिए, खाना खा लिजिए ।
रंडि । भोजनमु चेयंडि ।
రండి ! భోజనము చేయండి.
ఛలియే ఖానా ఖా లీజిఏ.
COME ! HAVE MEALS.

14) खाना बहुत स्वादिष्ट है ।
भोजनमु चाला रुचिगा उंदि ।
భోజనము చాలా రుచిగా ఉంది.
ఖానా బహుత్ స్వాదిష్ట్ హై.
THE MEALS ARE VERY TASTY / THE FOOD IS VERY TASTY.

15) और ले लिजिए शर्माइये मत,इसे अपना ही घर समझिए ।
इंका वेसुकोंडि,सिग्गुपडकंडि । मी इल्ले अनुकोंडि ।
ఇంకా వేసుకోండి,సిగ్గుపడకండి,మీ ఇల్లే అనుకోండి.
ఔర్ లే లీజియే షర్మాయియే మత్,ఇసే ఆప్నా హీ ఘర్ సమఝియే.
HAVE SOME MORE. DO NOT FEEL SHY. FEEL AT HOME.

सेवक से बातचीत　　పనివారితో సంభాషణ

CONVERSATION WITH SERVANT

1) एक कप कड़ी चाय ले आओ ।
ओका कप्पु स्ट्रांग टी तीसुकुनि रा ।
ఒక కప్పు స్ట్రాంగ్ టీ తీసుకుని రా.
ఏక్ కప్ కడి ఛాయ్ లే ఆవో.
BRING ME A CUP OF STRONG TEA.

2) क्या तुमने कपड़े धो लिए ?
नीवु बट्टलु उतिकेसावा ?
నీవు బట్టలు ఉతికేసావా ?
క్యా తుమ్‌నే కపడే ధో లియే ?
DID YOU WASH CLOTHES ?

3) बाजार जाकर दो किलो आलु ले आओ ।
बजारुकेल्लि रेंडु किलोल बंगालदुंपलु तीसुकुनिरा ।
బజారు కెళ్లి రెండు కిలోల బంగాళదుంపలు తీసుకుని రా.
బాజార్ జాకర్ దో కిలో ఆలు లే ఆవో.
BRING 2 Kgs OF POTATOES FROM MARKET.

4) कुत्ते को बाहर घुमा लाओ ।
कुक्कनि बयटा तिप्पि तीसुकुनिरा ।
కుక్కని బయట తిప్పి తీసుకుని రా.
కుత్తే కో బాహర్ ఘుమా లావో.
TAKE THE DOG FOR A STROLL.

5) आज रात के खाने में आलु पराठा बनाना ।
रात्रि भोजनम् लोकि आलू पराठालु चेयि ।
రాత్రి భోజనంలోకి ఆలూ పరాఠాలు చేయి.
ఆజ్ రాత్ కే ఖానేమే ఆలూపరాఠా బనానా.
MAKE ALOO PARATTAS FOR TODAY'S DINNER.

6) मेरे जूते पालिश कर दो ।
ना बूट्लु पालिष चेयि ।
నా బూట్లు పాలిష్ చేయి.
మేరే జూతే పాలిష్ కర్ దో.
POLISH MY SHOES.

7) मेरा चश्मा टेबल पर रख दो ।
ना कळ्ळजोडु मेजाबल्ला मीद पेट्टु ।
నా కళ్ళజోడు మేజాబల్ల మీద పెట్టు.
మేరా ఛష్మా టేబల్ పర్ రఖ్ దో.
PUT MY SPECTACLES ON THE TABLE.

8) मुझे बाहर जाना है कार निकालो ।
नेनु बयटिकि वेळ्ळालि । कारू तीयु ।
నేను బయటికి వెళ్ళాలి కారు తీయు.
ముఝె బాహర్ జానా హై కార్ నికాలో.
I HAVE GOT TO GO OUT. TAKE OUT THE CAR.

9) मेरा सामान टेक्सी में रख दो ।
ना सामान्लु टेक्सीलो पेट्टु ।
నా సామాన్లు టేక్సీలో పెట్టు.
మేరా సామాన్ టేక్సి మే రఖ్ దో.
PUT MY LUGGAGE IN THE TAXI.

10) मेरा तौलिया स्नानघर में रख दो ।
ना तुवालु स्नानाला गदिलो पेट्टु ।
నా తువ్వాలు స్నానాల గదిలో పెట్టు.
మేరా తౌలియా స్నాన్ ఘర్ మే రఖ్ దో.
KEEP MY TOWEL IN THE BATHROOM.

11) नहाने के लिए पानी गर्म कर दो ।
स्नानमु चेयाटानिकि नीळ्ळु वेडि चेयि ।
స్నానము చేయటానికి నీళ్ళు వేడి చేయి.

నహానే కే లియే పానీ గర్మ్ కర్ దో.
HEAT THE WATER FOR TAKING BATH.
12) चाय के साथ बिस्कुट भी लाना ।
टी तो पाटु बिस्केट्लु कूड़ा तीसुकोनि रा ।
టీ తో పాటు బిస్కెట్లు కూడా తీసుకుని రా.
ఛాయ్ కే సాత్ బిస్కిట్ భీ లానా.
BRING BISCUITS ALONG WITH TEA.

13) थोड़ा समय पर आया करो ।
कोंचेमु टैमुकु वस्तुंडु ।
కొంచెము టైముకు వస్తుండు.
థోడా సమయ్ పర్ ఆయాకరో.
COME ON TIME.

14) कल समय पर आ जाना ।
रेपु सरैना समयानिकि वच्चेयि ।
రేపు సరైన సమయానికి వచ్చెయి.
కల్ సమయ్ పర్ ఆ జానా.
COME ON TIME TOMORROW.

15) बर्तन अच्छे से साफ करो ।
अंट्लु सरिग्गा शुभ्रम चेयि ।
అంట్లు సరిగ్గా శుభ్రము చేయి.
బర్తన్ అచ్ఛేసే సాఫ్ కరో.
WASH THE DISHES PROPERLY.

16)कैसे पोछा लगया है । कमरा अभी भी गंदा दिख रहा है ।
इल्लु एला तडिबट्टातो तुडिचावु । गदि इंका अशुभ्रंगाने कनिपिस्तुंदि ।
ఇల్లు ఎలా తడిబట్టతో తుడిచావు, గది ఇంకా అశుభ్రంగానే కనిపిస్తుంది.
కైసే పోచా లగాయా హై, కమరా అభీ భీ గందా దిఖ్ రహా హై.
HOW DID YOU MOP THE FLOOR ? IT STILL LOOKS DIRTY.

टेलिफोन पर बात తెలిఫోనులో సంభాషణ

CONVERSATION OVER TELEPHONE

1)हैलो/जय श्री कृष्णा/राधे-राधे ।
हेलो/जय श्री कृष्णा/राधे-राधे ।
హలో !జయ శ్రీ కృష్ణ ! రాధే–రాధే.
హేలో ! జయ్ శ్రీ కృష్ణ ! రాధే–రాధే.
HELLO ! JAYA SRI KRISHNA/RADHE RADHE.

2) क्या मैं सुरेन्द्र जी से बातें कर सकता हूँ ?
नेनु सुरेन्द्र गारितो माट्लाडवच्चा ?
నేను సురేంద్ర గారితో మాట్లాడవచ్చా ?
క్యా మై సురేంద్ర జీ సే బాతేం కర్ సక్తా హూ ?
CAN I SPEAK TO Mr. Surendra?

3) हाँ,कहिए मैं सुरेन्द्र ही बोल रहा हूँ ।
आ,चेप्पंडि नेनु सुरेन्द्र ने माट्लाडुतुन्नानु ।
ఆ! చెప్పండి నేను సురేంద్రనే మాట్లాడుతున్నాను.
హా, కహియే మై సురేంద్ర హీ బొల్ రహా హూ.
YES, TELL ME, I AM SURENDRA SPEAKING.

4) मै आपसे मिलना चाहता हूँ । किस समय आऊँ ?
नेनु मिम्मल्नि कलुद्दामनुकुंटुन्नानु । ए समयमंलो रम्मन्टारु ?
నేను మిమ్మల్ని కలుద్దామనుకుంటున్నాను! ఏ సమయంలో రమ్మంటారు ?
మై ఆప్‌సే మిల్‌నా చాహతా హూ! కిస్ సమయ్ ఆవూ ?
I WANT TO MEET YOU. AT WHAT TIME SHALL I COME ?

5) आप चार बजे आ सकते है ।
मीरु नालुगु गंटलकु रागलरु ।
మీరు నాలుగు గంటలకు రాగలరు.
ఆప్ చార్ బజే ఆ సక్తే హై.
YOU CAN COME AT 4'O CLOCK.

6) हैलो आपकी आवाज़ अच्छे से सुनाई नहीं दे रही है ।
हलो मी माटा सरिग्गा विनिपिंचटम्लेदु ।
హలో మీ మాట సరిగ్గా వినిపించటం లేదు.
హెలో ఆప్‌కీ ఆవాజ్ అచ్ఛే సే సునాయి నహి దే రహి హై.
HELLO ! YOUR VOICE IS NOT AUDIBLE PROPERLY.

7) यहाँ सिगनल की थोड़ी समस्या है ।
इक्कड़ा कोंचेम सिगनलु समस्या उंदि ।
ఇక్కడ కొంచెము సిగ్నలు సమస్య ఉంది.
యహా సిగ్‌నల్ కీ తోడీ సమస్య హై.
THERE IS A PROBLEM WITH SIGNAL HERE.

8) मैं दूसरे नंबर से कॉल करता हूँ ।
नेनु वेरे नंबरु नुंचि काल चेस्तानु ।
నేను వేరే నంబరు నుండి కాల్ చేస్తాను.
మై దూస్‌రే నంబర్ సే కాల్ కర్‌తా హూ.
I WILL CALL FROM ANOTHER NUMBER.

9) हां, इसमे आवाज साफ आ रही है ।
आ, इंदुलो बागाने विनबडुतुंदि ।
ఆ, ఇందులో బాగానే వినబడుతుంది.
హా, ఇస్‌మే ఆవాజ్ సాఫ్ ఆ రహీ హై.
YES ! I CAN HEAR CLEARLY IN THIS.

10) बहुत दिनों से आपसे बातें नहीं हुई । क्या हाल है ? घर मे सब कैसे है ?
चाला रोजुला नुंडि मीतो माट्लडाटम् कुदरलेदु । एला उन्नारू ? इंट्लो अंता एला उन्नारु ?
చాలా రోజుల నుండి మీతో మాట్లాడటం కుదరలేదు ! ఎలా ఉన్నారు ? ఇంట్లో అంతా ఎలా ఉన్నారు ?
బహుత్ దినో సే ఆప్‌సే బాతే నహి హుయి ! క్యా హాల్ హై ? ఘర్ మే సబ్ కైసే హై ?
WE DIDN'T HAVE A TALK FOR A LONG TIME. HOW ARE YOU ? HOW ARE EVERYONE AT HOME?

11) ठीक है मैं भी लगाने सोच ही रहा था ।
बागाने उंदि । नेनु कूड़ा वेयिंचुदामनुकुंटुन्नानु ।

బాగానే ఉంది ! నేను కూడా వేయించుదామనుకుంటున్నాను.
ఠీక్ హై మై బీ లగానే సోచ్ హీ రహా థా.
OK, EVEN I WAS THINKING TO CALL YOU.
12) आजकल कैसे चल रहा है ?
प्रस्तुतम् एला उंदि ? एम चेस्तुन्नारु ?
ప్రస్తుతం ఎలా ఉంది ? ఏం చేస్తున్నారు ?
ఆజ్‌కల్ కైసే చల్ రహా హై ?
HOW ARE THINGS GOING ON NOW A DAYS ?

13) ठीक है काम की थोड़ी व्यस्तता है इस कारण कहीं आ जा नहीं रहा हूँ ।
फरवालेदु कास्ता पनि एक्कुवगा उंदि.दानि वलना एक्कडिकि वेल्लटमु लेदु ।
ఫరవాలేదు కాస్త పని ఎక్కువగా ఉంది. దానివలన ఎక్కడికి వెళ్ళటము లేదు.
ఠీక్ హై కామ్ కీ థోడీ వ్యస్తతా హై ఇస్ కారణ్ కహీ ఆ జా నహి రహా హూం.
GOOD. I AM A BIT BUSY WITH WORK. THAT IS WHY I AM NOT GOING ANYWHERE.

14) आप जिस एयरटेल सबसक्राइबर से बातें करना चाहते है वह किसी अन्य कॉल पर व्यस्त है ।
मीरु ए एयरटेल विनियोगादारुनितो माट्लाडालनुकुंटुन्नारो वारु वेरे कॉल लो उन्नारु ।
మీరు ఏ ఎయిర్‌టెల్ వినియోగదారునితో మాట్లాడాలనుకుంటున్నారో వారు వేరే కాల్ లో ఉన్నారు.
ఆప్ జిస్ ఎయిర్‌టెల్ సబ్‌స్క్రయిబర్ సే బాతే కర్‌నా చాహతే హై వహ్ అన్య కాల్ మే వ్యస్త్ హై.
THE AIRTEL SUBSCRIBER YOU WANT TO CONTACT IS BUSY WITH ANOTHER CALL.

15) कृपया थोड़ी देर बाद प्रयास करें ।
दया चेसि कासेपागि प्रयत्निंचंडि ।
దయ చేసి కాసేపాగి ప్రయత్నించండి.
కృపయా థోడీ దేర్ బాద్ ప్రయాస్ కరే.
PLEASE TRY AFTER SOMETIME.

ट्रेन/बस अड्डे पर वार्तालाप రైల్వేస్టేషన్/బస్టాండ్‌లో సంభాషణ

CONVERSATION AT RAILWAY STATION/BUS_STAND

1) यहां से विशाखपट्टणम कितनी दूर है ।
इक्कडिनुंचि विशाखपट्टणम् एंता दूरम ।
ఇక్కడి నుంచి విశాఖపట్నం ఎంత దూరం.
యహా సే విశాఖపట్నం కిత్‌నీ దూర్ హై.
HOW FAR IS VISAKHAPATNAM FROM HERE?

2) यही कोई लगभग बीस किलोमीटर ।
इंचुमिंचु इरवै किलोमीटरलु ।
ఇంచు మించు ఇరవై కిలోమీటర్లు.
యహీ కొఈ లగ్-బగ్ బీస్ కిలోమీటర్.
AROUND 20KMS FROM HERE.

3) यहाँ से जाने की क्या-क्या सुविधा है ?
इक्कडि नुंचि वेळ्ळडानिकि एमेमि सौकर्यालु उन्नायि ?
ఇక్కడి నుంచి వెళ్లడానికి ఏమేమి సౌకర్యాలు వున్నాయి ?
యహా సే జానే కేలియే క్యా క్యా సువిదా హై ?
WHAT ARE FACILITIES AVAILABLE TO LEAVE FROM HERE ?

4) बस व ट्रेन दोनों से जा सकते है ।
बस्सु लेदा ट्रैन मीदा वेळ्ळवच्चु ।
బస్సు లేదా ట్రైన్ మీద వెళ్లవచ్చు.
బస్ వ ట్రైన్ దోనోంసే జా సక్‌తే హై.
YOU CAN GO EITHER BY BUS OR TRAIN.

5) बस से कितना समय लगेगा ?
बस्सु मीदा एंता समयमु पडुतुंदि ?
బస్సు మీద ఎంత సమయము పడుతుంది ?
బస్ సే కిత్‌నా సమయ్ లగేగా ?
HOW LONG WILL IT TAKE BY BUS?

6) यही कोई एक घंटा ।
दादापु ओका गंटा ।
దాదాపు ఒక గంట.
యహీ కోఈ ఏక్ ఘంటే .
ALMOST ONE HOUR.

7) गरीब रथ कितने बजे आती है ।
गरीब रथ एन्नि गंटलकु वस्तुंदि ।
గరీబ్ రథ్ ఎన్ని గంటలకు వస్తుంది.
గరీబ్ రథ్ కిత్‌నే బజే ఆతీ హై.
AT WHAT TIME GARIBRATH TRAIN ARRIVES.

8) आपको कहाँ जाना है ?
मीरु एक्कडिकि वेल्लालि ?
మీరు ఎక్కడికి వెళ్లాలి ?
ఆప్‌కో కహా జానా హై ?
WHERE DO YOU HAVE TO GO?

9) मुझे हैदराबाद जाना है ।
नेनु हैदराबाद वेल्लालि ।
నేను హైదరాబాద్ వెళ్లాలి.
ముఝే హైదరాబాద్ జానా హై.
I HAVE TO GO TO HYDERABAD.

10) विशाखा रेल किस प्लेटफार्म पर आती है ?
विशाखा रैलु ए प्लेटफार्म मीदकु वस्तुंदि ?
విశాఖ రైలు ఏ ప్లాట్ ఫామ్ మీదకు వస్తుంది ?
విశాఖ రేల్ కిస్ ప్లాట్ ఫామ్ పర్ ఆతీ హై ?
ON WHICH PLATFORM THE TRAIN VISAKHA COMES?

11) हैदराबाद के लिए टिकट कितने की मिलेगी ?
हैदराबाद कु टिकट एंता उंटुंदि ?
హైదరాబాద్‌కు టికెట్ ఎంత వుంటుంది ?
హైదరాబాద్ కే లియే టికెట్ కిత్‌నే కీ మిలేగీ ?

HOW MUCH WILL A TICKET TO HYDERABAD COST?

12) पांच सौ बयालिस रूपये की ।
ऐदु वंदला नलाभै रेंडु रुपयलु ।
ఐదు వందల నలభై రెండు రుపాయిలు.
పాంచ్ సౌ బయాలిస్ రుపయే.
IT IS FIVE HUNDRED AND FORTY TWO RUPEES ONLY.

13) यहाँ रेल कितनी देर रुकती है ?
इक्कडा रैलु एंता सेपु आगुतुंदि ?
ఇక్కడ రైలు ఎంత సేపు ఆగుతుంది?
యహా రేల్ కిత్నే దేర్ రుక్తీ హై?
FOR HOW LONG WILL THIS TRAIN STOP HERE?

14) सिर्फ पांच मिनट रुकती है.
केवलम् ऐदु निमिशालु आगुतुंदि.
కేవలం ఐదు నిమిషాలు ఆగుతుంది.
సిర్ఫ్ పాంచ్ మినట్ రుక్తీ హై.
IT STOPS FOR 5 MINUTES ONLY.

15) यहाँ से रेल्वे स्टेशन कैसे जाना है ?
इक्कडिनुंचि रेल्वे स्टेशनु कु एला वेल्लालि ?
ఇక్కడి నుంచి రైల్వేస్టేషనుకు ఎలా వెళ్లాలి ?
యహా సే రైల్వేస్టేషన్ కైసే జానా హై ?
HOW DO WE GO TO RAILWAY STATION FROM HERE?

16) आप बस या आटो किसी से भी जा सकते है.
मीरु बस्सु लेदा आॅटो एलागैना वेल्लोच्चु.
మీరు బస్సు లేదా ఆటో ఎలాగైనా వెళ్లొచ్చు.
ఆప్ బస్ యా ఆటో కిసీ సే భీ జా సక్తే హై.
YOU CAN EITHER GO BY BUS OR AUTO.

17) जल्दी जाइये, वक्त नहीं है ।
त्वरगा वेल्लंडि, समयमु लेदू ।
త్వరగా వెళ్లండి.సమయము లేదు.
జల్దీ జాయియే వక్త్ నహీ హై.
GO QUICKLY YOU DO NOT HAVE MUCH TIME.

18) ठीक है, मैं ऑटो से ही चला जाता हूँ।
सरे अइते, नेनु ऑटो लोने वेल्तानु।
సరే అయితే, నేను ఆటోలోనే వెళ్తాను.
ఠీక్ హై, మై ఆటో సే హీ చలా జాతా హూ.
OK THEN, I WILL GO BY AUTO.

19) किराया कितना हुआ ?
बाडुगा एंता अइंदि ?
బాడుగ ఎంత అయింది ?
కిరాయా కిత్‌నా హుఆ ?
HOW MUCH IS THE CHARGE?

20) आप कहाँ तक जाएंगे ?
मीरु एक्काडिदाका वेल्तारू ?
మీరు ఎక్కడిదాకా వెళతారు ?
ఆప్ కహ తక్ జాయేంగే ?
TILL WHERE WILL YOU GO?

21) मैं विजयवाड़ा तक जाऊँगा।
नेनु विजयवाड़ा वरकु वेलतानु।
నేను విజయవాడ వరకు వెళ్తాను.
మై విజయవాడ తక్ జావూంగా.
I WILL GO TILL VIJAYAWADA.

22) भाड़ा पचास रुपए हुए।
किराइ याभै रूपायलयिंदि।
కిరాయి యాభై రుపాయలయింది.
భాడా 50 రుపయే హుఎ.
THE CHARGES ARE RS 50/-.

23) आप विजयवाड़ा क्यों जा रहे हो ?

मीरु विजयवाड़ा एंदुकु वेलुतुन्नारु ?

మీరు విజయవాడ ఎందుకు వెళుతున్నారు ?

ఆప్ విజయవాడ క్యోం జార హే హై ?

WHY ARE YOU GOING TO VIJAYAWADA?

24) मैं विजयवाड़ा कुछ खरीद दारी करने जा रहा हूँ।
नेनु विजयवाड़ा एदो कोनुगोलु कोसम् वेलुतुन्नानु ।
నేను విజయవాడ ఏదో కొనుగోలు కోసం వెళుతున్నాను.
మై విజయవాడ కుఛ్ ఖరీద్‌దారీ కర్‌నే జారహ హూ.
I AM GOING TO VIJAYAWADA TO MAKE SOME PURCHASES.

25) आप कहाँ से आ रहे हैं ?
मीरु एक्कडि नुंचि वस्तुन्नारु ?
మీరు ఎక్కడి నుంచి వస్తున్నారు ?
ఆప్ కహాసే ఆ రహేహై ?
WHERE ARE YOU COMING FROM?

26) मैं गाजुवाका से आ रहा हूँ।
नेनु गाजुवाका नुंचि वस्तुन्नानु ।
నేను గాజువాక నుంచి వస్తున్నాను.
మై గాజువాక సే ఆ రహ హూ.
I AM COMING FROM GAJUWAKA.

27) यह बस कहाँ तक जाएगी ?
ई बस्सु एक्कडि वरकू वेलुतुंदि ?
ఈ బస్సు ఎక్కడి వరకు వెళుతుంది ?
యహ బస్ కహ తక్ జాయేగీ ?
TILL WHERE WILL THIS BUS GO ?

28) यह बस विजयनगरम् तक जाती है ।

ई बस्सु विजयनगरम् वरकु वेलुतुंदि ।
ఈ బస్సు విజయనగరం వరకు వెళుతుంది.
యహ బస్ విజయనగరం తక్ జాతీ హై.
THIS BUS WILL GO TO VIJAYANAGARAM.

29) धन्यावाद, फिर मिलेंगें ।
धन्यावादमुलु, मळ्ळी कलुद्दाम् ।
ధన్యవాదములు,మళ్లీ కలుద్దాం.
ధన్యవాద్,ఫిర్ మిలేంగే.
THANKS, WE WILL MEET AGAIN.

स्कूल मे बातचीत　　　　స్కూలు సంభాషణ

CONVERSATION IN THE SCHOOL

1) नमस्ते मैडम,मैं राम की मां हूँ । मेरा नाम आहुति है ।
नमस्ते मैडम,ना पेरू आहुति,नेनु रामु अम्मानंडि ।
నమస్తే మేడమ్,మై రామ్ కీ మా హూ ! మేరా నామ్ ఆహుతి హై.
నమస్తే మేడమ్, నా పేరు ఆహుతి,నేను రాము అమ్మనండి.
HELLO MADAM, MY NAME IS AAHUTI. I AM RAM'S MOTHER.

2) राम कक्षा में कैसा रहता है, ठीक से पढ़ता है न ?
राम क्लासुलो एला उंटाडु,सरिग्गा चदुवुतुन्नाडा ?
రామ్ కక్షా మే కైసా రహతా హై, ఠీక్ సే పఢ్‌తా హై నా ?
రాము క్లాసులో ఎలా వుంటాడు, సరిగ్గా చదువుతున్నాడా ?
HOW IS RAM IN THE CLASS ? IS HE STUDYING WELL ?

3) हाँ ठीक है पर थोड़ी समस्या है ।
बाने उंटाडंडि कानि चिन्ना समस्या उंदि ।
హా ఠీక్ హై పర్ థోడీ సమస్య హై.
బానే వుంటాడండి కాని చిన్న సమస్య వుంది.
HE IS OK. BUT THERE IS SMALL PROBLEM.

4) ठीक है,पर कक्षा में बहुत बातें करता है ।
अंता बाने उंटाडु कानि क्लासुलो एक्कुवगा माट्ललाडुतू उंटाडु ।
ఠీక్ హై,పర్ కక్షా మే బహుత్ బాతే కర్‌తా హై.
అంతా బానే వుంటాడు కాని క్లాసులో ఎక్కువగా మాట్లాడుతూ వుంటాడు.
HE IS FINE, BUT TALKS A LOT IN THE CLASSROOM.

5) कक्षा मे बहुत शांत रहता है ।
क्लासुलो चाला निशब्दंगा उंटाडु ।
కక్షా మే బహుత్ శాంత్ రహతా హై.
క్లాసుతో చాలా నిశ్శబ్దంగా వుంటాడు.
HE IS VERY QUIET IN THE CLASS.

6) गणित में थोड़ी और ध्यान देने की आवश्यकता है ।

मेथ्सुलो इंकोंच्म श्रध्दा अवशरमु ।
గణిత్ మే థోడీ ఔర్ ధ్యాన్ దేనే కీ అవశ్యకతా హై.
మేథ్స్‌లో ఇంకొంచెం శ్రద్ధ అవసరము.
MORE ATTENTION IS NEEDED IN MATHS.

7) पढ़ता तो ठीक है पर लिखता बहुत धीरे-धीरे है ।
बाने चदुवुताडु कानि चाला नेम्मदिगा रास्ताडु ।
పఢతాతో ఠీక్ హై పర్ లిఖ్‌తా బహుత్ ధీరే ధీరే హై.
బానే చదువుతాడు కాని చాలా నెమ్మదిగా రాస్తాడు.
HE STUDIES WELL BUT HE WRITES VERY SLOWLY.

8) राम तो बहुत तेज बच्चा है । हम सब को इस पर गर्व है ।
रामु चाला तेलिवैना पिल्लवाडु । अतनंटे मा अंदरकि अभिमानमु ।
రామ్ తో బహుత్ తేజ్ బచ్చా హై ! హమ్ సబ్ కో ఇస్ పర్ గర్వ్ హై.
రాము చాలా తెలివైన పిల్లవాడు ! అతనంటే మా అందరికీ అభిమానము.
RAM IS A CLEVER BOY. WE ALL ARE PROUD OF HIM.

9) इसके सामाजिक विज्ञान मे अंक अच्छे नहीं आए । उसके लिए क्या करना है ?
वीडिकि सोशल स्टडिसलो मार्कुलु सरिग्गा रा लेदु दानिकोसम मेमेमि चेयालि ?
ఇస్‌కే సామాజిక్ విజ్ఞాన్ మే అంక్ అచ్చే నహి ఆయే ! వుస్‌కే లియే క్యా కర్‌నా హై ?
వీడికి సోషల్ స్టడీసులో మార్కులు సరిగ్గా రాలేదు దాని కోసం మేమేమి చేయాలి ?
HE DIDNOT GET GOOD MARKS IN SOCIAL STUDIES. WHAT SHOULD WE DO ABOUT IT.

10)आप रोज टिफिन बदल - बदलकर दीजिए ।
मीरु रोजू रकारकाला टिफिन्स इस्तुवुंडंडि ।
మీరు రోజూ రకరకాల టిఫిన్స్ ఇస్తూవుండండి.
ఆప్ రోజ్ టిఫిన్ బదల్-బదల్‌కర్ దీజియే.
GIVE HIM VARITIES OF SNACKS EVERYDAY.

11)आजकल मैं ध्यान दे रही हूँ कि यह बोर्ड पर मेरा लिखा हुआ ठीक से नहीं देख पा रहा है । एक बार इसकी आँख चेक करा दीजिए ।
नेनु ई मध्यना गमनिंचानु इतनु नेनु बोर्ड मिदा रासिंदि चूसि चदवालेका पोतुन्नाडु ओकासारि अतड़ि कल्लु चेक चेयंचंडि ।
ఆజ్‌కల్ మై ధ్యాన్ దే రహి హూ కి యహ్ బోర్డ్ పర్ మేరా లిఖా హుఆ ఠీక్ సే నహి దేఖ్ పా రహా హై.
ఏక్ బార్ ఇస్‌కీ అంఖ్ చెక్ కరా దీజియే.
నేను ఈ మధ్యన గమనించాను ఇతను నేను బోర్డ్ మీద రాసింది చూసి చదవలేక పోతున్నాడు. ఒకసారి అ

తడి కళ్ళు చెక్ చేయించండి.
I OBSERVED RECENTLY THAT HE IS UNABLE TO READ WHAT IS WRITTEN ON THE BLACK BOARD. GET HIS EYES CHECKED ONCE.

12)कक्षा में कुछ बच्चे इसे चिढ़ाते है । वह आपको बताने से डरता है ।
क्लसुलो वीडिनि कोंता मंदि पिल्ललु एड़िपिस्तुन्नारु । मितो चेप्पडानिकि भय पडुतुन्नाडु ।
క్లాసులో వీడిని కొంతమంది పిల్లలు ఏడిపిస్తున్నారు. మీతో చెప్పడానికి భయ పడుతున్నాడు.
కక్షా మే కుచ్ బచ్చే ఇసే చిఢాతే హై. వహ్ ఆప్‌కో బతానే సే డర్‌తా హై.
SOME CHILDREN ARE TEASING HIM IN THE CLASS. HE IS AFRAID TO REPORT THAT TO YOU.

13)मोहन इसका खाना रोज छीनकर खा लेता है । यह रोज भुखा रह जाता है ।थोड़ा ध्यान दीजिए ।
मोहनने पिल्लवाडु विडि टिफिन लाक्कुनि तिनेस्तुवुंटाडटा वीडु आकलितो उंडिपोतुन्नाडु मीरु कास्ता चूडंडि ।
మోహననే పిల్లవాడు వీడి టిఫిన్ లాక్కుని తినేస్తువుంటాడటా వీడు ఆకలితో ఉండిపోతున్నాడు ! మీరు కాస్త చూడండి.
మోహన్ ఇస్‌కా ఖానా ఛీన్‌కర్ ఖా లేతా హై ? యహ్ రోజ్ భూకా రహ్ జాతా హై ? థోడా ధ్యాన్ దీజా యే.
MOHAN SNATCHES EATS HIS FOOD EVERY DAY. HE REMAINS HUNGRY. PLEASE TAKE CARE

14)राम थोड़ा शर्मीला लड़का है । उत्साहित करने से बहुत अच्छा कर लेता है । हम लोग तो घर मे उत्साहित करते रहते हैं । आप भी थोड़ा ध्यान दीजिए ।
रामुकि कास्ता सिग्गु एक्कुवा,प्रोत्साहिस्ते बागा चदुवुताडु । इंटलो मेमु चेप्तूने वुंन्टामु,मीरू कूड़ा कास्ता श्रध्दा वहिनचंडि ।
రాముకి కాస్త సిగ్గు ఎక్కువ ప్రోత్సాహిస్తే బాగా చదువుతాడు.ఇంట్లో మేము చెప్తునే వుంటాము.మీరు కూడా కాస్త శ్రద్ధ వహించండి.
రామ్ థోడా షర్మీలా లఢ్‌కా హై ! ఉత్సాహిత్ కర్‌నే సే బహుత్ అచ్చా కర్ లేతా హై ! హమ్ లోగ్ తో ఘర్ మే ఉత్సాహిత్ కర్‌తే రహ్‌తే హై !ఆప్ భీ థోడా ధ్యాన్ దీజివి.
RAM IS A SHY BOY. HE CAN STUDY EVEN BETTER IF WE ENCOURAGE HIM. WE KEEP TELLING HIM AT HOME. KINDLY YOU ALSO PAY ATTENTION TO HIM.

15)टीवी व विडियोगेम पर थोड़ा नियंत्रण कीजिए ।
टीवी विडियोगेम लु कोंचम् कंट्रोलु चेयंडि ।
టీవీ, విడియోగేములు కొంచెం కంట్రోలు చేయండి.
టీవీ వ విడియోగేమ్ పర్ థోడా నియంత్రణ్ కీజియే.
PUT TABS ON HIS TV WATCHING AND VIDEO GAMES.

सब्जी बाज़ार मे बातें   కాయగూరల దుకాణంలో సంభాషణ

CONVERSATION AT VEG. MARKET

1) घर में कुछ सब्जी नहीं है । सब्जी मंडि जाना है । सरिता तुम मेरे साथ चलेगी क्या?
इंट्लो कायागूरलु एमी लेवु।कायागूरला मारकेट वेल्लालि । सरिता नुव्वु नातो वस्तावा?
ఇంట్లో కాయగూరలు ఏమీలేవు. కాయగూరల మార్కెట్టుకు వెళ్లాలి. సరితా, నువ్వు నాతో వస్తావా ?
ఘర్ మే కుఛ్ సబ్జీ నహీ హై. సబ్జీ మండి జానా హై. సరితా తుమ్ మేరే సాథ్ చలేగీ క్యా ?
WE DO NOT HAVE ANY VEGETABLES AT HOME. WE SHOULD GO TO THE VEGETABLE MARKET. SARITA, WILL YOU COME WITH ME?

2) माँ, मेरा थोडा गृह कार्य बाकी है,पाँच मिनिट के बाद चलें क्या?
अम्मा, नाकु कोंचमु होमवर्कु उंडिपोइंदि,ऐदु निमिशालु तरुवता वेलदामा?
అమ్మ, నాకు కొంచెము హోమ్‌వర్కు ఉండిపోయింది, ఐదు నిమిషాలు తరువాత వెళదామా ?
మా, మేరా థోడా గృహ్ కార్య్ బాకీ హై, పాంచ్ మినిట్ కే బాద్ చలే క్యా ?
MOTHER, I HAVE SOME WORK TO DO. CAN WE GO AFTER 5 MINUTES?

3) ठीक है,मै इंतजार कर रही हूँ ।
सरे, नेनु वेयिट चेस्तुन्नानु ।
సరే, నేను వెయిట్ చేస్తున్నాను.
ఠీక్ హై, మై ఇంతజార్ కర్ రహీ హూం.
OK I AM WAITING.

4) आओ चलें ।
पदा वेलदामु ।
పద వెళ్దాము.
ఆవో చలే.
LET US GO.

5) नमस्ते मेडम आइये, ताजी सब्जियां है, आज ही आई है,ले लिजिए ।
नमस्ते मेडम, रंडि, ताजा कायागुरलु इवाले वच्छायि, तीसुकोंडि ।
నమస్తే మేడమ్ రండి, తాజా కాయగూరలు ఇవాళే వచ్చాయి, తీసుకోండి.
నమస్తే మేడమ్ ఆఇయే, తాజీ సబ్జీయా హై, ఆజ్ హీ ఆయి హై, లే లిజియే.

HELLO MADAM, COME, FRESH VEGETABLES HAVE ARRIVED TODAY. TAKE THEM.

6) प्याज और आलू कैसे दे रहे हो ?
उल्लिपायलु,बंगालदुंपलु एला इस्तुन्नावु ?
ఉల్లిపాయలు, బంగాళదుంపలు ఎలా ఇస్తున్నావు ?
ప్యాజ్ ఔర్ ఆలూ కైసే దే రహే హో ?
WHAT ARE THE RATES OF ONION AND POTATOES ?

7) प्याज बीस रुपए और आलू पंद्रह रुपए किलो है ।
उल्लिपायलु इरवै रुपयलु,बंगालादुंपलु पदिहेनु रुपायलु केजी ।
ఉల్లిపాయలు ఇరవై రుపాయలు, బంగాళదుంపలు పదిహేను రుపాయలు కేజీ.
ప్యాజ్ బీస్ రుపయే ఔర్ ఆలూ పంద్రహ్ రుపయే కిలో హై.
ONIONS RS.20/-KG AND POTATO RS.15/- KG.

8) बहुत ज्यादा दाम बता रहे हो ।
चाला एक्कुवा धरा चेप्पतुन्नावु ।
చాలా ఎక్కువ ధర చెప్తున్నావు.
బహుత్ జ్యాదా దామ్ బతా రహే హో.
YOU ARE SAYING HIGH RATES.

9) ऐसी बात नही है । आजकल दाम बढ़ गया है। आप कहीं भी पूछ लिजिए ।
अलांटिदेमी लेदु. ई मध्या धरलु पेरिगायी । मीरु एक्कड़ेना अड़गंडि ।
అలాంటిదేమీ లేదు. ఈ మధ్య ధరలు పెరిగాయి. మీరు ఎక్కడైనా అడగండి.
ఐసీ బాత్ నహీ హై. ఆజ్‌కల్ దామ్ బఢ్ గయా హై. ఆప్ కహీం భీ పూఛ్ లిజిఏ.
IT IS NOT LIKE THAT. THE PRICES HAVE GONE UP. YOU CAN ENQUIRE ANY WHERE.

10) ठीक है, दोनो एक-एक किलो दे दो ।
सरे, रेंडु चेरोका किलो इव्वु ।
సరే, రెండు చెరొక కిలో ఇవ్వు.
ఠీక్ హై దోనో ఏక్-ఏక్ కిలో దేదో.
OK, GIVE ONE KILO EACH.

11) माँ बहुत दिनों से मशरूम नही बनाई हो । मै एक पेकेट ले लूं क्या ?

अम्मा मसरूम वंडि चाला रोजुलइंदि,वका पेकेट तीसुकोना ?

అమ్మ మష్‌రూమ్ వండి చాలా రోజులయ్యింది, ఒక పేకెట్ తీసుకోనా ?

మా బహుత్ దినో సే మష్‌రూమ్ నహీ బనాఇ హో. మై ఏక్ పేకెట్ లే లూం క్యా ?

MOM, IT IS A LONG TIME SINCE YOU PREPARED MUSHROOMS. SHALL I TAKE ONE PACKET?

12) ठीक है ले लो ।

सरे तीसुको ।

సరే తీసుకో.

ఠీక్ హై లే లో.

OK, TAKE IT.

13) मिर्ची अदरक भी एक-एक पाव दे दो ।

पच्चिमिर्चि,अल्लम कूडा चेरोका पावु किलो इव्वु ।

పచ్చిమిర్చి, అల్లం కూడ చెరొక పావుకిలో ఇవ్వు.

మిర్చి, అదరక్ భీ ఏక్-ఏక్ పావ్ దే దో.

ALSO GIVE ME GREEN CHILLIES, GINGER 250g EACH.

14) टमाटर कैसे किलो दे रहे हो ?

टमाटालु किलो एला इस्तुन्नावु ?

టమాటాలు కిలో ఎలా ఇస్తున్నావు ?

టమాటర్ కైసే కిలో దే రహే హో ?

WHAT IS THE RATE OF TOMATO PER Kg

15) तीस रुपए किलो ।

केजी मुप्पै रुपयलु ।

కేజీ ముప్పై రుపాయిలు.

తీస్ రుపయే కిలో.

30 RUPEES PER KILO.

16) थोड़ा कम कीजिए बहुत ज्यादा बता रहे है ।

कोंचेमु तग्गिनचंडि एक्कुवा चेप्पुतुन्नारु ।

కొంచెము తగ్గించండి ఎక్కువ చెప్తున్నారు.

థోఢా కమ్ కీజియే బహుత్ జ్యాదా బతా రహే హై.

REDUCE IT SLIGHTLY. YOU ARE ASKING TOO MUCH.

17) ठीक है पाँच रूपए कम ही दे दीजिए ।

सरे अयिते ऐदु रुपयिलु तक्कुवा इव्वंडि ।

సరే అయితే ఐదు రుపాయిలు తక్కువ ఇవ్వండి.

ఠీక్ హై పాంచ్ రుపయే కమ్ హీ దే దిజిఏ.

OK, YOU GIVE RS.5/- LESS.

18)भिंडी,झिगी,फूलगोभी,लौकी सब आधा-आधा किलो ठीक दाम लगा के दे दो,मैं बार-बार मोल भाव नहीं करुंगी। बेंडाकायालु,बीरकायालु,कॉलीफ्लावर,अनपकाया अन्नि अरा किलो चोप्पूना सरैना धरलो इव्वु नेनिंका माटि-माटिकि बेरंम आड़नु ।

బెండకాయలు, బీరకాయలు, కాలీఫ్లవర్, ఆనపకాయ అన్ని అర కిలో చొప్పున సరైనా ధరలో ఇవ్వు నేనింక మాటి మాటికీ బేరం ఆడను.

భిండీ,ఝింగీ,ఫుల్‌గోభీ,లౌకీ సబ్ ఆధా,ఆధా కిలో ఠీక్ దామ్ లగాకే దే దో. మై బార్–బార్ మోల్ భావ్ నహీ కరూంగీ.

GIVE LADY FINGERS, BOTTLE GOURD, CAULIFLOWER, GOURD HALF KILO EACH AT A REASONABLE RATE. I WILL NOT BARGAIN AGAIN.

19) मै ज्यादा नही बोल रहा हूँ, कम करके ही लगा रहा हूँ ।

नेनु एक्कुवा चेप्पलेदु, तग्गिंचे इस्तुन्नानु ।

నేను ఎక్కువ చెప్పలేదు, తగ్గించే ఇస్తున్నాను.

మై జ్యాదా నహీ బోల్ రహా హూం, కమ్ కర్‌కే హీ లగా రహా హూం.

I AM NOT TELLING MORE. I AM GIVING AT REDUCED PRICES.

20) साग भी ताजा ही है ले लिजिए ।

आकु कूरलु कूडा ताजागा उन्नाइ तीसुकोंडि।

ఆకుకూరలు కూడ తాజాగా ఉన్నాయి. తీసుకోండి.

సాగ్ భీ తాజా హీ హై లే లిజియే.

THE LEAFY VEGETABLES ARE ALSO FRESH. TAKE THEM.

21) ठीक है भाजी साग और पालक दस-दस रुपए का दे दो और धनिया व करीपत्ता पाँच-पाँच रुपए का दे दो ।
सरे तोटाकूरा पालकूरा चेरोका पदि रुपयिलदि इव्वु,कोत्तिमिरा करिवेपाकु चेरो ऐदु रुपायिलदि इव्वु ।
సరే తోటకూర, పాలకూర చెరొక పది రుపాయిలది ఇవ్వు, కొత్తిమీర, కరివేపాకు చేరొ ఐదు రుపాయిలది ఇవ్వు.
ఠీక్ హై భాజీ సాగ్ ఔర్ పాలక్ దస్-దస్ రుప్‌యే కా దే దో ఔర్ ధనియా వ కరీపత్తా పాంచ్-పాంచ్ రుప్‌యే కా దే దో.
OK GIVE SPINACH, AMARANTHUS EACH FOR RS 10/- GIVE CORIANDER LEAVES, CURRY LEAVES EACH FOR RS 5/-

22) दस रुपए मे कितने नींबू दे रहे हो ?
पदि रूपायिलकि एन्नि निम्माकायलु इस्तुनावु ?
పది రుపాయిలకి ఎన్ని నిమ్మకాయలు ఇస్తున్నావు ?
దస్ రుపయే మే కితనే నీంబు దే రహే హో ?
HOW MANY LEMONS YOU ARE GIVING FOR RS TEN RUPEES.

23) चार ले लिजिए ।
नालुगु तिसुकोंडि ।
నాలుగు తీసుకోండి.
చార్ లే లిజియే.
TAKE FOUR NOS.

24) छः दोगे क्या ?
आरु इस्तवा ?
ఆరు ఇస్తావా ?
ఛే దోగే క్యా ?
CAN YOU GIVE ME 6 NOS

25) ठीक है ले लिजिए ।
सरे तिसुकोंडि ।
సరే తీసుకోండి.
ఠీక్ హై లే లిజిఏ.
OK. TAKE IT.

26) पूरे कितने हुए ।

मोत्तम एंता अयिंदि ।

మొత్తం ఎంత అయింది.

పూరే కితనే హుఎ.

HOW MUCH IS THE TOTAL.

27) एक सौ सत्तर रूपये हुए ।

नूटा डभ्भै अयिंदि ।

నూటఢభ్భై అయింది.

ఏక్ సౌ సత్తర్ రుపయే హుయే.

IT IS RS ONE HUNDRED AND SEVENTY.

28) ये ले दो सौ ।

ई रेंडु वंदलु तीसुको ।

ఈ రెండు వందలు తీసుకో.

యే లో దో సౌ.

TAKE THESE RS TWO HUNDRED.

29) ये आपके बचे तीस रुपए लिजिए ।

इदिगोंडि मिगिलिना मुप्पै रुपायलु ।

ఇదిగోండి మిగిలిన ముప్పై రుపాయిలు.

యే ఆప్‌కే బచే తీస్ రుపయే లిజియే.

TAKE THESE REMAINING RS 30/-

होटल मे बातें హోటల్‌లో సంభాషణ CONVERSATION IN THE HOTEL

1) स्वागत है । आइये कितने लोग है सर ?
स्वागतं रंडि,एन्ता मंदि सर ?
స్వాగతం రండి, ఎంతమంది సర్ ?
స్వాగత్ హై ఆయియే ! కిత్‌నే లోగ్ హై సర్ ?
WELCOME! HOW MANY PEOPLE ARE HERE, SIR?

2) आपका टेबल तैयार है । अंदर आइए ।
मी टेबुल तयारुगा उंदि । लोपलकि रंडि ।
మీ టేబుల్ తయారుగా వుంది.లోపలికి రండి.
ఆప్‌కా టేబల్ తైయార్ హై, అందర్ ఆయియే.
YOUR TABLE IS READY. PLEASE COME IN.

3) इधर अंधेरा है, हमें दूसरी जगह चाहिए ।
इक्कडा चीकटिगा उंदि माकु वेरे चोटा कावालि ।
ఇక్కడ చీకటిగా ఉంది,మాకు వేరే చోట కావాలి.
ఇధర్ అంధేరా హై, హమే దూసరీ జగహ్ చాహియే.
IT IS DARK HERE. WE WANT ANOTHER PLACE.

4) बच्चों के लिए ऊँची वाली कुर्सी चाहिए ।
पिल्ला कोसम एत्तुगा उन्ना कुर्ची कावालि ।
పిల్లల కోసం ఎత్తుగా ఉన్న కుర్చీ కావాలి.
బచ్చోం కే లియే వూంచీ వాలి కుర్సీ చాహియే.
WE WANT A HIGH CHAIR FOR THE CHILDREN.

5) क्या मैं अब ऑर्डर ले सकता हूँ ?
नेनु इप्पुडु ऑर्डरु तीसुकोवच्चा ?
నేను ఇప్పుడు ఆర్డరు తీసుకోవచ్చా ?
క్యా మై అబ్ ఆర్డర్ లే సక్‌తా హూం ?
SHALL I TAKE ORDER NOW?

6) आपके होटल मे क्या विशेष है ?
मी होटल लो एवि बागुंटायि ?
మీ హోటలులో ఏవి బాగుంటాయి ?
ఆప్‌కే హోటల్ మే క్యా విశేష్ హై ?
WHAT ARE THE SPECIALS IN YOUR HOTEL?

7)हमारे यहाँ मलाई कोफ्ता विशेष है ।
मा दग्गरा मलाई कोफ्ता प्रत्येकमु ।
మా దగ్గర మలాయి కోఫ్తా ప్రత్యేకము.
హామారే యహాం మలాయి కోఫ్తా విశేష్ హై.
MALAI KOFTA IS OUR SPECIALITY.

8) थोड़ा तीखा कम डालना ।
कोद्दिगा कारमु तग्गिंचि वेयंडि ।
కొద్దిగా కారము తగ్గించి వేయండి.
థోడా తీఖా కమ్ డాల్‌నా.
MAKE IT LESS SPICY.

9) रोटी में क्या-क्या है ?
रोटीलु एमेमि उन्नाई ?
రోటీలు ఏమేమి వున్నాయి ?
రోటీ మే క్యా-క్యా హై ?
WHAT ARE THE VARIETIES OF ROTIES AVALIABLE?

10) सभी नान बहुत अच्छे है इस होटल के ।
अन्नी नानलु चाला बावुंटायि होटललो ।
అన్ని నాన్‌లు చాలా బావుంటాయి ఈ హోటల్‌లో.
సభీ నాన్ బహుత్ అచ్ఛా హై ఇస్ హోటల్ కా.
ALL THE FLAT BREADS ARE GOOD IN THE HOTEL.

11)स्टार्टर मे क्या-क्या है ?
स्टार्टलु एमेमि उन्नाई ?
స్టార్టర్లు ఏమేమి వున్నాయి ?
స్టార్టర్ మే క్యా-క్యా హై ?
WHAT ARE THE STATERS AVAILABLE?

12)बेबी कार्न चिलि के साथ हॉट एंड सॉर सूप चार ले आओ ।
बेबी कार्न चिलि तो हॉट एंड सॉर सूपु नालुगु तीसुकूरा ।
బేబీ కార్న్ చాల్లీ తో హాట్ అండ్ సోర్ సూపు నాలుగు తీసుకురా.
బేబీ కార్న్ చిల్లీ కే సాథ్ హాట్ ఎండ్ సోర్ సూప్ చార్ లే ఆవో.
BRING FOUR HOT AND SOUR SOUPS ALONG WITH CHILLI BABY CORN.

13) आप लोगों को और कुछ चाहिए ?
मीकिंकेमैना कावाला ?
మీకింకేమైనా కావాలా ?
ఆప్ లోగోం కో ఔర్ కుచ్ చాహియే ?
DO YOU WANT ANYTHING ELSE?

14) यह सब्जी उतनी खास नहीं । दूसरी ले आओ ।
ई कूरा अंता बागो लेदु, इंकोकटि तीसुकुरा ।
ఈ కూర అంతా బాగోలేదు,ఇంకొకటి తీసుకురా.
యహ్ సబ్జి వుత్నీ ఖాస్ నహి దూస్రీ లే ఆవో.
THIS CURRY IS NOT SO GOOD. BRING ANOTHER ONE.

15) नॉन थोड़ा कच्चा लग रहा है ।
नानु कोंचेमु पच्चिगा उंदि ।
నాను కొంచెము పచ్చిగా ఉంది.
నాన్ థోడా కచ్చా లగ్ రహా హై.
NAAN(FLAT BREAD) SEEMS TO BE A BIT UNCOOKED .

16) सब्जी थोड़ी चटकदार बनाना ।
कूरा कोंचेमु रुचिकरमगा चेयि ।
కూర కొంచెము రుచికరంగా చేయి.
సబ్జి థోడీ చటక్‌దార్ బనానా.
MAKE THE CURRY A LITTLE TANGIER.

17) गर्म गर्म गुलाब जामुन होगा क्या ?
वेडि वेडि गुलाब जामुन उंदा ?
వేడి వేడి గులాబ్ జామున్ ఉందా ?
గరమ్ గరమ్ గులాబ్ జామున్ హోగా క్యా ?
DO YOU HAVE HOT GULABJAMUNS?

18) पानी का बोतल ले आना ।
मंचिनीटि बाटिल तीसुकुरा ।
మంచినీటి బాటిల్ తీసుకురా.
పాని కా బోటల్ లే ఆనా.
BRING A BOTTLE OF WATER.

19) यहाँ टिस्यू पेपर नहीं है ।
इक्कड़ा टिस्यू पेपरु लेदु ।
ఇక్కడ టిష్యు పేపరు లేదు.
యహా టిష్యు పేపర్ నహి హై.
THERE IS NO TISSUE PAPER HERE.

20) टेबल थोड़ा गंदा है,साफ करवा दो ।
टेबुलु कोंचेमु आपरिसुभ्रंगा उंदि,शुभ्रम चेयिंचंडि ।
టేబులు కొంచెము అపరిశుభ్రంగా ఉంది, శుభ్రం చేయించండి.
టేబుల్ థోడా గందా హై,సాఫ్ కర్ వాదో.
THE TABLE IS DIRTY. GET IT CLEANED.

21)आपकी सर्विस बहुत अच्छी है । धन्यवाद ।
मी सर्विसु चाला बावुंदि । धन्यवादमुलु ।
మీ సర్వీసు చాలా బావుంది. ధన్యవాదములు .
ఆప్‌కీ సర్వీస్ బహుత్ అచ్ఛీ హై. ధన్యవాద్.
YOUR SERVICE IS GOOD. THANKYOU.

22) सौंफ के साथ मिसरी नहीं है क्या ?
सोपुतो पाटु पटिकबेल्लम मुक्कलु लेवा ?

సోపుతో పాటు పటిక బెల్లం ముక్కలు లేవా ?
సోంఫ్ కే సాథ్ మిస్‌రీ నహి హై క్యా ?
DON'T YOU HAVE SUGAR CRISTALS WITH ANISEEDS?

23) हाथ धोने के लिए फिंगर बाऊल है ना ?
चेतुलु कडुगु कोवटानिकि फिंगर बाऊलु उंदा ?
చేతులు కడుగుకోవటానికి ఫింగర్ బౌలు ఉందా ?
హాథ్ ధోనే కే లియే ఫింగర్ బౌల్ హై నా ?
DO YOU HAVE FINGER BOWL FOR WASHING HANDS?

24) बिल ले आओ । स्वाइपिंग मशीन है ना ?
बिल्लु तीसुकुरा । स्वाइपिंग मशीनु उंदिकदा ?
బిల్లు తీసుకురా !స్వైపింగ్ మిషను ఉందికదా ?
బిల్ లే ఆవో ! స్వైపింగ్ మిషిన్ హై నా ?
BRING THE BILL. DO YOU HAVE SWIPING MACHINE?

25) सर पैसे कार्ड मे या कैश देंगे ?
सर डब्बुलु कार्ड द्वाराना लेदा कैश इस्तारा ?
సర్, డబ్బులు కార్డు ద్వారానా లేదా క్యాష్ ఇస్తారా ?
సర్ పైసే కార్డ్ మే యా కేష్ దేంగే ?
SIR, HOW DO YOU PAY? THROUGH CARD OR CASH?

26) ये तुम्हारे टिप के पैसे ।
इविगो नी टिप्पु डब्बुलु ।
ఇవిగో నీ టిప్పు డబ్బులు.
యే తుమ్‌హారే టిప్ కే పైసే.
HERE IS YOUR TIP MONEY.

27) यहाँ टिप लेने की अनुमति नहीं है ।
इक्कड़ा टिप्पु तीसुकोवाटानिकि अनुमति लेदु ।
ఇక్కడ టిప్పు తీసుకోవటానికి అనుమతి లేదు.

యహాం టిప్ లేనే కీ అనుమతి నహి హై.
WE ARE NOT ALLOWED TO TAKE TIP HERE.

28)सर फिडबेक लिख दीजिए ।
महोदय, फिडबेक व्रायंडि ।
మహోదయ, ఫీడ్‌బేక్ వ్రాయండి.
సర్ ఫీడ్‌బేక్ లిఖ్ దీజియే.
SIR, GIVE YOUR FEEDBACK.

अभ्यास (बड़े वाक्य) వాక్యాల అభ్యాసం *PRACTICE SENTENCES*

1) हमारी संस्कृति विश्व विख्यात है ।
मना संस्कृति विश्वा विख्यातम् ।
మన సంస్కృతి విశ్వవిఖ్యాతం.
హమారీ సంస్కృతి విశ్వ్ విఖ్యాత్ హై.
OUR CULTURE IS WORLD FAMOUS.

2) हमारे देश के प्रथम प्रधान मंत्री जवाहर लाल नेहरू थे ।
मना देश तोलि प्रधान मंत्री जवाहर लाल नेहरू ।
మన దేశ తొలి ప్రధాన మంత్రి జవహర్‌లాల్ నెహ్రూ.
హమారే దేశ్ కే ప్రథమ్ ప్రధాన్ మంత్రి జవహర్ లాల్ నెహ్రూ థే.
JAWAHARLAL NEHRU WAS THE FIRST PRIME MINISTER OF OUR COUNTRY.

3) श्वेता हिंदी व तेलुगु दोनो भाषाओ मे प्रवीण है ।
श्वेता हिंदी तेलुगु रेंडु भाषाल्लो प्रवीणुरालु ।
శ్వేత హిందీ,తెలుగు రెండు బాషల్లో ప్రవీణురాలు.
శ్వేతా హిందీ వ తెలుగు దోనో భాషావోం మే ప్రవీణ్ హై.
SWETHA IS AN EXPERT IN BOTH HINDI AND TELUGU.

4) राहुल सदैव दूसरों की मदद करता है ।
राहुल एप्पुडू इतरुलकु सहायम् चेस्ताडु ।
రాహుల్ ఎప్పుడూ ఇతరులకు సహాయం చేస్తాడు.
రాహుల్ సదేవ్ దూస్‌రో కీ మదద్ కర్‌తా హై.
RAHUL ALWAYS HELPS OTHERS.

5) जनसंख्या वृद्धि देश की बहुत बड़ी समस्या है ।
जनाभा वृध्दि देशानिको पेद्दा समस्या ।
జనాభా వృద్ధి దేశానికో పెద్ద సమస్య.
జనసంఖ్య వృద్ధి దేశ్ కీ బహుత్ బఢీ సమస్య హై.
POPULATION RISE IS A BIG PROBLEM IN OUR COUNTRY.

6) **सैनिकों** के प्रति सबके मन मे सम्मान होना चाहिए ।

सैनिकुला पट्ला प्रजलंदरि मनसुलो गौरवमु उंडालि ।
సైనికుల పట్ల ప్రజలందరి మనసుల్లో గౌరవము ఉండాలి.
సైనికోం కే ప్రతి సబ్‌కే మన్ మే సమ్మాన్ హోనా ఛాహిఎ.
EVERY ONE SHOULD HAVE RESPECT TOWARD SOLDIERS IN THEIR HEARTS.

7) ज्यादा टीवी देखने से आँखें खराब हो सकती है ।
टीवी एक्कुवगा चूस्ते कल्लु पाडववच्चु ।
టీవీ ఎక్కువగా చూస్తే కళ్లు పాడవవచ్చు.
జ్యాదా టీవీ దేఖ్‌నే సే ఆంఖే ఖారాబ్ హో సక్‌తీ హై.
WATCHING TV FOR LONG TIME MAY SPOIL YOUR EYES.

8) खेलकूद स्वास्थ के लिए अतिआवश्यक है ।
आटपाटलु आरोग्यानिकि चाला मुख्यमैनवि ।
ఆటపాటలు ఆరోగ్యానికి చాలా ముఖ్యమైనవి.
ఖేల్‌కుద్ స్వస్థ్ అయకే లిఎ అతి ఆవష్యక్ హై.
GAMES ARE VERY IMPORTANT FOR HEALTH.

9) बच्चों को खेलकूद व योगाभ्यास की शिक्षा देनी चाहिए ।
पिल्ललकु आटपाटलु लेका योगाभ्यासमुलो शिक्षणा इव्वालि ।
పిల్లలకు ఆటపాటలు లేక యోగాభ్యాసములో శిక్షణ ఇవ్వాలి.
బచ్చోం కో ఖేల్‌కుద్ వ యోగాబ్యాస్ కి శిక్ష దేనీ చాహియే.
TRAINING IN EITHER SPORTS AND GAMES OR YOGA SHOULD BR GIVEN TO CHILDREN.

10) स्वस्थ शरीर मे ही स्वस्थ दिमाग रहता है ।
आरोग्यवंतमैना शरीरमुलोने मंचि बुध्दि उंटुंदि ।
ఆరోగ్యవంతమైన శరీరములోనే మంచి బుద్ధి ఉంటుంది.
స్వస్థ్ శరీర్ మే హీ స్వస్థ్ దిమాగ్ రహేతా హై.
HEALTHY BRAIN RESIDES IN HEALTHY BODY.

11) मेरे स्टेशन पहुंचते ही गाड़ी चली गई ।
नेनु स्टेशनु चेरिना वेंटने बंडि वेल्लिपोयिंदि ।
మేరే స్టేషన్ పహుంచ్‌తే హీ గాఢీ చలీ గఈ.
నేను స్టేషను చేరిన వెంటనే బండి వెళ్లిపోయింది.
AS SOON AS I REACHED THE STATION, THE TRAIN LEFT.

1) अधजल गगरी छलकत जाए ।
निंडुकुंडा तोणकदु ।
నిండుకుండ తొణకదు.
అధ్‌చల్ గగరీ ఛల్‌కత్ జాయే.
A FULL POT WOULD NOT SPILL(AN EMPTY VESSEL MAKES MORE NOISE).

2) अंधों में काना राजा ।
वृक्षम् लेनिचोटा आमुदम् वृक्षमे महावृक्षम।
వృక్షం లేని చోట ఆముదం వృక్షమే మహావృక్షం.
అంధో మే కానా రాజా.
BEST AMONGST THE WORST LOT.

3) नाच न जाने आँगन टेढ़ा ।
आडालेनम्मा मद्देलु ओडंदटा ।
ఆడలేనమ్మ మద్దెలు ఓడందట.
నాచ్ నా జానే ఆంగన్ టేడా.
A BAD CARPENTER BLAMES HIS TOOLS.

4) बंदर क्या जाने अदरक का स्वाद ।
गाडिदकें तेलुसु अटुकुला रुचि ।
గాడిద కేం తెలుసు అటుకుల రుచి.
బందర్ క్యా జానే అదరక్ కా స్వాద్.
A THING IS VALUED WHERE IT BELONGS.

5) आगे कुँवा पीछे खाई ।
मुंदु नुय्यि वेनुका गोय्यि ।
ముందు నుయ్యి వెనుక గొయ్యి.
ఆగే కూంవా పీచే ఖాయి.
TO BE BETWEEN THE DEVIL AND THE DEEP SEA.

6) एक कान सुन दूसरे से उड़ाना ।
ओका चेवि नुंचि विनि रेंडोव चेवि नुंचि वदिलेयटम् ।
ఒక చెవి నుంచి విని రెండోవ చెవి నుంచి వదిలేయటం.
ఏక్ కాన్ సున్ దూస్‌రే సే వుఢానా.
TO LISTEN FROM ONE EAR AND LEAVE IT FROM OTHER (PRETENDING TO LISTEN AND NOT LISTENING).

10) सावन के अंधे को सब हरा ।
पच्चा कामेर्ल वाडिकि लोकमंता पच्चगा कनबडिनट्टु ।
పచ్చకామెర్లవాడికి లోకమంతా పచ్చగా కనబడినట్లు.
సావన్ కే అంధేకో సబ్‌హారా.
THE WORLD LOOKS ALL YELLOW TO THE JANDICED EYE.

11) आग से खेलना ।
निप्पुतो चेलागाटं ।
నిప్పుతో చెలగాటం.
ఆగ్ సే ఖేల్‌నా.
PLAYING WITH FIRE.

14) आसामान से गीरा खजुर में अटका ।
पेनव मीदा नुंचि पोय्यिलो पड़डट्टु ।
పెనం మీద నుంచి పొయ్యిలో పడ్డట్టు.
ఆస్‌మాన్ సే గిరా ఖజురా మే అటక్.
OUT OF THE FRYING PAN STRAIGHT INTO THE FIRE.